Convoy to
AUSCHWITZ

Women's Life Writings from Around the World
Edited by Marilyn Yalom

Convoy to
AUSCHWITZ

~mm~

Women of the French Resistance

CHARLOTTE DELBO

Translated by Carol Cosman
Introduction by John Felstiner

NORTHEASTERN UNIVERSITY PRESS
BOSTON

Northeastern University Press

Copyright 1965 by Les Editions de Minuit, Paris
Translation copyright 1997 by Carol Cosman

Library of Congress Cataloging-in-Publication Data
Delbo, Charlotte
    [Convoi du 24 janvier. English]
    Convoy to Auschwitz : women of the French resistance / Charlotte
Delbo ; translated by Carol Cosman ; introduction by John Felstiner.
        p.   cm. — (Women's life writings from around the world)
    ISBN 1-55553-313-2 (cloth : alk. paper)
    1. Auschwitz (Poland : Concentration camp)   2. World War,
1939–1945—Personal narratives. French.   3. Women political
prisoners—France—Biography.   4. World War, 1939–1945—Underground
movements—France.   I. Title.   II. Series.
D805.P7D4313   1997
940.54′7243′094386—dc21   96-37825

Designed by Diane Levy

Composed in Jenson by G & S Typesetters, Inc., Austin, Texas
Printed and bound by Maple Press, York, Pennsylvania. The paper
is Sebago Antique, an acid-free stock.

MANUFACTURED IN THE UNITED STATES OF AMERICA
01   00   99   98   97   5   4   3   2   1

This is how it all happened,
and I invent nothing.

Electra, Act II, scene 9
Jean Giraudoux

Contents

Acknowledgments

I COULD NOT HAVE WRITTEN this book without the help of my friends. They have opened their hearts and their memories. Hélène Bolleau looked up the women from Charente; Cécile, often joined by Lulu, explored the area around Paris; for the North and the East, Madeleine Doiret methodically followed trails and clues. Hélène Fournier managed to find the families from Tours, Gilberte Tamisé traced the women from Bordeaux. Marie-Elisa Nordmann deserves credit for reconstructing from memory the list of Auschwitz deportees. Hélène Avenin, secretary of the Auschwitz Association, gave us access to her archives; Olga Wormser made her documentation available to me. Thanks to all of them, and to all the women too numerous to name here.

C. D.

Foreword

THE BOOK YOU HAVE IN YOUR HANDS, *Convoy to Auschwitz*, is one of a kind—a collective biography of the 230 Frenchwomen who were deported from Compiègne to Auschwitz on January 24, 1943. Almost all of these women were involved in resistance against the Nazis (only a couple were Jews). Twenty years later one of the few survivors from that convoy, Charlotte Delbo, assembled the stories of every one of her comrades, publishing *Le Convoi du 24 janvier* in 1965. Now that book has been translated into English for the first time, adding a unique form of witness to our sense of the mid-century cataclysm.

"Tell them we existed!" Nazism's European victims always said or would have said, and two striking examples of such testimony come to mind. Primo Levi, liberated from Auschwitz and returning to an Italy he doubted would (or even could) acknowledge the unheard-of reality of his wartime experience, wrote a poem he called "Shema" ("Listen!" or "Hear!"), which begins:

> *You who live secure*
> *in your warm houses, . . .*
> *Consider whether this is a man,*
> *Who labors in the mud . . .*
> *Who dies at a yes or a no.*
> *Consider whether this is a woman,*
> *With no hair and with no name*
> *With no strength left to remember.*

And the survivor-poet Paul Celan, years after the catastrophe that left him utterly destitute except for his mother tongue, ended a poem this way:

Niemand   No one
zeugt für den   witnesses for the
Zeugen.   witness.

Those lines themselves are of course bearing witness, even in Celan's despairing heart-cry, and we have had many other witnesses for what transpired in Nazi-ridden Europe between 1933 and 1945. Yet the survivors' need to tell, along with the world's incomprehension and forgetfulness, still persists.

Charlotte Delbo, born near Paris in 1913, was traveling in South America when she learned in September 1941 that a Communist friend had been guillotined by Marshal Pétain's police. Germany had invaded France in May 1940 and by June had granted an armistice, whereby northern France fell under German control and Pétain's collaborationist, anti-Communist, anti-Semitic, authoritarian regime ruled from Vichy. Internal resistance by the Maquis in France began immediately, and was later augmented by the Free French movement, headed by de Gaulle from London.

To support her comrades, Charlotte returned to France, rejoined her husband, Georges Dudach, and worked with him in the Resistance for four months, until they were both arrested; he was subsequently shot. She herself, after five months in the fortress at Romainville, was transported to Birkenau-Auschwitz in a trainload of 230 women. Within six months, three-quarters of them perished, mostly from deprivation and disease. Charlotte Delbo survived—as a political prisoner, not a Jew—more than two years of what has been called *l'univers concentrationnaire*, the other world of the camps.

"Twenty years later"—Delbo is speaking of a fellow deportee but the words hold for her as well—"she suffers from the indifference, the ignorance, the incomprehension she meets with among those who were not deported. Who still thinks about the Jewish children from Paris burned at Auschwitz?" In 1965 Delbo published the first volume of what became a trilogy (now available as *Auschwitz and After*, Yale University Press, 1995) recounting her sense of that "other" world.

"*O vous qui savez*," she writes, much like Primo Levi,

O you who know
did you know that hunger makes the eyes shine
   that thirst dulls them
did you know that one can see one's mother dead
and have no tears.

And, somewhat like the surrealist Magritte's painting of a pipe, captioned "This is not a pipe," Delbo describes reaching Auschwitz by rail: "The station is not a station." Given the strange and estranging narrative styles of such predecessors as Albert Camus and Samuel Beckett (who were also active in the Resistance), Delbo's Auschwitz trilogy finds a way to make us imagine the unthinkable. In a chapter called "The Mannequins," she looks from her barrack at bodies lying in a snow-covered yard: "Naked. Laid one next to the other. White, a bluish white against the snow. Heads shaved, pubic hair stiff. The corpses are frozen. White with brown nails. Frankly speaking, the toes sticking up are ridiculous. Terrifyingly ridiculous." She remembers as a young girl seeing some mannequins left outside a fancy shop and feeling oddly disturbed by these undressed figures. But "Now the mannequins are bedded in the snow . . . our comrades from yesterday. . . . Yesterday they gulped down filthy soup. They had diarrhea and got beaten. Yesterday they were suffering." How to square human experience as we know it with this other world? Such degradation defies conventional narrative.

Although Charlotte Delbo's Auschwitz trilogy is intensely admired, *Convoy to Auschwitz* is much less well known. For twenty years I have thought there is no other work like it, and have wanted it available in English. Charlotte Delbo simply took it upon herself to account for each and every one of the 230 women who left Compiègne by train for Birkenau on January 24, 1943—to memorialize them, I would say, to commit them to memory and commit us to them.

Only 49 of 230 were still alive at Liberation. (Charlotte Delbo herself went from Auschwitz to the camp at Ravensbrück, and was repatriated by the Red Cross via Sweden. She died in 1985.) From these 49 women Delbo elicits some sense of their postwar existence. But everyone on the transport receives the biographic gift of factuality, exactness, understatement—in effect, a carefulness and caring, *des petits soins*, as the French say.

Just this solicitude, I think, is also what distinguished the behavior of Delbo and her fellow prisoners, enabling an unusually high proportion of them to survive. Compared to them, the Jews at Auschwitz suffered more overcrowding, severer roll calls, worse punishments. What's more, Charlotte Delbo's cohort of 230 women had known each other in the Romainville prison during the months before they were deported; many of them had been militants, and they shared the same nationality and a common language. (Delbo also notes that the younger the women, the better their chances; of the fifty-four prisoners older than forty-four, not one survived.) Above all, there were the small things that perhaps come more naturally to women than to men: "holding each other's arms while walking, rubbing each other's backs during roll call. . . . Each of the survivors knows that without the others, she would not have returned."

What sort of book is *Convoy to Auschwitz*? Not really a memoir, and not strictly sociology or history either, but the best of each, a collective biography for which there is no precedent. Delbo's French publisher, Les Editions du Minuit, which originated clandestinely during the Occupation, issued *Le Convoi du 24 janvier* under the rubric "Great Documents," and it is certainly that. After

Charlotte Delbo's informative, sensitive, and pensive introduction, each vignette comes in a revealing format: the name, the life before, the arrest, then in its own space the prisoner's Auschwitz number cutting into her years, followed by the camp experience and its aftermath, if any.

A tragic coincidence brought all these lives through 230 arrests in 1942 to the fortress at Romainville and then the Compiègne railway station. Yet these disparate stories, recovered and recounted by Charlotte Delbo with the help of several comrades, render a richly diverse canvas of prewar French life: laundress, hairdresser, concierge, dressmaker, knitter, cook, charwoman, farmer, furrier, tanner, housewife, oyster farmer, factory hand, ironer, bartender, upholsterer, shopkeeper, civil employee, nurse, enameler, typist, welfare worker, singer, proofreader, dentist, pharmacist, teacher, doctor, professor, photojournalist, midwife, secretary, student. They range from someone with no schooling at all to Marie-Claude Vaillant-Couturier, wife of the editor of *L'Humanité* and a member of Parliament after the war.

All walks of life led to Romainville because all sorts of Frenchwomen became engaged in activities that Vichy meant to suppress: supplying arms and food, distributing newspapers and leaflets, furnishing liaison, monitoring broadcasts, harboring activists, and so on. Half of the women were Communists, whether party members or not, others were in Gaullist networks, while some were arrested for crossing the Demarcation Line and a few for reasons having nothing to do with the Resistance—including one or two women who'd denounced Jews or Communists and been picked up anyway.

To enter the world of Charlotte Delbo's comrades, it helps to recall France's political and economic situation after World War I, much of which was fought on French soil. There were two million killed or seriously wounded, and devastation in the north and east. Resentment focused on Germany, yet financial crisis and labor unrest in the late Twenties and early Thirties turned French conservatives more sharply against the Left. What's more, the country's first Popular Front government, in 1936–37, was led by a Jew, Léon Blum. Despite the Nazi menace, anti-Communists and many French Catholics were more comfortable with Germany than with Soviet Russia. The women in Delbo's convoy to Auschwitz stemmed from one side of a divided France.

If one were to assemble just the first halves of all their vignettes, the part before the Auschwitz tattoo, a vivid complex of wartime resistance would emerge: the FTP (Sharpshooters-and-Partisans), the National Front, the Communists, the Gaullists, the various labor organizations, and so on. And opposite them the SS and Gestapo, the French special brigades and gendarmes, many members of the municipal police, plus informers and denouncers. Then after the tattoo number come a hundred ways of perishing but also the countless small heroisms you will come upon in this book. One woman recalls: "When I was there, I used to think, 'If I get back, I'll read all the books Charlotte talked to me about.' And I have."

Finally, after the last vignette, Charlotte Delbo adds another, "Mado . . ."—no full name, no life story, no number: "She must have died in the first few days. No one had time to get acquainted with her. None of the women surviving today remembers her." And that ends *Convoy to Auschwitz*.

"No one / witnesses for the / witness," Paul Celan wrote. "And some there be that have no memorial, That are perished as though they had never been," the Bible tells us. Yet Charlotte Delbo's great document gives us an act of loyal and specific witness. Even Mado has her memorial.

—John Felstiner

Convoy to
AUSCHWITZ

Departure and Return

ON THE MORNING of January 24, 1943, a damp cold enveloped Ile-de-France with low-lying clouds and wisps of fog trailing through the trees. It was early Sunday morning. As we came into town, we noticed a few pedestrians. Some were walking their dogs, others hurried by. Perhaps they were going to early Mass. They hardly glanced at the trucks we were standing in. We sang and called out, trying to startle them: "We're Frenchwomen! Political prisoners! We're being deported to Germany!" They would stop for a moment at the edge of the sidewalk, raise their eyes, quickly lower them, and continue on their way. We continued on ours and soon lost sight of them. The trucks stopped near a railroad siding far from the docks. The freight cars formed a long train. The cars in front were already shut. They contained twelve hundred men who had left the Royallieu camp the evening before, boarded the train, and spent the night in the Compiègne station. They must have been cold. The last four cars were empty. As we jumped down, German soldiers directed us into the train. Sixty to seventy women in each of the first three cars, twenty-seven in the last one, where I found myself. There were two hundred and thirty of us. We had been counted the previous evening for the food distribution: each of us got one loaf of bread and a piece of sausage ten centimeters long. The amount of food told us nothing about the length of the journey.

The train car contained half a bale of straw. Scattered about, it did not form a litter, but seemed more like a mess that needed sweeping up. In the middle, a tar barrel. The soldiers slid the doors shut and bolted them. We settled down in the darkness. We had our suitcases, our purses. Most of the women—two hundred and twenty-two—came from the fort at Romainville and had been transported to Compiègne in two groups, one on January 22, the other on the twenty-third. Six came from the prison at Fresnes, two from the cells at the armory.

We settled in for a long journey, friends sitting together. I was with Yvonne Blech, Yvonne Picard, Viva, and Madame Van der Lee, who carefully placed her black hat on her suitcase, unfolded her blanket, and tucked her unfashionable otterskin coat around her legs. It was cold.

The train did not move. We took paper and pencils out of our bags and wrote notes: "Would the person who finds this be kind enough to notify —— in —— that her daughter" — or "his wife" or "her sister" — "Christianne" or "Suzanne" or "Marcelle" — has been deported to Germany. We are in good spirits. See you soon." Viva always ended with "I will return," underlined. Each woman put several addresses in her message, asking her relatives to contact the families of the others, in case only one note should reach its destination. Many of these notes were collected by the railway workers at Compiègne, who sent them on.

The train set off. We sang. At every jolt, the barrel slid rapidly from one end of the car to the other. We made a doorstop with a suitcase. Luckily, the contents of the barrel quickly froze. Otherwise, we would have been splashed at every vibration. The train rolled along; we were singing. We examined the partitions of the cattle car. With a nail file or a penknife, we pried out the knotholes in the wood. We took turns peering through a hole to read the names of the stations. When the train slowed down periodically, we knew that we were approaching a switchpoint, where there would be a wait, and we quickly prepared notes which we slipped under the doors, weighting them with coins for stamps. At Châlons-sur-Marne, a railway worker walked alongside our car, whispering: "They were beaten. They lost Stalingrad. You'll come back soon. Be strong, girls." We shouted with joy and sang again at the tops of our lungs.

We also tried to dislodge the floor planks. In my car, nothing budged. In Madeleine Dechavassine's, they succeeded, and the opening would have been big enough to get through. The most reasonable among them argued that while some might escape, the others would be shot. If only they could have seen what was coming . . .

After Metz, which we reached at nightfall, we no longer threw pieces of paper. Jeanne Humbert said: "My brother-in-law is a railway worker here."

We huddled against one another to sleep. On Monday, we kept taking turns at the knotholes. The names of the stations no longer meant anything to us. The following night there was a stop at Halle. They unhooked our cars from the front of the train, where the men were. They were going to Oranienburg. The survivors learned this in 1945.

Tuesday morning, the train stopped at a large station. Breslau. The soldiers opened the doors and distributed tepid water. We had drunk nothing since the departure. Nor had we eaten anything, apart from some barley soup they had given us at the Weimar station; the bread had frozen. A soldier closed the door again, saying: "We're leaving you here. Now the SS will take over." The journey continued. The train stopped that evening and stood still all night. It was much colder.

The next morning—Wednesday, January 27, 1943—the cars were opened. Cries, shouts, incomprehensible orders, dogs, SS, machine guns, the clanging of weapons. A roadside that was not a station. The cold was piercing. Where were we? We found out only two months later. A hundred and fifty women died without knowing they were at Auschwitz.

Along the road, men stood in line at attention. We accosted them. No one answered us, not so much as a gesture or a glance.

The SS made us line up. In front. Walking was painful. We were numb, the ground was covered with ice, the suitcases were heavy.

Halfway along, we crossed a line of women, a long column. The *kapos** ordered them to let us pass. They were nearly blue with cold. As we came near, we smelled an odor that we hesitated to attribute to them, the smell of a badly neglected stable, the smell of cows soiled with their own filth. Lulu thought: "They could at least wash." Who knew that there was no water in the camp? Who imagined that the toilets were simply an open trench you reached by crossing a swamp of diarrhea? "They smell so bad." Cécile said: "Eight days from now you'll smell just as bad and you won't notice anymore."

Turning off the road, we were suddenly faced with barbed wire and watch towers. Barbed wire white like sugar crystals, watch towers black against the snow. This was when the women at the head of the line sang "la Marseillaise." Near the entrance, a sign made from a board nailed to a spindly post, the kind used in the countryside to warn, "Private Preserve" or "Private Property," said: "*Vernichttunglager.*" "You know German—what does it mean?"—*Nichts* means 'nothing, nothingness.' 'Toward nothing, nothingness.' In other words, 'Extermination Camp.'"—"Oh, that's cheerful."

This was Birkenau, the women's camp, situated two kilometers from Auschwitz proper, where the men's camp stood. It had been opened the previous summer on the site of a mass grave of Russian prisoners. This too we learned only later.

We entered the gate. Female SS stood on each side. The first we had seen. High black boots, long black capes, high hoods above their military caps. Silhouettes sharply etched against the snow.

We traced the outlines of barracks, low, as though hidden in the snow: these were the blockhouses. We had to step over corpses. Twisted faces, bloody

---

*In camp language, a male or female prisoner supervising a work detail. (Trans.)

bones. Seeing them, we understood that death was not gentle here. Nor the life spent awaiting it.

We entered a long, narrow barracks. Sitting on our suitcases, we waited a long time. Prisoners filed toward us, asking us to give them our things. "They're going to take everything from you anyway." They also asked to keep our jewelry, which they promised to return after we'd been searched. Yvonne Picard gave them a favorite signet ring set with a diamond. Afterward, she looked in vain for the woman she had given it to.

Noon. Soup. The inmates distributed red enamel pails shaped like salad bowls, filled with an evil-smelling soup. One of the women said: "This soup is inedible. It smells like a sewer." Madeleine Doiret answered: "The soup will always smell like a sewer, we'll just have to eat it or die of hunger. Might as well start now." Several ate that first soup. Others did not, nor any soup afterwards. Later, we understood why the soup stank: everyone had diarrhea and to go out at night for your needs was to risk a beating; what's more, those women with diarrhea had no time to leave the block. The pails were used as chamber pots.

The door at the end of the barracks opened. On the threshold stood SS men and women. One asked if there was a dentist among us. Danielle Casanova stepped forward. Another called our names. He read and pronounced them badly. Marie-Claude helped him. Beside each name was written, "Anti-German activities." This was the chief accusation.

As we were called up, we undressed and put our clothes in our suitcases, which we had marked with our names. Once naked, we entered a room where another prisoner cut our hair with scissors. Short. Down to the scalp. Another shaved our pubic hair. A third wiped our heads and pubic areas with a cloth soaked in gasoline. The disinfection. Then, to the shower. There was no water. Besides, we'd left our toiletries in the suitcases. Then to the steam room. The women who had gone first were already sitting on wooden slats in the steam. I looked for my friends and recognized no one. Naked and shaved, no one looked the same. I was naked and shaved too. Viva recognized me: "Come here. Come sit with us," she sang out in a joyful voice, the way you hail someone in the crowd at a village fair. I can still hear her voice.

Again we waited. Some prisoners were sitting at small tables at the bottom of a row of steps. They called us up one by one. Dipping her stiletto into a little bottle, a Jewish woman tattooed me, saying: "Don't be afraid. It doesn't hurt," and in a scarcely audible voice: "Where did you come from? Paris? Will the war be over soon?"—"Yes, we won Stalingrad." She looked at me with gratitude. She spoke good French. Naked, shaved, tattooed, we went into another room where there were piles of clothing along the wall. A prisoner threw us a shirt, underwear, a scarf, a bibbed apron, socks or stockings—but nothing to keep them up, a dress, and a striped jacket. The shirts and underwear were stained with blood, pus, diarrhea. The dresses, too. There were lice in the seams. The dresses and jackets were damp and hot. They had come out of the bathhouse. The disinfection. They dried on us as we came out of the steam and turned into coats of ice.

"Now, go take some shoes."

"Be very careful with the shoes. Try to find some that don't leak, even if they're too big or too heavy. Shoes are the most important thing," said Yvonne Blech. Where had she acquired such experience? She selected deliberately, examined meticulously. The hobnail boots she selected for herself and for me were in decent condition. Madeleine Doiret was allotted slippers of torn felt. Others got clogs with wooden heels. For months I watched over my hobnail boots. I kept them under my head when I slept. Going to roll call with naked feet meant certain death.

Another prisoner distributed calico numbers to sew on the sleeve of the dress and the front of the jacket. Someone asked the meaning of the red triangle next to the number. "Political. Political prisoner." Two girls protested: "We aren't politicals. We're whores." They wore the red triangle anyway.

One inmate handed us a threaded needle for sewing.

"How many of you are there?"

"Two hundred and thirty."

"There won't be thirty of you in a month."

She was a Dutch woman.

"A thousand of us arrived in October. I'm the last one."

We thought she'd been ordered to demoralize us.

"And why is that? Are they going to shoot us?"

"No. But roll call kills everyone."

"Why roll call?"

"Four hours standing outside every morning and nearly the same in the evening, sometimes all day."

We thought she wanted to discourage us. We were determined not to believe her. Hours standing? That's not something you die from. Our courage was based on great ignorance.

The final formality: filling out an identity card. The question "How many gold crowns do you have?" intrigued us.

When a group of thirty of us was ready, a *Lagerpolizei* (an inmate responsible for keeping order in the camp) led us into one of the blocks, number 14. We spent two weeks there in quarantine, exempted from outside work. We had only roll calls and fatigue duty. In the first eight days, ten women died. Mostly the elderly. It was usual for death to start with the elderly.

At first, we were very determined—doing gymnastics, washing ourselves.

Going for water was a perilous expedition. All the routes were staked out by polizei, kapos, SS armed with cudgels. The faucet was guarded by one of the German women criminals. Getting to it was almost impossible. And when you were lucky enough to gather a little water in the bottom of the pail, it was rusty, nauseating, with an oily skin on the surface like grease drops on asphalt. It was undrinkable, and fetid in a few hours.

On February 12 we left Block 14 for Block 26. Our air shafts faced the courtyard of Block 25. We soon knew all about Block 25.

Block 26 was full to bursting. It sheltered a thousand women: Poles and ourselves. We were lodged eight to a tier. The tiers were compartments strung together (imagine a large rabbit hutch without doors), 1.8 meters per side, on three levels. The first was at ground level, on muddy earth swimming with urine, diarrhea, and melted snow. You could sit on the third level, under the roof. Nowhere else: the compartment ceilings were too low. The young women took the third level, where the older and less agile could not climb. Eight to a tier, squeezed together. We could lie down only head to foot, on our sides. Marie-Claude went to see Stenia, the block chief—she was called the *blockova* in the camp dialect influenced by the Poles, who numbered in the thousands— and appealed to her that we were too crowded. "It will be better in a few days." Marie-Claude told us what Stenia had said, without understanding what she meant. We did not understand, either. But we soon did.

In one day at the end of February, we had nine deaths. On April 10, 1943— seventy-three days after our arrival—there were only seventy of us left, and that was when the typhus epidemic surged again with a vengeance.

People we tell this to now cannot understand how so many of us could die so quickly. Our explanations make no sense.

We had been abruptly transported from a temperate climate to an inland one in the dead of winter, wearing our comfortable coats, our woolens, our rayon dresses, unlined jackets, and open shoes. And, of course, acute nephritis can set in during roll call—when you're scantily dressed, standing still with your feet in snow for hours on end, the thermometer at minus fifteen degrees centigrade; you can catch pneumonia in an hour and die of it in a few days; dysentery can kill in three weeks, or even less. And there were women who did not eat at all. From the moment they arrived, they couldn't swallow a thing. Some couldn't sleep. When the work began in the marshes, hauling bricks or sand, felling trees, pushing heavy handcarts, they were already exhausted. Death from exhaustion was quick, too. Then there were accidents, dog bites, the selection on February 10, beatings that fractured the skull or vertebrae, frostbite that became gangrened. In the filth and cold, everything was fatal, even a fleabite.

By August 3 there were fifty-seven of us left.

On that date something extraordinary happened. The survivors of the convoy were placed in quarantine.

Symbolically situated outside the barbed wire, facing the entrance to Birkenau, was a wooden barracks: the quarantine block. German female criminals were isolated there before being released. This news was so extraordinary that a rumor soon spread: the Frenchwomen would be freed.

The Frenchwomen—that was our convoy. We were by no means the only Frenchwomen at Birkenau, but we were the only ones under the rubric "political." The others were "Jews." A Jew might be taken in combat, gun in hand, or in a roundup; it made no difference. To the Gestapo, he was a Jew, never a political prisoner. Jews no longer had a nationality. Since Jews and non-Jews were all at Auschwitz, what was the difference? The difference was enormous from the first. On arrival, the Jewish convoys faced a selection. Only young people able to work entered the camp. The others were gassed right away. Often there was no selection: the entire convoy was sent to the gas chamber.

At Birkenau, conditions for Jews and non-Jews were nearly the same. Nearly. But that slight difference led to a higher mortality rate among the Jews. The blocks of Jewish women were more overcrowded than the others. Not everyone could lie down for the night. Those who did not find a place on the planks of the tiers spent the night standing in the aisles. The Jews suffered general punishments more often than we did, doing roll call on their knees with their arms in the air, for example: something we never experienced. Moreover, these Jewish women, thrown together on the eve of deportation, rarely formed cohesive, supportive groups. Their blocks were a mixture of Jews from different countries without a common language or much basis for friendship and mutual aid. If our convoy had so many survivors—and for Birkenau in 1943, fifty-seven out of two hundred and thirty after six months was exceptional, unique in the history of the camp—this was because we already knew each other (having spent weeks, and sometimes months, together at Romainville) and had formed small, tightly knit units within a large, homogeneous group, helping each other in all sorts of ways, often quite small: holding each other's arms while walking, rubbing each other's backs during roll call; and, of course, we could talk to each other. Speech was self-defense, comfort, hope. By talking about who we were before, about our lives, we perpetuated the time before, we maintained our reality. Each of the survivors knows that without the others, she would not have returned.

The quarantine was our salvation. No more roll call, no more hard labor, no more marching, a quarter liter of milk per day, the possibility of washing, of writing once a month, of receiving parcels and letters.

Seventeen of us were at Raisko and stayed there, probably because conditions of life there were similar to those in quarantine. What was Raisko? In

Ukraine and Belorussia, the Germans had seen fields of *koksaghiz*, a kind of dandelion whose root was discovered by a Russian botanist in Pamir to contain a high proportion of latex. The Germans commandeered books and scientists to try and cultivate this plant in the swampy fields of Auschwitz, and the camp made a contract with I. G. Farben. SS Doctor Caesar was made director of the laboratory. In February 1943, shortly after our arrival, a secretary asked us during a morning roll call if any of us were botanists, biologists, or chemists. Five candidates were enlisted: Madeleine Dechavassine, Marie-Elisa Nordmann, Hélène Solomon, Laure Gatet, and Alice Loeb. The last two died before the unit was formed. Jacqueline Dissoubray was recruited a little later as a botanist. On March 21, 1943, the four women left Birkenau to live at the staff house, a barracks-like building situated near the men's camp. There were showers. Roll call lasted only a few minutes. Subsequently, this advance guard was able to get others admitted, claiming they needed lab assistants or gardeners to help with planting and weeding. They could do this thanks to Annie Binder, a Czech woman, Caesar's secretary, and to Claudette Bloch, a Frenchwoman who had known Marie-Elisa before the war. The assay office was not ready until July. Beginning in May, instead of going to the marshes, the lab assistants and gardeners went to Raisko, two kilometers from Birkenau. This was a considerable distance, since at the time most of them were recovering from typhus. On the first of July 1943, Dr. Caesar's entire team moved into a new, clean, wooden barracks where there were hot showers, straw mattresses on individual beds, and toilets. Not to have to smell the stench from the crematoria was a deliverance. We saw the smoke that formed a thick cloud above the fourteen chimneys across one side of the horizon. We sometimes got hold of the *Volkischer Beobachter*. Reading this communiqué raised our spirits and our courage. The women at Raisko could also write and receive parcels.

For twenty years we've tried to guess the reason for this measure, which was such a blessing. Why were we so blessed by the Gestapo? Some thought that Berlin had conceded to a broadcast by Fernand Grenier from Radio London. But this broadcast took place on August 17, 1943,[1] whereas the quarantine took effect on August 3. Fernand Grenier, Communist deputy with the Gaullist government in exile, had received an August 1943 issue of *Etoiles* describing the conditions of "a hundred" Frenchwomen who had been in the Resistance and had left the fort at Romainville on January 22, 1943. The text suggests either that the person who wrote it knew little about Birkenau and our convoy, or that those who recopied the transmission at different stages did not want to believe it and corrected it. They may have read: "There is one water faucet for ten thousand women," but judged it more likely to read "for five hun-

---

1. Fernand Grenier, *C'était ainsi* (Edition sociales, 1959).

dred women." One faucet for five hundred—that would have been marvelous. Those who stayed in Block 26 went sixty-seven days without washing. At first, we would rub ourselves with snow. But snow doesn't wash, and it soon turned to fetid mud. In a short time, our bodies were covered with lice: white lice, fat and soft. When our hair grew back, we had them on our heads: nervous black lice that crunched dryly. And when our pubic hair grew back, a third variety appeared, less agitated, more encrusted. Lice carry typhus. I washed myself for the first time at the beginning of April in a stream, during the midday break. Until then, the streams had been frozen. The blast of the whistle interrupted me before I could attack my knees, using a handful of sand for soap.

In the radio broadcast, they also said that at the slightest misstep, the inmates were sent "into the salt mines and never returned." The myth of the salt mine. As if there were or could be something worse than Birkenau. At Birkenau, there was only one punishment: Block 25, death.

Where had the information come from? Very likely from a Pole who had escaped from Auschwitz in April 1943 and had managed to reach Switzerland, where he met a journalist. This Pole was probably ill-informed about our convoy because communication between the men's camp, where he was, and Birkenau had to pass through several intermediaries and various languages.

Even in its watered-down version, this broadcast created a great stir. It was the first time anyone had spoken about Auschwitz. Those who heard it were astonished.

Why this blessing? We have to admit we still don't know. Some speak of an effort by the Red Cross. It's true that the International Red Cross had been alerted by our families, desperate for news of us since our departure, and that the German Red Cross was asked to locate us. But not until 1944 did the Red Cross seek authorization to visit the concentration camps, and authorization was given only in March 1945. One thing is certain: at the end of June 1943, Marie-Claude Vaillant-Couturier was called to the *Politische Abteilung* (the camp's political police), where she was told that her family was asking for news of her through the Red Cross and was given permission to write them, then and there. Several days later, at the beginning of July 1943, we were all given the right to send letters. The men deported in July 1942—only those considered Frenchmen, not Jews—got the same privilege.

One can always guess. Or simply imagine that one fine day some bureaucrat discovered that, contrary to regulations, non-Jewish French citizens were being held at Auschwitz (no convoy of "politicals" was sent to Auschwitz after ours), and the Gestapo then decided to transfer us to Ravensbrück, figuring it was a good idea to prepare us by putting us in quarantine.

In the first four months of quarantine, from August to November 1943, five died. For them, the reprieve had come too late. If the quarantine had begun in September, not one of us would have left Birkenau. At Raisko, no one was lost.

On January 7, 1944, ten women from the Raisko group were chosen by the commandant of Auschwitz to be transferred to Ravensbrück. Only eight left, when two were detained at the last moment because they were down with fever. Why this detachment to Ravensbrück? We do not know. They left Auschwitz in a third-class train car, escorted by four young SS. For the journey they were given back their suitcases, the same ones they had labeled the day of their arrival on January 27, 1943. The suitcases were almost empty, but they were definitely theirs. Isn't this impressive?

The camp at Ravensbrück was not far from the train station. Standing under tall pines with its surrounding wall painted green, there was nothing terrifying about it. Not for those of us coming from Birkenau, at any rate. When we saw prisoners with gray hair and tired faces, when we saw the bathrooms and the water—a dozen faucets—in each barracks, we thought this would be tolerable. After Birkenau.

Yet we lived in fear. The streets of the camp were constantly being blocked by police sweeps. Women found on the scene were caught in a net. Whole blocks were emptied for transport. To leave in a transport meant you were sent to work in a factory. You did not know where you were going or what would happen. The eight women from Raisko used American Indian methods to conceal themselves and avoid being caught. But six were caught: Marie-Jeanne Pennec, who was sent to a factory in Czechoslovakia, and Lulu, Cécile, Carmen, Gilberte, and Poupette, who went to Beendorf, a salt mine that housed a munitions factory.

On August 4, 1944, our friends who had been in quarantine with us arrived at Ravensbrück (all except two, Marie-Jeanne Bauer and Marcelle Mourot, who had been kept in the Birkenau *revier*;[2] the sick were not moved). The quarantine had lasted ten months. In June 1944, doubtless following the Normandy landing, the quarantine had been lifted and the women were sent back to work, mending clothes left behind by Jews entering the showers.

Those thirty-five women who arrived on August 4, 1944, were classified "NN" (*Nacht und Nebel*—"Night and Fog"), which meant they would not be sent to work outside the camp or on another transport. This meant, too, that they had no right to send letters or receive parcels. This didn't much matter, however, because communication with France had been cut since June 1944. Yet not all the women were "NN," as if there was not room enough in the "NN"

---

2. Abbreviation for *Krankenrevier*, quarters for the sick in a military precinct. We do not translate this word, which the French pronounced as *revir*, because it was neither a hospital, an ambulance, nor an infirmary. It was a filthy place where the sick lay rotting on three floors.

block for the women at the bottom of the list. The SS administration operated with a logic that often escaped us.

Then, on August 16, 1944, the Raisko women arrived. There were seven and they were not "NN." At that time, fifty-two of us were alive. None of us died at Ravensbrück.

On March 2, 1945, all the "NN" and several others who had joined their ranks so as not to be separated from the group—to be separated from the group was a constant fear—thirty-three in all, left Ravensbrück. The sick stayed behind, six of them, plus three of those in the revier and two of the eight who'd come from Raisko in January. They were working at Siemens (in workshops adjoining the camp, making radio coils), where they had signed on so as not to risk being sent on another transport.

Leaving Ravensbrück on March 2, 1945, the thirty-three arrived at Mauthausen on March 5, after a very strenuous journey. From Mauthausen, they were sent to clear the tracks at the switchpoint station, at Amstetten, some distance from the camp. They were transported there during the night. This station was bombed daily by the American Air Force. On March 21, 1945, three of these women (Charlotte Decock, Olga Melin, Yvonne Noutari), who had jumped for joy at the planes' approach, were killed in a bombing attack.

When the evacuation of the camps began, the survivors of the convoy were scattered. Thirty were liberated at Mauthausen on April 22, 1945, and taken to Switzerland in vans of the International Red Cross. From Saint Gall they traveled to Paris by train and arrived there on April 30, 1945.

Eight of the women who had remained behind left Ravensbrück (some on April 23, 1945, the others on April 25) and were brought to Sweden by the Swedish Red Cross. The five from Beendorf, also taken in hand by the Red Cross, rejoined them in May. All those in Sweden were repatriated by air in the last week of June 1945.

One woman who was critically ill could not be evacuated without an ambulance. The Red Cross was going to return with the necessary equipment but could not because the route north was cut on April 27, 1945, when the two fronts met. Marie-Claude Vaillant-Couturier and Heidi Hautval stayed behind with her. All three were liberated by the Soviet army on April 30, 1945, and returned to Paris on June 25.

Hélène Solomon was liberated by the American army and managed to get back via Lille on May 15, 1945. Marie-Jeanne Pennec returned around the same date from Czechoslovakia. Marie-Jeanne Bauer, who had stayed at Auschwitz, was the last to arrive in Paris, on July 15, 1945.

Of the two hundred and thirty who sang in the train cars as we left Compiègne on January 24, 1943, forty-nine returned, after a deportation lasting twenty-seven months. For all of us, this is still a miracle we cannot fathom.

The Women

JEANNE ALEXANDRE, NÉE BORDERIE ("MUGUETTE")

Born on March 27, 1912, at Chambon-par-Anglars-de-Salers, Cantal, where her parents had a little farm. When her father died at the front in the First World War, her mother had no resources and was forced to leave their land. She went to work in a factory near Paris; Jeanne and her sister were sent as boarders to a convent school in Senlis.

At the age of fourteen, Jeanne became an apprentice at Christofle's in Saint-Denis, where she worked steadily until 1939. There she became quality controller in silverware and met her husband, Maurice, a precision-tool maker and fitter.

In 1942 Maurice Alexandre, called "Robert," became the *Francs-Tireurs et Partisans* [FTP] technician responsible for the Ile-de-France region. He prepared derailment boxes for the railroads, invented an explosive suitcase, manufactured bomb cases, etc. Jeanne transported weapons and dynamite and arranged contacts between him and the political and military leaders responsible for Ile-de-France. They entrusted their three-and-a-half-year-old son to Jeanne's sister.

On December 15, 1942, Maurice and Jeanne Alexandre arrived, by different routes, at the Porte des Lilas entrance into Paris, where they had an appointment at eleven in the morning to meet Suzanne Lasne, who was to introduce them to a comrade from the MOI (the immigrant labor organization that included foreigners: many Spaniards, veterans, the Manouchian group,* among others). They waited a few minutes. Suzanne Lasne did not show up. They were about to leave when they were surrounded by a large police force. Suzanne

---

*A group of Jewish immigrants who were part of the anti-Nazi resistance. (Trans.)

Lasne had been arrested the evening before. On a piece of paper in her pocket, the names of her next contacts were written. . . .

Jeanne and Maurice Alexandre joined Suzanne Lasne at police headquarters. They remained there until December 24, 1942, and were interrogated continuously. Jeanne was in one room, Maurice in the next. Policemen tortured Maurice for hours, several times a day, while others said to Jeanne: "You hear him? That's your husband. You'd better talk if you want them to stop." Neither of them said a word. No one in their group said anything. And for nine days at police headquarters, Maurice Alexandre, with shackles on his wrists and ankles, was attached to the wall by a chain around his waist.

On December 24, 1942, they were transported to Fresnes, and from there Jeanne was taken on January 23, 1943, to Compiègne where she joined the convoy leaving the next morning.

Auschwitz # 31779

Jeanne Alexandre did not last long. She died of dysentery, in the revier at the end of February 1943. Killed in four weeks, she was thirty-one years old.

Maurice Alexandre remained chained in a cell in Fresnes, in solitary confinement, until his departure for Struthof on July 9, 1943 (one hundred seventy-two men left that day, seven survived). Three months later, he was sent to Dachau. He returned—disabled—in July 1945. At the end of 1945, he learned of his wife's death from the women in the convoy who had returned.

Marie ALIZON ("Mariette")
and her sister, Simone ("Poupette")

Both women were born in Rennes: Marie on May 9, 1921, Simone on February 24, 1925.

There was a small hotel near the Rennes station with a dozen rooms for travelers. The young girl at the reception desk was Mariette, the daughter of the house. After years of work and savings, the parents, both from poor peasant families, had managed to acquire this business. They were comfortably well-off, but still frugal and cautious. If only they had known what was going to happen. Mariette helped them at the hotel after leaving the religious school where she completed her elementary education. In 1942 she was twenty-one and engaged to be married. Her fiancé was in the Resistance, in the Johnny network of the Free French forces that depended for information on clandestine runs to London, where they met with General de Gaulle. When the members of his resistance network had business in Rennes or needed a hiding place, he sent them to Mariette, who put them up at the hotel.

One group of the Johnny network was caught in March 1942. Mariette was arrested on March 13, 1942, by *feldgendarmes*,* who handed her over to the Gestapo. She was imprisoned in the Tower in Rennes.

Three days later, Poupette was also arrested as she was leaving the house to go to school (she was studying at the religious school where her sister had been a student). Poupette was seventeen. She was slender and still looked like a child. She was a courier for the Johnny network.

The two sisters were taken separately to the Santé prison in Paris. Each was held in solitary confinement. After several days they discovered, communicating through the pipes, that they were not far from each other. They were transferred to Fresnes in October 1942, still in solitary, without having seen each other. Eight months alone, inactive, bored, and hungry, they were reunited at Romainville on November 6, 1942. There they were permitted to write and receive letters (two per month). Their father wrote to them that their mother had died in July, while they were at the Santé.

Auschwitz # 31777: Mariette

Auschwitz # 31776: Poupette

Mariette died at Birkenau on June 3, 1943. Holding on as long as she could, exhausted by dysentery, with swollen glands in her groin that prevented her from walking, she reluctantly entered the revier. There she contracted an inflammation of the ear and finally gave up.

We saw her lying dead on a heap of corpses taken from the revier. A rat had eaten her ear.

During those first three months, the two sisters never left each other. Mariette watched over her little sister, who turned eighteen in Birkenau. When her mother died, Hélène Brabander joined them. They were an inseparable trio.

After Mariette and Hélène died, everyone wondered if Poupette would hang on. She was very frail and had been sickly as a child. Her friends managed to get her signed up for the Raisko unit in July 1943. She was saved.

Along with seven others chosen for no apparent reason, she was transferred from Raisko to Ravensbrück on January 7, 1944. From there she was sent, on August 7, 1944, to Beendorf—a former salt mine that housed a V-1 and V-2 factory located at various levels underground, between 400 and 600 meters deep. The work and discipline were very hard; the food was similar to what we had at the camp. On April 21, 1945, the mine was evacuated. The prisoners were piled into open freight cars, except for the one carrying Poupette, Cécile, Gilberte, Carmen, and Lulu. The other cars carried as many as two hundred

---

*Military police. (Trans.)

and forty individuals, but theirs had only a hundred and ten, plus three SS escorts. They quickly realized that to survive the journey, a firm rule would have to be established: they divided themselves evenly—fifty-five on each side— and took turns lying down. The order was strict: five women lay down at one end of the car for a hour, twenty sat stacked against one another with their legs open, like inverted commas, while the rest stood squeezed together. They rotated, taking turns in these positions. Thanks to this, they all got there alive. In the other cars, things did not go so well. The kapos, most of them criminals, wrapped the sickest prisoners in blankets and sat on them, suffocating them. All they had to do was shake out the blankets over the rails to make room.

The train proceeded slowly, continually held up by bombing raids and damaged tracks. There were long stops. Then the SS would make the prisoners get down and dig holes to bury the dead. When their task was done, they would stretch out between the tracks. Then the train would start off again. One night, taking advantage of a stop, all the Russian prisoners in one car escaped. The SS raked the train with machine gun fire, then took three hundred men and shot them on the spot.

When at last, after a journey of ten days—covering 180 kilometers—the convoy arrived at Neuengamme, the camp had just been evacuated. The last inmates had left that very morning. The women climbed back into their train and arrived two days later at Zazel, a little camp near Hamburg, guarded by feldgendarmes. These feldgendarmes came to them behind the barbed wire and said over and over:"Don't blame us, it's not our fault. We're gendarmes, not SS." The Allies were getting closer. The noise of cannons grew louder and louder. During the journey, the women had even seen the first American tanks enter the town of Stendhal.

They were exhausted. From the time they were evacuated from the mine until they arrived at Zazel, they had eaten only a piece of sugar and a packet of noodles. They had eaten the noodles uncooked. Dozens of prisoners died every day. Poupette was in a gravedigger unit, she buried corpses all day long, transporting them, digging their graves. She was twenty years old. On May 1, 1945, the SS came to transport them by truck to the Danish border. They were liberated on May 3, 1945, and taken to Sweden by the Red Cross.

Poupette was repatriated by air from Stockholm on June 28, 1945. What did she find when she arrived in Rennes? Her father had remarried, to a much younger woman who was not happy to see the girl they thought had died with her sister. The father had learned of Mariette's death from a letter Poupette had written from Raisko in July 1943.

With no mother, no sister, a strange stepmother, and a father who had never been very kind and had now become a stranger, Poupette married in September 1946. She soon saw that she had made a mistake. Her husband moved into the hotel and wanted to share the management with Monsieur Alizon. Son-in-law and father-in-law did not get along. Their disputes over money provoked others between husband and wife.

Monsieur Alizon, whose young wife had left him, died. Poupette divorced. She ran the hotel and raised her two daughters, who were born in 1947 and 1950. When asked how she readapted to life, she answered: "All the women who came out of the camps proved their determination. They still needed luck. You can't say that other people were very understanding. I don't think I was a special case, yet I thought I was treated like someone abnormal, sick. No member of the family took the deportation seriously since I had come out of it alive. We haven't been spared the thousand difficulties of daily life; they were just added to past sufferings." She told me: "Yet I have no regrets. You see, in my world, limited to the hotel, I would never have met women like you." She added: "When I was there, I used to think: 'If I get back, I'll read all the books Charlotte talked to me about.' And I have."

Simone Alizon was named sublieutenant in the French Fighting Corps [FFC]. She received the Legion of Honor in March 1966.

Maria ALONSO ("Josée")

Born on August 20, 1910, at Santa-Fé de Mondujar, she was four years old when her parents, who were agricultural laborers, left Spain to come to Paris.

Maria Alonso attended the elementary school in Rue Tiquetonne, in the eleventh arrondissement; then she took courses with the National Assistance Board and finished her nursing degree.

During the occupation she worked as a nurse at the Tenon Hospital. She secretly nursed combatants who were living underground and could not see a doctor or walk into a hospital for help. She assisted a woman doctor at Saint-Louis Hospital performing minor surgery. Through one of her patients, she was put in contact with the group of post office employees that included Marie-Thérèse Fleury, and she became "Josée."

The postal workers needed a mimeograph machine, and Josée's brother had one. Josée asked him for it. He took it to his sister at 25 Rue Orfila, where Gabriel Laumain and Charles Bévillard came to pick it up. Bévillard was arrested, the mimeograph was seized. Where did he get this machine? After hours of torture, he gave the names and addresses of Josée and Laumain. Other members of the group were subsequently arrested at the beginning of October 1941.

Josée was taken to police headquarters. The examining magistrate told her it was Laumain who had given their names, but that night an agent told her in confidence that they had found the mimeograph at Laumain's place. . . . When they interrogated him, Laumain took everything on himself, hoping to protect his comrades. Josée was released after twenty-four hours.

Several days later Laumain, who was at the Santé, slipped a note into his laundry bag: "Alonso will be called as a witness at the trial." Laumain's wife understood that she should warn Josée. She quickly transmitted the message. To dodge or run away was not in Josée's nature. When the Gestapo knocked, she was at home.

Coming home from school one day in November 1941, her eldest son (Josée had married in 1929 and divorced in 1936) found a note on the table: "Two gentlemen came looking for me. Go to Tonton's. Mama." Josée's brother took in his sister's two sons.

The group of postal workers was tried by a German tribunal on June 18, 1942. Gabriel Laumain, regional treasurer of the Paris PTT [the postal service], and Charles Bévillard were condemned to death and executed on June 29, 1942; Jean Escaré of Perpignan and Louis Sabini, condemned to the hardships of prison, died in the deportation; René Pape, René Vialaneix, and Antoinette Weibel were deported and returned. Josée Alonso, like Marie-Thérèse Fleury, was acquitted. From the courtroom, she was, nonetheless, taken back to prison and transferred, on August 1, 1942, to the Romainville fort. At Romainville, Josée was named head of the camp. She was responsible for transmitting instructions, distributing parcels and letters. She had such authority, such dignity that the sergeant who accompanied her when she made her rounds in the fortress seemed to be under her orders.

Auschwitz # 31778

At Birkenau, Josée could not stand it when the kapos—prisoners like us— beat her. At the first slap, she punched back. The kapo nearly knocked her out. One day, very near the beginning, when we were still exempt from outside work, she wanted to fill her pail with water from the only faucet in the camp. A polizei armed with a cudgel was guarding the faucet. She let only Germans through. Josée tried to pass. The polizei beat her black and blue and doused her. Josée returned to the block shivering. She died of double pneumonia in the revier on the fourteenth or fifteenth of February 1943.

Her brother and sister learned of her death from Henriette Mauvais, when we returned.

Named sergeant in the RIF [French Internal Resistance], Maria Alonso was considered a political deportee, as if she had not been part of the Resistance and had been deported by chance or circumstance.

At the Tenon Hospital, a plaque reads: "Maria Alonso, nurse 3rd class, died for France."

"Political Deportee"/"Resistance Deportee"

When they returned from the camps, the survivors passed through selection centers where they were given, according to their statements, deportation cards that were supposed to be temporary. Later, when verifications had been made, all deportees—provided they had not been arrested for a misdemeanor—were issued a blue card identifying them as political deportees. Deportee associations then felt it was important to distinguish between those deported because they belonged to a resistance network and those who were Jewish or had been caught haphazardly in a roundup. For those belonging to recognized resistance networks and who had fought against the occupiers, a card identifying them as "resistance deportees" was created (a pink card). Deportees established their right to this resistance card with a certificate of membership in a network and by the testimony of their resistance commanders. A number of deportees who otherwise deserved it were not given the title of "resistance deportees." Some will ask, "What difference does it make?" A considerable one, because political deportees were lumped together with civilian victims, meaning that their disability pension—and who returned from the camps unscathed?—was based on the income of civil pensions, which are lower than military pensions by around 60 percent.

This injustice was redressed in 1970: political deportees and resistance deportees now receive the same pension.

Hélène ANTOINE, née Demangeat

Born in Thaon in the Vosges on July 24, 1898, she left her native region after completing her primary education and went to work in a textile factory in Troyes. René Antoine, a mechanic from Bordeaux, worked in this factory as well. They married and soon left to settle in the area around Bordeaux. During the occupation, Hélène and René Antoine were in the FTP. They dug a hole in their garden for hiding weapons and they sheltered resisters. They were arrested at their home in August 1942 by the French police.

Hélène and her son Michel, age ten, were imprisoned in the Boudet barracks. A few days later, the police moved the child to Haut-L'Evêque, in Alouette, Pessac, a sanatorium where children who were not sick occupied one wing. When he discovered where the boy was, René Antoine's brother went to find him and, with the cooperation of the director, withdrew him. Rumor had it that these children were to be deported. Little Michel, hidden in his uncle's truck, was driven to some friends in the Pyrénées.

René Antoine was executed at Souge on September 21, 1942. Hélène was transferred from Bordeaux to Romainville on October 14, 1942.

"Died at Auschwitz between February and June 1943," according to the Veterans Ministry. No eyewitness report. All the women in her small group died, too. The uncle received a notice in French from the Mayor's office: "Hélène Antoine died of a boil," without further details.

Today [1965], Michel Antoine is married and the father of five children. He is a worker. He did not arrange in time for his parents to be confirmed in the RIF. He does not have the card that was sent to the rightful claimants, and can no longer obtain one. Consequently, he has not received reparations from the Germans. The ministry has pronounced the case "closed."

Marie-Jeanne BAUER, née Gantou

Born on July 14, 1913, in Saint-Affrique, to a family of four children. The parents, modest peasants, held a small piece of land that became inadequate as the family grew larger. So they started a small business as well.

Marie-Jeanne went to school in Saint-Affrique, completing middle school; then she studied to be a nurse and, after obtaining her State degree, worked in Paris hospitals. In 1937, she married Jean-Claude Bauer, a doctor who had an office in Saint-Ouen.

They were both communists and were in the Resistance from the beginning of the occupation. In 1942, they belonged to the National Front: they served as letter drops, transported leaflets, and arranged safehouses for guerilla fighters, whom they provided with food and money.

Dr. Bauer was arrested on March 1, 1942, in Paris. On March 6, Marie-Jeanne was taken to police headquarters. It did her no good to deny anything or to claim alibis (she hadn't stopped living a normal life or working at her hospital): there was a dossier verifying her affiliation with the CGTU [Confédération Générale du Travail Unifiée].* After a few days at police headquarters, she was sent to the station, and from there to the Santé on April 30, 1942 (to be put in isolation in the German section, which meant no letters, no parcels, no walks). She left her cell only twice: once to be interrogated by the Gestapo in Rue des Saussaies and the second time, on May 23, 1942, to say good-bye to her husband, imprisoned in another wing, just before he was executed at Mont-Valérien.

On August 24, 1942, she was transferred to the fort at Romainville, which she left on January 22, 1943, for Compiègne and Auschwitz.

---

*The umbrella organization for affiliated unions. (Trans.)

Auschwitz # 31651

On February 24, 1943, she was assigned to the revier as a nurse. Attached to the block of patients with contagious diseases, she witnessed the death of a number of women from the convoy. She had a lengthy bout of typhus, alternating between delirium and lucidity. Whenever she regained consciousness, she had a different bedmate. One day, Marie-Jeanne found she was the only person alive amidst four corpses.

Recovered from typhus, she went to work making cellophane tape. This was a convalescence unit. They braided strips of cellophane to make into tape for reinforcing the army stretchers. The work itself was not particularly tiring—seated on stools, the women were sheltered; but they had to turn out 1,600 kilometers to fill their quota, and to the women recovering from typhus (several weeks of fever, a weight loss of more than twenty-five kilos), it seemed three times longer.

Her convalescence ended. Marie-Jeanne returned to work in the gardening units. On August 3, 1943, she benefited with the others from the quarantine measure. But soon after, at the beginning of October, she was sent back to the revier with double conjunctivitis, keratitis, and abscesses. These were the worst days: no contact with friends, no one to talk to. Froura, a Polish doctor, cared for her and worked a miracle. Cured, Marie-Jeanne could return to the quarantine block. She soon reentered the revier with another case of conjunctivitis. This is why she did not leave for Ravensbrück with the others on August 2, 1944, and saw the Soviet army arrive at Auschwitz.

Most of the inmates had been evacuated to other camps, with the sick simply abandoned on the spot. On January 27, 1945, the Russian advance guard came, stayed a few hours, and left again in pursuit of the German army. Other regiments came after them and assumed the direction and organization of the camp. The spectacle they encountered has been described: walking skeletons, talking corpses, etc. They gathered the survivors at the men's camp and left Birkenau. Marie-Jeanne slept on the floor of a Russian truck strewn with straw. Those women who were strong enough to stand looked after the others, made a fire, helped the Soviet doctors and nurses distribute rations and medicine. They took over the kitchen. Soldiers came there to warm their dinner pails. One evening a soldier (a Pole with the Soviet army) arrived completely drunk. He had just learned that his family was dead, his house destroyed. In despair, he got drunk. He entered the room where Marie-Jeanne was sitting among the others, looked at her, and said, "Deutsch," and, pulling out his enormous revolver, he aimed at her and fired. Marie-Jeanne had no time to be frightened. They carried her out and took the soldier away. She got better: the bullet had passed through the crook of the aorta and exited under the shoulder blade, without touching either the heart or the lung. Marie-Jeanne testified in the soldier's defense; he was not executed. She knew that people can go mad with sorrow.

Time dragged by at Auschwitz waiting for the war to end, waiting to be repatriated. The prisoners wanted their freedom. They were granted permission to leave, on condition they return before nightfall. One day Marie-Jeanne and two of her friends took advantage of a Polish Red Cross van and went to visit Cracow. The Russians let them take blankets from the "Canada" [the storehouse of booty taken from prisoners upon arrival—see more below] to sell at the market and make some money. Someone also gave them zlotys.

They entered the first store where they saw something for sale—apples— and asked for a large bunch. When they showed their zlotys, the shopkeeper took back all the apples and wouldn't hand over even one unless the customers had exact change (she weighed and reweighed them). Frustrated, they bought and shared one apple three ways. Then they sold their blankets at the market to make some money—quite a lot, they thought. They bought lard, bread, eggs, and a chicken, which they planned to take back to the camp for the others. They sat down on the edge of the sidewalk and gradually ate all the provisions. Soon they had no money, no food, and no way back to Auschwitz. They had one resource left: the public soup kitchen. Several days passed. At last they found a ride in a car, full of Russian officers, which dropped them several kilometers from Auschwitz. They still had to cross a guarded bridge over the Vistula river, and the soldiers, thinking they were spies, refused to let them pass. They took them to the town mayor's quarters, a peasant house where the cow shared the only room while pigs grunted under the bed. They explained what had happened, everything was cleared up, and they got back to the camp on foot.

At last, the repatriation was arranged. On the road to Odessa by truck and train.

Marie-Jeanne arrived at Gare du Nord on July 15, 1945. No one was waiting for her. Her building had been bombed, her apartment looted. She learned that her brother had been executed in Saint-Affrique on August 13, 1944. She was dazed, ill, with no incentive or stamina; what should she do? A medical exam revealed that she still tested positive for typhus, and the doctors wouldn't believe that she'd had it two years ago. She lost the sight in her right eye, and her left eye was badly damaged.

She had difficulty readapting. She had to fight against the feeling that all these sacrifices had been useless, and when she looked around and saw the opportunists and eleventh-hour partisans, she came close to despair. To help herself forget, she took long trips.

Named adjutant in the RIF.

The "Canada"

The expression *Canada* in German means something like *Peru* in French: "riches, gold." "Canada" was what they called the sorting house for booty, the piles of baggage left on the platform by Jews gassed upon arrival. Inmates—the *Effecktskommando*—sorted, classified, inventoried, and piled up clothes, furs, jewelry, lingerie, medicine, glasses, toys, cosmetics, blankets, eiderdowns, prostheses, dollars, gold coins, diamonds, pieces of fabric—everything people had brought with them, whatever was most precious when they were allowed "thirty kilos of baggage" or all their goods when they were told: "You are being settled in a new town." The prisoners handled these fabulous riches. Theft was tempting, but the risk was great since there was only one punishment, whatever the magnitude of the crime, and that was death. Yet the kapos managed to wangle something for themselves, and whatever they took out of the "Canada" was precious currency.

Gabrielle BERGIN, née Richoux

Born on December 19, 1894, in Bourges, father unknown. Her mother was a domestic. As soon as she left school, she too entered domestic service. At twenty, she married a man from Vierzon and moved to that town.

Gabrielle Bergin kept a café on the grounds of the Bois d'Yevre, near the Cher, in the quarter of Vierzon within the occupied zone. The river served as the demarcation line. From the beginning of the occupation, she helped escaped prisoners, Jews, and resisters hunted by the Gestapo cross to the unoccupied zone.

This was an era when the envious and the ne'er-do-wells, debtors and jealous women, those who coveted an inheritance and those too cowardly to settle their own accounts took advantage of a formidable power. Gabrielle Bergin was denounced by her husband's mistress.

She was arrested by the Gestapo of Vierzon on September 15, 1942, and arrived at Romainville at the end of October 1942.

Auschwitz # 31 . . .

She died at Birkenau on March 23, 1943.

Eugenia, called "Jeanne," BESKINE

Born on March 7, 1889.

We nicknamed her "Jeanne-the-Russian" because she was Russian and we didn't know her last name.

She arrived at Romainville on January 15, 1943. Where had she come from? Why had she been arrested?

Auschwitz # 31837

She was caught in "the race" on February 10, 1943, and died several days later in Block 25.

"The Race"

After the morning roll call, which had lasted as it always did from four to eight hours, the SS made all the inmates leave in columns, a thousand women already numb from standing still. It was minus eighteen degrees centigrade. Five by five abreast in a field on the other side of the road facing the entrance to the camp, the women remained standing, without food or drink, until the end of the day. The SS, posted behind machine guns, were guarding the edges of the field. Heoss, the commandant, came on horseback to review the square formations, to check their alignment; as soon as he came in sight, all the SS shouted garbled orders. Women were falling in the snow and dying. The others, tapping their feet, rubbing each other's backs, beating their arms so as not to freeze, watched the trucks pass loaded with the living and the dead on their way from Block 25 to the crematorium.

Around five o'clock in the evening, the whistle blew. The order to return. The columns reformed, five abreast. "When you get to the gate, run." The order was passed back through the ranks. Yes, we had to run. On either side of the camp's main street, in a tight hedge, stood all the SS, male and female, all the kapos, the polizei, everyone with any rank. Armed with sticks, lashes, canes, and belts, they beat the women as they went by. We had to run to the other end of the camp. Swollen from the cold, chattering with fatigue, we had to run the gamut of blows. Those who could not run fast enough, who tripped or fell, were pulled out of the line, grabbed by the neck with a fist gripping a cane, and tossed aside. When the race was finished and all the inmates were back in the blockhouses, the women who had been pulled aside were taken to Block 25. Fourteen of us were taken that day. In Block 25, you got almost nothing to eat or drink. People died there after a few days. Those not dead when the *Sonderkommando* (prisoners who worked in the crematorium) came to empty Block 25 left with the corpses for the gas chamber.

"The race"—this is what we called it—took place on February 10, 1943, exactly two weeks after our arrival at Birkenau. Rumor had it we were being made to pay for Stalingrad.

Antoinette BESSEYRE, née Tressard

She was born on July 7, 1919, in Quimperlé, in Brittany, but she was a Parisian who had some secondary education and became a secretary. Shortly before the war, she left her parents to marry Mary Besseyre, a militant communist. She too was a militant. They were arrested on May 13, 1942, in Paris in the fifteenth arrondissement, where they were living under false identities.

Mary Besseyre was tried by a German court on September 30, 1942, sentenced to death, and executed at the shooting range at Issy-les-Moulineaux on October 21, 1942.

Antoinette was in the cells from May until October 27, 1942, and then sent to Romainville until the departure.

Auschwitz # 31763

Antoinette followed the itinerary of the largest group of survivors: Birkenau, quarantine, the sewing workshop, Ravensbrück, Mauthausen. She returned to Paris at the end of April 1945.

Her father, arrested in March of 1940 and interned in various camps in France (Ile de Ré, Riom), was deported to Buchenwald and returned shortly after she did.

She remarried but had no children because she did not feel she had the strength for motherhood: she was seriously ill. For seventeen years, she suffered anniversary reactions of typhus symptoms. Every year in April, she would suddenly come down with a high fever and general aches and pains without any apparent organic cause. Blood tests were all negative. She summoned her characteristic energy and did not coddle herself.

She was named sergeant-major in the RIF.

Antoinette BIBAULT, née Méterreau

Born on July 18, 1893, at Mayet, in Sarthe, where her parents were farmers. She learned needlework and married a carpenter-cabinetmaker established in Tours. They lived at 33 Rue Bernard-Palissy, in the same block of buildings as Franciska Goutayer [see this name].

Her neighbors accused Madame Bibault of having been responsible for the arrest of around thirty members of the Resistance during the summer of 1942, including her brother. The prefect of the region, Tracou, had promised a reward of 50,000 francs to informers. Was it to avoid paying her that the Gestapo arrested Madame Bibault on August 8 or 10, 1942? Indeed, it was only after imprisonment in Tours until November 7, 1942, that she found herself in

Romainville with one of her victims, Franciska Goutayer, who formally accused her.

Auschwitz # 31771

Antoinette Bibault died in the first ten days, February 5 or 6, 1943. She was found dead on her tier before roll call.

Her husband, deported at the same time as she was, died at Mauthausen. Her brother died in 1945 at Buchenwald.

Félicienne BIERGE, née Pintos

Born on June 9, 1914, in Spain, to a family of eight children. Félicienne was six years old when her parents settled in Bordeaux. She left school at thirteen and worked in a factory until her marriage.

In 1942, Félicienne and her husband, who was a layout carpenter working in aviation, had a secret printing press in their home and distributed their publications in various places. Félicienne was arrested at home on July 30, 1942, by Commissioner Poinsot of Bordeaux.[3] Her son, aged four, was crying as the police questioned her. They took mother and child. That day they placed the boy with a neighbor, and his paternal grandmother came to fetch him.

Raymond Bierge, Félicienne's husband, was arrested the same day at the factory where he was working. He was executed by firing squad in Souge on September 21, 1942. From the Boudet barracks in Bordeaux, Félicienne was transferred to Romainville on October 14, 1942.

Auschwitz # 31734

She had typhus in April 1943 and left the revier only when the group was quarantined on August 3, 1943. Ravensbrück from August 4, 1944, to March 2, 1945; Mauthausen from March 5, 1945, until the Liberation, April 22, 1945.

---

3. Pierre Poinsot, thirty-eight years old, commissioner of General Information in 1940; in Bordeaux administration until 1943, then commissioner of Jewish affairs and involved in the Administration of Political Affairs [SAP] under direct orders from the Gestapo; finally posted to Vichy. In August 1944, he fled with Darnand's militia, but was arrested on April 24, 1945, in Switzerland, carrying 500,000 francs. His wife was arrested two days later at the Dijon station; she was carrying a million francs.

At his trial, which began on June 15, 1945, at Moulins, Poinsot, sleeves rolled up, blackjack in hand, said: "When I meet a communist, I see red." Nine hundred and forty patriots had been arrested in Bordeaux by him or under his orders, and seven hundred shot. "I believed in collaboration, and for that reason I put my whole heart into the work. I have no crime on my conscience," he told the judges. Sentenced to death and to national degradation, he was executed at Riom on July 16, 1945, along with his associates, the policemen Evrard and Célérier.

On her return, Félicienne studied hairdressing at the reeducation center. She remarried, to the driver of a gasoline truck. She had a daughter in 1950. She does not work outside the home. What she doesn't do today she puts off until tomorrow. She seems to have no money worries, which helps a lot. But like all the others, she often thinks of Birkenau, and at night she is in the camp again with her comrades and the SS.

Rosette BLANC

Born on September 24, 1919, in Elru, Pyrénées-Orientales, the youngest of eight children. Her parents owned a small farm.

Rosette left elementary school after completing her basic education and went to work on a farm in the vicinity. At the age of eighteen, she left Rousillon to come to Paris. She was a maid at the home of a police inspector. It was a hard job, and she left after four months. She wanted to do something else. With the help of an uncle she took time off from work and learned stenography at the Pigier school. Two of her brothers belonged to the Young Communists. She joined as well. During the Spanish Civil War she was back in the Pyrénées-Orientales, where she helped the Spanish republicans. In 1937 she founded the Perpignan branch of the Union of French Girls.

She became a militant and in 1940 joined the clandestine sector of the Communist Party. She lived in Paris under the name of Amélie Garrigue. There she was arrested at the beginning of March 1942, caught in a dragnet by the special brigades, which apprehended almost the entire leadership of the University chapter of the National Front (Politzer, Jacques Solomon, etc.), for whom Rosette was a liaison agent.

She spent several days in the General Intelligence offices at police headquarters. When the interrogators were done, she was sent to the cells until March 23, 1942, from there to the Santé until August 24, 1942, and from there to Romainville until the departure.

Auschwitz # 31652

She died of typhus in April 1943. One of her brothers, a militant like her, died in the deportation.

There is a plaque at 18 Rue Chabrière in Paris, in the fifteenth arrondissement, where she was arrested.

Claudine BLATEAU, née Pinet

Born on March 23, 1911, in Niort, Deux-Sèvres, she was an orphan who never knew her parents. She was raised in Deux-Sèvres, in Scondigny, where she went to elementary school. In 1928, she married Marcel Blateau, sector chief of the rural Electrical Union. Two children were born, in 1929 and 1932. In 1942, Claudine and her husband were members of the FTP (since May 1941, in the Saint-Just company under orders from Captain Poilane, in charge of liaisons and broadcasts). They guaranteed contacts between different points in Charente, transported weapons for the Marianne and France groups, lodged combatants, and hid resisters hunted by the Gestapo.

They were both arrested on August 12, 1942, at their home in Matha by the police commissioner of Bordeaux, after being denounced by Vincent [see *Marguerite Valina*]. The police searched the premises, rummaged around, and found the weapons that Marcel Blateau had hidden in a transformer.

Claudine was imprisoned in the Boudet barracks in Bordeaux until October 14, 1942, and transferred from there to Romainville.

The paternal grandmother took in the two children.

Auschwitz # 31737

She completed the entire journey: Birkenau, quarantine, Ravensbrück, Mauthausen, where she was liberated on April 22, 1945.

Marcel Blateau was executed in Bordeaux on September 21, 1942. He was forty-two years old.

Claudine remarried in January 1946. In precarious health, very easily tired, she readapted thanks to her second husband, who spared her any worry or work.

Named soldier second-class in the RIF.

Yvonne BLECH, née Vauder

Born January 25, 1907, in Brest, to a solidly middle-class family with local roots.

At the age of eighteen, she was sent to Paris to finish her secondary education, and after receiving her baccalaureate she decided to stay. Employed at Gallimard for several years, she got to know the young writers who published with that house: Pierre Unik, Drieu La Rochelle, Saint-Exupéry.

In 1934 she was with the Association of Revolutionary Writers and Artists [AEAR], which planned to set up workers' libraries in the factories. Yvonne took an active part in these libraries. At this period she broke with her father, an extreme right-wing city council official in Brest.

She left Gallimard in 1937 to become editorial secretary of *Visages du Monde*, where Roger Pillement was editor-in-chief, and married the writer René Blech, a member of the Communist Party. In 1938 she was editor of *Regards*, an illustrated weekly, and joined the Communist Party.

Regards was outlawed in 1939. Yvonne Blech worked at home as a copy editor for Gallimard, reading the proofs for the *Pléiade* volumes. The Paul Valéry volume was her last assignment.

In 1942 René Blech, who had become part of the clandestine organization at the beginning of the war, was living elsewhere under an assumed name. His wife led what seemed to be an ordinary life, with nothing to hide. This way she could supply him with provisions and run errands for him.

On March 3, 1942, the special brigades allowed René Blech to escape. They went to his known residence, discovered Yvonne, searched the apartment, but found no trace of René Blech, no incriminating papers. Yvonne claimed that she was separated from her husband, that she was filing for divorce and didn't know where he was. They were about to leave when they recognized her umbrella. For her meetings with her husband, Yvonne had taken a thousand precautions: she had used different make-up, another hairdo, other clothes. But she had not thought to change her umbrella.

From the General Intelligence offices, she was sent to the cells on March 10, and to the Santé on March 23, where she was held in isolation for five months. She was transferred to Romainville on August 24, 1942.

Auschwitz # 31 . . .

She died on March 11, 1943.

She had contracted dysentery during the journey. She held out as long as she could, with her back straight, her chin up. Then she said: "I know we'll win. But the war will last another two years, and I won't last two months." She went into the revier. She gave up fighting on her feet. Before she died, she said to Madeleine Dechavassine, her neighbor in the revier: "If you return, tell my husband I curse him." René Blech died without being told.

She knew that to go into hiding René Blech had gone to live with his mistress. Out of pride, and because the demands of the struggle prevailed over personal feelings, Yvonne had remained in her husband's resistance group.

Hélène BOLLEAU and her mother, Emma BOLLEAU, née Laumondais

Hélène Bolleau was born on April 6, 1924, in Royan, where her parents settled in 1936, when her father was named head of the Pontaillac post office.

Before the war, Roger Bolleau had been a militant with the Communist Party. In 1940, though at this time he had no contact with the party, he knew they should prepare to fight the occupiers. He stockpiled weapons that the French had abandoned in their flight. Aided only by his wife, he continued to publish *La Voix des Charentes*, printed on the mimeograph, and distributed many issues under the counter. Then the Resistance took shape, the FTP was formed. The Bolleaus collected money for prisoners and their families, and created the Germain group, the first FTP group in Charente-Maritime.

Roger Bolleau, called "Germain," was arrested on March 7, 1942, on his way back from Saintes, where he had met with Octave Rabaté at the home of the Lemassons. At the same time, the police arrested his daughter, Hélène, not yet eighteen years old, who acted as secretary and typed the stencils (she had completed elementary school and a commercial certificate).

Hélène was released six days later. She did not go home. She belonged to the National Front youth group. From then on she lived clandestinely, assuming responsibility for the Germain group's contacts with other groups. But she was not on firm ground in Charente. She went to Deux-Sèvres and the Vendée. Her tasks included distributing tracts, taking up collections to help the militants, and running the printing operation (*La Voix des Charentes* and *Jeunesse libre de Charente-Inférieure*). She was then seen in Angers, where she participated in the campaign to block delivery of grain to the Germans, and her leaders decided to transfer her to Paris. Before setting off, she went to Royan to collect clothes and ration coupons. She was arrested there on August 7, 1942, by a patrol of German and French police. Immediately imprisoned in La Rochelle, she notified her mother, who since her husband's arrest had tried to appear innocent of any suspect activity.

Emma Bolleau was arrested on September 15, 1942, carrying a parcel to her daughter in prison. During her examination, a prisoner said that he hadn't dealt with the daughter but with the mother.

Emma Bolleau joined her daughter at Lafond prison (La Rochelle), and both were transferred to the prison in Angoulême on October 30, then to Romainville on November 18, 1942.

Auschwitz # 31806

Emma Bolleau held on fifty-two days; that was a long time at Birkenau. She was only forty-two years old. If no mother returned, it was because the mothers suffered doubly: for themselves and for their daughters, whom they were unable to help. They had to stand by unflinchingly while the girls were beaten; they could no longer protect them and felt they were a burden to them.

Emma Bolleau died on March 20, 1943. She had contracted dysentery and died of dehydration. "In the field I saw her drink the muddy water that seeped into the horses' tracks," said her daughter. She was so dehydrated, she couldn't eat. She became a skeleton.

Hélène Bolleau entered the revier in April 1943. After recovering from typhus, she did convalescent duty braiding cellophane tape; she was then sent back to the swamps, the bricks, the ashes from the crematorium. (The ashes, mixed with charred bones, were carried to the edge of the marshes by truck. After the mud and slime had been removed, this human bonemeal had to be spread on the bottom of the marshes with rakes to form a thick layer that created a drainage bed.)

She, too, was saved by the quarantine.

At Ravensbrück, where she arrived with her companions on August 4, 1944, she broke a leg doing soup duty. That was on January 27, 1945. The soup buckets were very heavy, the paths from the kitchen were slippery. The fracture was set in a cast only at the beginning of April. She was in the revier when the others left for Mauthausen on March 2, 1945. She stayed behind at Ravensbrück, where she was liberated on April 23, 1945, by the Red Cross, taken to Sweden, and repatriated from Stockholm by air on June 23, 1945.

She was twenty-one years old when she returned. Her father had been executed at Mont-Valérien on September 21, 1942; her grandfather had died in 1943; her apartment house had been razed in the bombing of Royan, January 5, 1945; her grandmother, wounded in the bombing, was paralyzed. Luckily, she found her fiancé again, back from Dachau. They were married at the end of 1945.

"I was very ill when I returned, and I suffered from nervous depression. I had three operations. I put all my hope in my children. I made a home, hoping to become normal again, capable of raising a family. This wasn't easy, but my determination allowed me to overcome the hardest moments. Meetings with former deportees and our struggle so that our children shouldn't spend their twenties the way we did sustained me when my morale weakened," she said in 1965.

Named soldier second-class in the RIF, she received the Legion of Honor on July 14, 1977.

Josée BONENFANT

A woman in her forties who joined the convoy at Compiègne on January 23, 1943, on the eve of departure. She came from the prison at Fresnes.

She had been arrested in mid-December 1942, in the same roundup as Jeanne Alexandre. Her husband was a resister who stored materiel for the FTP in his workshop—he was a garage mechanic—in a Paris suburb. She knew nothing about it. Others remember she had a daughter about ten years old and that her husband was deported to Oranienburg; that's all.

Auschwitz # 31848

She died at the end of February 1943. No eyewitness report.

Yvonne BONNARD

Born on August 5, 1899. We found her at Romainville, where she'd been since August 7 or 8, 1942, and nicknamed her "Grandma Yvonne" when she told us she'd married very young, already had a married daughter, and had just become a grandmother.

Auschwitz # 31 . . .

We do not know her number because we have no photograph.[4]

One evening after the roll call, she fell in the mud. Friends carried her back to the block. She died during the night. Around February 15, 1943.

We have not been able to locate her family.

Yvonne B., née T.

Born January 15, 1908, in Saint-E . . . , in Indre-et-Loire, where her parents were farmers. After elementary school, she helped on the farm and married a farmer, and the young couple settled in with Yvonne's parents.

She was denounced by a field hand who accused her of concealing weapons. The arms in question were her husband's hunting rifle. She was arrested by

---

4. The Photographs: We know the numbers of the dead from the photographs. A week after our arrival at Birkenau, on February 3, 1943, we were taken—in columns five abreast, our only way of moving from one place to another—to the men's camp at Auschwitz, about two kilometers from Birkenau. We walked through the gate that has become so famous, with its motto: *Arbeit macht frei*—"work makes you free." Five by five, we passed through for body measurement. Those women in the revier (Marguerite Coringer), already dead (Madame Bouillard), or employed in the revier (the doctors Heidi Hautval and Mai Politzer, and the dentist Danielle Casanova) were not photographed. When the Poles took possession of Auschwitz again in 1945, after the Soviets liberated it, they searched the camp and the areas attached to it looking for documents and papers. They found little to flesh out the historical record, since the SS had burned everything before evacuating. In a shallow ditch, however, they found the photographic plates of the "anthropometer." The "F" (for French) and the numbers allowed our convoy to be identified, and the Soviets gave us access to the photographs. Thanks to the cooperation of Monsieur Smolen, curator of the Auschwitz museum, we obtained newly printed photos. Thirty or so were still missing: the plates had been broken. There are spots on some because their surfaces had deteriorated in the ground.

French gendarmes on October 1, 1942, at her home, incarcerated in Tours, and later transferred to Romainville on November 7, 1942. She was pregnant. If she had made her condition known, she would not have been deported since at the time—July 1942 until January 1943—pregnant women were removed from Romainville before the departure for Auschwitz. Some were actually freed, others hospitalized at Val-de-Grâce and deported to Ravensbrück after their delivery. Yvonne B. said nothing, embarrassed and ashamed. Her husband had been a prisoner of war in Germany since 1940.[5]

Auschwitz # 31792

She must have been taken in "the race" on February 10, 1943. Through the window of Block 26, where we were sent on February 12, we could see her corpse lying naked in the snow in the courtyard of Block 25, still pregnant with the fetus.

Her family learned of her death through Hélène Fournier upon her return in May 1945.

Léona Clémence BOUILLARD, née Raveau

Born on April 26, 1885, in Eteignères, in the Ardennes, she was married in 1902. Her husband had a small contracting business. They lived at "Mon idée," some distance from Tremblois.

They were both arrested on May 19, 1942, by the Gestapo. "You were denounced for distributing tracts," said the interpreter. Tracts for the National Front.

Madame Bouillard was incarcerated in the Charleville prison, then the prison in Rethel, and finally in Nancy. She was transferred to Romainville on November 21, 1942.

A helpful little grandmother, who immediately made friends among the young women. They called her "Nana Bouillard."

Auschwitz # 31 . . .

She died in the first three days, one morning at roll call. Four of us carried her corpse back to the blockhouse.

The Veterans' Ministry noted the date as February 15, 1943, a date probably supplied by one of the survivors from memory. But such remembered dates are rarely accurate. At Birkenau, time flowed differently. Her family learned of her death only in 1945.

---

5. Out of concern for family feelings, I have decided not to give the name of this comrade.

Her husband, deported on the same train, died at Oranienburg in 1943. He was sixty-six years old.

Alice BOULET, née Paris

Born October 8, 1914, in Grury, Saône-et-Loire, where her parents were farmers. She completed elementary school and then worked on her parents' farm.

In 1932, at the age of eighteen, she married Marcel Boulet, a customs officer posted on the French-Belgian border.

In 1939, the Boulets, both members of the Communist Party, came to live in Paris, in the twentieth arrondissement. Then they were separated by the struggle. Each had his own tasks. In 1941, Alice Boulet was a liaison agent for the National Front. At this period, a liaison agent was someone who transported printed material, transmitted messages and instructions, etc. She lived alone under an assumed name in the fifteenth arrondissement, where she was arrested on June 17, 1942, by five inspectors of the special brigades, the same inspectors who arrested Madeleine Doiret a few hours later.

Alice Boulet was detained in the cells from June 20 to August 10, 1942, then transferred to Romainville until the departure.

Auschwitz # 31 . . .

She died at the beginning of March 1943. She had entered the revier because of dysentery. When it became known that a selection would take place at the revier, she left and died the following day in Block 26 after returning from work.

Her husband, Marcel Boulet, arrested on July 23, 1944, and deported in one of the last convoys, died on January 4, 1945, in Wilhemshafen.

The Boulets had no children. Alice's parents learned of her death when the survivors returned.

Sophie BRABANDER
and her daughter, Hélène

Born on July 4, 1887, in Lublin, this young girl of the Polish bourgeoisie came to Paris in 1909 to do her law degree; had she remained in Poland, she would have had to do this at a Russian university. She finished her degree and, in 1916, married her countryman François Brabander, a medical student who had left Poland for the same reason.

In 1914 François Brabander had joined the French army for the duration of the war. After the armistice, he joined the campaign to liberate Poland (the Weygand army). Once demobilized, he completed his studies, and since he would have had to pass exams again to practice medicine in Poland had he returned, he stayed in France and in 1920 obtained French citizenship.

Dr. Brabander had an office in Paris; he opened another in Lens, where he cared for Polish miners. Keeping up his contacts with Polish emigrants in France (those who came in 1926 and in 1939), he was president of the Sokols, an athletic association of Poles from France, Belgium, and Holland. In 1939 the Sokols made up the Polish regiment formed in France by General Sikorski.

After the defeat, Dr. Brabander thought of going to London to join the Polish government in exile. With his wife and two children (Hélène, born in 1923, and Romuald, his youngest), he left for Toulouse and tried to arrange passage to Spain, without success. The Brabanders returned to Paris.

All the activities of the Polish organizations ceased, but networks were created. François Brabander belonged to the Powon (Monika) network, and his wife helped him. The Monika network formed the first Polish underground forces in France.

In October 1941, Dr. Brabander was arrested by the Gestapo after a search of his residence turned up a tract. He was sentenced to two months in prison in the Cherche-Midi, then in Hauteville, near Dijon. After completing his sentence, he was released on Christmas Eve, 1941. He must have thought he could continue with his clandestine work by taking greater precautions. On September 29, 1942, the Gestapo arrested François Brabander and his wife at home and, a few hours later, their sixteen-year-old son, Romuald. They were taken to Rue des Saussaies, put in separate cells for several hours, then interned the same evening in Romainville after a brief interrogation. Father and son were quartered with the men. The following day, Sophie Brabander saw the arrival of her daughter Hélène: she had slept at a friend's house, where she had gone to dinner, and had been arrested going home the next morning.

Dr. Brabander and Romuald left Romainville in November after spending a night in the pillbox, where they put men who were to be shot the next day. But they were not shot. They were both in the camp at Compiègne when we arrived there on January 23, 1943. Seeing his wife and daughter, Brabander, the camp doctor, asked the commandant for permission to speak to them. Permission was not granted.

Father and son left in the same deportation by the same train we did. They went to Oranienburg-Sachsenhausen.

Auschwitz # 31694: Sophie Brabander

Auschwitz # 31695: Hélène Brabander

Madame Brabander was called first for the shower and the shearing. As ordered, she stripped and sat on a stool to have her hair cut by another inmate.

Hélène, standing naked, too, was waiting her turn. She sat down in her mother's place, her mother took the scissors and cut her daughter's hair herself.

Sophie Brabander was caught in "the race" on February 10, 1943. She died several days later in Block 25.

Hélène died in the revier on May 12 or 13, 1943. She had contracted typhus. Madeleine saw her on May 1, 1943, the day the chief SS doctor of the revier ordered that all patients be given baths in the same rapidly cooling water. A disinfection. Naked under a blanket, Hélène Brabander hadn't the strength to stand. She was so thin that her clavicles and hip bones protruded from her skin.

GEORGETTE BRET, née FOURCADE

Born on October 6, 1905, in Sainte-Foy-la-Grande, Gironde, where her parents worked in a grocery store and where she completed elementary school. She became a seamstress, making jackets and waistcoats.

In 1930 she married Robert Bret, a worker in the tramway workshops in Bordeaux and a militant communist.

Robert Bret was arrested on November 22, 1940. He was already a member of a clandestine organization that became the Special Organization for sabotage [OS] and had then joined the FTP.

After her husband's arrest, Georgette continued to hide and distribute propaganda material. Her husband was executed on October 24, 1941, in Souge. She did not interrupt her activities. All the same, in July 1942, when she saw comrades from her group fall into the hands of Poinsot, she left Bordeaux to go to Dax, to her sister's. Her refuge was not secret enough: Poinsot found her there and arrested her on August 28, 1942.

The Hâ fortress until October 14, 1942; Romainville until the departure.

Auschwitz # 31747

She died on May 20, 1943. She held on a long time, suffering from pain difficult to describe because shortly before her arrest she had been operated on for plantar warts. In prison, the wounds healed poorly; standing at roll call and walking to the marshes were unbearably painful. At Birkenau we had to stand about sixteen hours a day. She held on. At the end of April, when the typhus epidemic intensified, she fell ill and should have gone to the revier. Again, during the first days of the fever, she resisted. Her comrades thought she had recovered. A relapse of typhus carried her off.

Her daughter, Janine, who was nine years old in 1942 and had been taken in by an aunt, learned of her death through the survivors of the convoy upon their return.

Simone Victorine BRUGAL, née Pichon

Born on July 2, 1897, in Saint-Denis, an only daughter. Her father, originally from Luxembourg, was general representative to Holland and Belgium for the Baccarat crystal company. She spent her childhood in Amsterdam, Brussels, and finally Paris, where she went to school but did not continue her studies. She was married very young to Joseph Damgé of Luxembourg, whom she divorced after their daughter was born. At a certain period—which we haven't been able to pinpoint—she was a hairdresser on the *La Fayette*, a transatlantic liner that sailed between Le Havre and New York.

In 1922, she set up housekeeping with Captain Gougenheim, a cavalry officer and Jew from Alsace, with whom she had four sons. She left the boys with him when she separated from him in 1936; and on November 26, 1940, in Toulon, she married Raoul Brugal, thought to be a fishmonger.

She was arrested in Paris on May 15, 1942. She was leaving her mother's home, at 78 Rue d'Hauteville, and traveling by bicycle down Rue des Messageries. The Gestapo were waiting for her at the corner of the street. Why? The Gestapo had searched her mother's place without finding anything.

Simone Brugal was imprisoned in Fresnes until October 2, 1942, the day she arrived at Romainville. None of the women who shared her barracks thought she was a resister. They remembered that she had offered to pay another woman to take her turn sweeping up; they remembered her carrying on with the German soldiers who guarded the fort: when the door of the room was opened for the women to walk into the courtyard, she hurried toward the adjutant, batting her eyelashes. She wanted to make conversation. Unfortunately for her, the Germans of the fort were military, not Gestapo. They did not understand her advances.

Auschwitz # 31705

Simone Brugal died in Birkenau at the beginning of February 1943.

Captain Gougenheim (who took the name "Garnier" in the Resistance) was arrested in Limoges by the Gestapo on April 10, 1943. From prison in Limoges, he was sent to Compiègne on July 22, 1943, but was deported from Drancy (they had discovered that he was a Jew) to Auschwitz and gassed when he came out of the train car on September 1 or 2, 1943.

Marcelle BUREAU

Born April 7, 1923, an only child, in Etaules, Charente-Maritime, where her parents were oyster farmers. After completing elementary school, she worked with her parents in the oyster beds.

Beginning in 1941, Marcelle's father was part of the Germain group with Roger Bolleau. After her father's arrest, Hélène Bolleau [see this name] reorganized the group and helped to found a National Front cell. She made contact with Bureau, who said: "I'll talk to my daughter about it." And this is how Marcelle became involved in the Resistance.

She was arrested on August 6, 1942: the police had seized inadequately coded documents on a young man arrested in Royan for having stolen a mimeograph meant for a print shop. Marcelle's father and one of her friends were also taken to command headquarters in Pontaillac, but released. Confronted with Marcelle, a member of her group named her after hours of torture.

Imprisoned in La Rochelle from August 7 to the end of October 1942, then in Angoulême, Marcelle Bureau arrived at Romainville on November 18, 1942.

Auschwitz # 31 . . .

She died on April 16, 1943. She had just turned twenty years old; she succumbed to typhus after several days of violent delirium. In August 1943, Hélène Bolleau wrote in a letter to her aunt: "Please tell Raymonde from Etaules that I certainly share the pain she must feel at the loss of her daughter." Hélène's aunt conveyed the message to Marcelle's mother.

Marcelle Bureau's young fiancé was arrested when she was. He came back from the camps of Sachsenhausen and Leipzig (he was one of the survivors of the flamethrowers of Leipzig: as Russian troops advanced, the SS set the camp on fire before leaving the city. The young man survived only because he was buried under a heap of corpses).

Marcelle Bureau's mother was broken by her daughter's death. She never attended any commemorative ceremony.

ALICE CAILBAULT, née Gardelle

Born on April 1, 1906, in Paris. Her father, originally from the Charente, worked at the Renault factory in Boulogne-Billancourt. In 1917 her mother left Paris with the four children—she was afraid of Big Bertha.* Taking refuge in Javrezac, in Charente, she sent Alice to a private school; when the war ended, she set up a small home-knitting business with her daughters.

In 1926, in Paris, Alice married Louis Cailbault, a worker at Renault and also a native of the Charente region, to which the couple returned in 1936.

---

*The huge guns the Germans used to shell Paris, which had a range of up to seventy-six miles. (Trans.)

Louis Cailbault renewed the lease on a farm in Saint-Laurent-de-Cognac, following in his father's footsteps. Alice, however, did not become a farmer. She had a knitting machine and worked first for stores, then for a private clientele that became quite substantial.

Louis Cailbault was taken prisoner at Dunkirk in June 1940, and Alice stayed alone in Saint-Laurent-de-Cognac with her daughter, Andrée, born in 1926, her father, Monsieur Gardelle, an elderly maid, and a boy who helped out. Wood was scarce. During this period, she worked as a farmer.

In July 1942, her childhood friend Margot Valina asked her if she would shelter resisters, if necessary. Alice was willing.

On August 12, 1942, at five in the morning, around forty Germans came in two trucks and searched the Cailbault farm. They found neither anything there nor anyone but the residents. Some members of the FTP had in fact slept there the previous night—on the eve of a sabotage operation.

Alice and her daughter, Andrée, were arrested and taken to the command headquarters of Cognac; the daughter was released the next morning. Several days later, Vincent [see *Margot Valina*] came to see Andrée; he told her he was with her mother at command headquarters. The young girl was very worried. Hadn't her mother told Vincent, after the arrest of Margot Valina, on the previous July 28, not to send anyone else to the Cailbault farm?

Alice Cailbault was imprisoned at Hâ until October 14, 1942, then sent to Romainville.

After her mother's arrest, Andrée Cailbault ran the farm with her maternal grandfather and an aunt, her mother's sister, who came from Paris. She regularly supplied goods to the families of resisters and took farm products to Saintes.

Auschwitz # 31738

Alice Cailbault died at Birkenau on March 8 or 9, 1943. By the time she entered the revier, her legs were so swollen she could hardly walk.

On April 1943, her parents received an official notice from Auschwitz through the mayor's offices of Saint-Laurent-de-Cognac: "Alice Cailbault deceased in a hospital on March 8, 1943, and interred in a cemetery in Germany."

Germaine CANTELAUBE, née Charles

Born March 27, 1908, in Paris. Her father was an office worker. Germaine was raised in Montigny-Beauchamp, in the Seine-et-Oise region, and attended school there, completing elementary school. In 1925 the family moved to Périgueux, their home province, and Germaine became a seamstress.

In 1932, in Chignac (Dordogne), she married Cantelaube, a railway worker, employed in maintenance, and a militant communist. The couple settled in Bordeaux.

In 1940, as soon as the Resistance was organized, Cantelaube was in on the action. He stored tracts at his home (his wife knew of this), made contacts, etc. He was arrested during the summer of 1941, and shot at Souge on October 24, 1941.

Germaine Cantelaube did not stop her activities, however. She transported materials and sheltered resisters.

She was arrested on August 28, 1942, by Poinsot's police, at her home, 31 Rue Delavaux in Bordeaux. The Boudet barracks until October 14, 1942, Romainville, Auschwitz.

Auschwitz # 31740

She died of dysentery at the Birkenau revier on March 31, 1943.

When they returned, the survivors from Bordeaux announced Germaine's death to the directress of the Belcier school, where Germaine had been employed. Germaine's brother informed her mother.

The mother, whom we found in Périgueux, is now [in 1965] eighty-six years old. She lives alone with her memories. She knows that her daughter spit in Poinsot's face during the interrogation; she remembers that when she asked why they had arrested her daughter, the police answered: "Your daughter said she wanted to avenge her husband."

Yvonne CARRE, née Calmels

Born April 1, 1897, in Montceau-les-Mines, where in 1871 her grandfather was mayor of the Montceau Commune.

She was married to Gaston Carré, former commander of the fourteenth International Brigade in Spain, FTP commander in the Resistance. They were both communists and left Aubervilliers in 1941 (where Yvonne was in the HLM) for Saint-Denis, where they were not known. They were active militants. Yvonne Carré was first arrested at the beginning of May 1942 and released, probably because her husband was the real target. They were arrested together on May 16, by the Gestapo at Saint-Denis, in the same dragnet as Raymond Losserand [see *Louise Losserand*] and France Bloch-Sérazin, members of the same resistance group.

Imprisoned in the cells until October 27, 1942, then at Romainville, Yvonne Carré knew that her husband was sentenced to death by a German court on September 30, 1942, and executed at the shooting range in Issy-les-Moulineaux, October 21, 1942.

She died at the beginning of March 1943. Like almost everyone else, she had dysentery and had left the column to relieve herself. The SS set a dog on her that tore a piece of flesh. The wound became infected. Yvonne entered the revier. In just a few days, gangrene consumed her entire leg.

We have not been able to find her family.

VINCENTELLA, CALLED "DANIELLE," CASANOVA, NÉE PERINI

Born on February 9, 1909, in Ajaccio, Corsica, to a family of five children. Her father was a teacher and a school principal.

She came to Paris to complete her studies in 1927, joined the Young Communists, and began her political career. Elected to the central committee of the Young Communists in 1934, married to Laurent Casanova, she was both professionally active (as a dental surgeon) and politically involved. In 1936 the Communist Party asked her to create a separate organization for girls, and she became secretary general of the Union of French Girls.

The Communist Party was outlawed in September 1939. She became part of the clandestine leadership. She edited *La Voix des Femmes*, led women against the occupation, and formed cells that would evolve into the Union of French Women. She also played an important role in the university branch of the National Front and in the Young Communists. Her husband was a prisoner of war. She lived in Paris under a false identity.

On February 14 of that cold winter of 1942, knowing that Georges and Maï Politzer [see this name] had no heating, Danielle decided to take them some charcoal. When she knocked on the Politzers' illegal residence with her basket of coal in her arms, she found herself face to face with inspectors from the special brigades who had just arrested Georges and Maï. She was soon identified at General Intelligence and sent to the cells until March 23, 1942, then to the Santé, where she was kept in isolation, in a cell she shared with two comrades. Punished with a week of solitary because she was passing news to the male prisoners (Politzer was in a wing across from hers) through the air vents, she came out having lost a lot of weight. From the Santé she was sent on August 24, 1942, to Romainville, where she carried on animated political discussions.

Auschwitz # 31655

At Birkenau, as we were waiting to be stripped, sheared, and tattooed, an SS officer asked if there was a dentist among us. Danielle identified herself. They put her through the induction process immediately. They tattooed her but did not cut her hair, made her dress in clean striped clothing, and set her up in a dental office, a barracks within the revier. This barracks was divided into three rooms: a waiting room warmed by a round stove, a room furnished with three low beds (for the dentist and each of her two assistants), and the office proper, which according to Danielle was very well equipped. Why a dental office? Who were the patients? An ordinary prisoner needed a great deal of luck and guile to gain access. The only inmates eligible for these services were the kapos, the column *führerines* (the directors of work, nearly all of them German criminals), and other privileged prisoners. We know how the Nazis organized the camps. By creating a small privileged elite who could eat their fill and exercise the right of life or death over the others, they got the results they wanted: ferocious discipline and rivalry between the prisoners. For our group, their strategy did not play out: Danielle stayed close to us and continued to champion our cause.

Without applying for the position but simply because the last dentist had just died of typhus, Danielle found herself in an unusually privileged position: no roll call, no outdoor work, no fatigue duty, no beatings. She spent her days in a warm place. She slept in a bed with a mattress, clean sheets, comfortable blankets. She had hot water to wash herself and also her clothes (woolens, lingerie, which she wore under her uniform), silk stockings, good thick ski boots which she put on to leave her barracks, while in her office she wore city shoes. All these things were brought to her by her patients, high ranking prisoners, the kapos, the Germans, who had large quantities of things from the "Canada" and wanted to get the best care by paying for it, since the dentist had orders only to pull teeth, not to treat them. In addition, Danielle was recognized almost immediately by the German communists, who, according to the tactic adopted from the beginning of the concentration camp system, occupied posts in the administration of the camp, enjoying a certain margin of initiative. Her job offered Danielle possibilities which she exploited: through the kapos of different commandos, through a woman who was responsible for the administration of the revier, she tried to alleviate the ghastly conditions suffered by the members of her convoy. She succeeded in getting Mai Politzer admitted as a physician at the very beginning, then a dozen of us as nurses, and Alida Delasalle and Marilou Colombain as seamstresses.

She often came to Block 26 to see us in the evenings after roll call, and distributed by rotation what she'd gathered through her connections: bread, woolens, a few precious packets of charcoal for the dysentery patients. The fact that she was protected comforted the others. "We'll all die here," each woman thought, "but Danielle will return. Danielle will tell what happened." And the patients she went to see in the revier gave her the wedding rings they'd managed to hide in their fists during induction, or a word for their loved ones. Danielle would return.

But she did not return. In April typhus, endemic at Birkenau, reached truly terrifying proportions. The normal camp mortality rate was three hundred per day. In April the number climbed to five hundred. The chief SS physician liked Danielle very much; she was a good worker. He had already lost the previous dentist and wanted to keep this one. He proposed to vaccinate her. She accepted and received two shots. It was probably too late, and Danielle fell ill on May 1, 1943. She was nursed in the little infirmary reserved for kapos (nine individual beds, white sheets, steps for getting down out of bed, slippers, bright quilts, tea with lemon—those lemon slices in a little dish fascinated me when I went to see Danielle, who did not recognize me. I was tempted to steal them, but I didn't. I don't know what stopped me). And her case was personally followed by Dr. Roder, an odd character in the SS—it was said that he committed suicide in November 1944—who gave her shots for her heart. Nonetheless, Danielle succumbed on May 9, 1943. The disease seemed to have been more violent than was usual in weaker patients. In a glass, on a stool covered with a napkin at the head of her bed, stood a bunch of lilacs brought by one of the gardening crew.

Friends carried her body on the litter and deposited it near the morgue, the little hangar where the corpses were heaped behind Block 25. She lay there, still beautiful because she was not so thin, her face framed by her abundant black hair, the collar of a white nightdress buttoned to her neck, her hands on the white sheet, two little branches of leaves near her hands. The only fine corpse we saw at Birkenau.

Danielle Casanova was posthumously awarded the Legion of Honor. All the workers' municipalities in the Parisian suburbs have named streets after her, and in Paris part of Rue des Petits-Champs was renamed Danielle-Casanova.

Hélène CASTERA, née Vervin

In Bègles, Gironde, there is a Rue des Quatre-Castéra:

- the mother, Hélène Castéra, born April 21, 1887, in Chiry-Ourscamp, in the Oise;
- the father, Albert Castéra, ship's carpenter;
- the eldest son, René Castéra, born October 17, 1909;
- the second son, Gabriel Castéra, born August 10, 1911.

Although married and the father of three children, Gabriel Castéra was not living at home in 1942. He was a "night fighter," as they were called at the time. When his comrades needed a place to stay, he sent them to his parents in Bègles. Madame Castéra liked these visitors: they brought news and interesting conversations. She listened and asked questions.

Gabriel Castéra was captured by the police on July 8, 1942. They arrested his parents the following day. On July 14, 1942, René Castéra, who tried to discover his family's whereabouts, was also arrested.

Madame Castéra, after being interned in the fortress at Hâ, was transferred to Romainville on October 14, 1942.

Auschwitz # 31719

She died of dysentery at the very beginning of March 1943.

Her two older sons, Gabriel and René, were executed by firing squad at Souge on September 21, 1942. Out of charity, her friends did not tell her. She died without knowing.

Her husband was deported to Mauthausen. He died there on February 12, 1944. He was sixty-two years old.

Marcel Castéra, the youngest son, was spared only because he was a fireman for the autonomous port of Bordeaux and assigned to his station during this period. He learned of his mother's death through a notice from Auschwitz, which he had to have translated: "Hélène Castéra deceased March 4, 1943, at 2:10 p.m., of acute stomach and intestinal catarrh."

NOTIFICATIONS OF DECEASE

After arriving at Birkenau, once we were sheared, tattooed, and dressed, we filled out forms on large, yellow sheets of bristol paper. We had to indicate family name, first name, date and place of birth; father's family name, first name, and date of birth; mother's first name and maiden name; the number of gold crowns we had in our mouth, if any; the name and address of someone to notify in case of accident.

At the revier, the corpses were piled up near the door. A sturdy pile that would not collapse. Getting the corpses down from the beds and putting them on the pile was the nurses' basic work. The secretary of every revier would pull out the left arms and record the tattooed number in the block book. The book of the dead. This secretary was always behind in her work. Furthermore, when a corpse was in the middle of the pile and difficult to reach, it was not recorded. Nor when the tattooed arm had been eaten away by a rat. Between the day of death and the day when the information arrived at the *Politische Abteilung*, a work crew of inmates (a good detachment, with shelter and clean work) spent their day moving forms from the "arrival" box to the "deceased" box. They established a notification of decease—a printed form—on which they recorded the date of decease as the time of transcription, the hour of death as whatever came to mind, the cause as one of the four or five admissible illnesses (noncontagious or benign). Sometimes, to avoid thinking about it, they would assign the same illness to all the dead on a given day, and another illness on the following day. There was the day of pneumonias, the day of catarrhs, and then they began all over again. So that (this happened for Madame Jacquat and for Madame Lambert) two families from the same town could be notified at the same time of their relative's death on the same day from the same illness. Certain notifications of decease indicated no cause, but sometimes—depending on the whim of the inmate filling it out or on the demands of a kapo who wanted careful work—the form bore the words: "died at the hospital at Auschwitz" or "on Kasernenstrasse" or "the body was interred in a cemetery in Germany." The *Politische Abteilung* was always behind in its work: for the hundred and seventy-eight women of our convoy who died at Auschwitz, only thirty notifications were sent.

Yvonne CAVE, née Richard

Born March 17, 1896, in Montrouge, Seine, where her parents, who had six children, ran a mushroom farm. Yvonne left elementary school in Montrouge at thirteen, without her certificate, and learned cardboard making. She married Henri Cavé, a widower with a grown daughter, who was a cardboard maker himself. The Cavés lived at 231 Rue de Vaugirard, in a building where Madame Richard, Yvonne's widowed mother, was the concierge.

During the occupation, Yvonne and her husband did not conceal their antipathy for the Germans, and several times shopkeepers said to Madame Richard that "her daughter ought to be careful." One day in September 1942, Yvonne passed a young man in the hall she'd known as a boy; he was preening in his splendid uniform of the *Chantiers de jeunesse* (a fascist youth group). "Aren't you ashamed to wear that outfit? The Germans won't always be here, you know."—"Watch out, I'll make you shut your trap," the young man said.

A few days later, the Gestapo. Interrogation. Some white paper—the size for tracts, they said—had attracted the Germans' attention. No, this paper was not meant for tracts; a neighbor woman gave it to the Cavés, thinking they might use it for their work. Fine. The police went over to the radio and turned it on. The needle still pointed to Radio London. The Cavés had been listening when they'd knocked on the door: "So, you listen to London?" They went away.

A week later, on September 26, 1942, the Cavés were summoned to the Gestapo on Rue des Saussaies, and they went as ordered. They never returned.

The following day, one of Yvonne's sisters went to Rue des Saussaies to inquire. "Yes, they're here. Come back tomorrow and bring them something to eat." The sister returned the next day with a basket of food. They laughed in her face: "This isn't a hotel. No one stays here." In October she received the card from Romainville, a pink card with the printed sentence, in French and

English: "I am in the fortress at Romainville. I am fine. Affectionately." Only the signature was handwritten. Then, no more news.

Yvonne and Henri Cavé left on the same train.

Auschwitz # 31 . . .

Yvonne Cavé died at Birkenau at the end of February 1943. Her shoes had been stolen during the night. In the morning, she had to go barefoot to roll call—four hours standing in the snow—and then to work. Her legs swelled visibly in the course of the day. She died three days later in the revier, from acute nephritis.

In March 1943 her sister was summoned to the Gestapo, Rue des Saussaies. An interpreter told her: "Your sister died of a heart attack."

Henri Cavé died at Oranienburg during the summer of 1944. He was wounded during the bombing of the Heinkel factory, April 18, 1944. With open wounds in both legs, he was sent to the revier of the main camp, where one of his comrades saw him for the last time on June 15, 1944.

Camille CHAMPION, née Chuat

Born June 1, 1898, in Huelgoat (Finistère), to a family of four children. Her parents were in the lumber business.

She went to elementary school until the age of fourteen in Saint-Victor-de-Réno, in Orne.

In 1921 she married Marcel Champion, a mailman.

In 1942, in Maison-Maugis, Orne, she was running a family boardinghouse for up to ten boarders. Why were Marcel and Camille Champion arrested at their home on the evening of March 3, 1942, by inspectors of the special brigades who had come expressly from Paris? Had they come to arrest some resisters who used the boardinghouse as their address? The Champions were not members of the Communist Party before the war, and yet they were taken in a roundup along with many communists (Pican, Politzer).

Luckily, neither their son, then aged eighteen, nor any boarders were at home.

Camille Champion was taken immediately to Paris, interrogated at General Intelligence, detained in the cells until April 30, 1942, transferred to the Santé—where she was held in isolation until August 24, 1942—and from there to Romainville.

Auschwitz # 31656

She died of typhus in April 1943.

Her son learned of her death from the survivors of the convoy.

Marcel Champion was executed by firing squad at Mont-Valérien on September 21, 1942. He was forty-seven years old.

Christiane CHARUA ("Cécile")

Born on July 18, 1915, in Calais; but in 1917, during the war, the family took refuge in Conflans-Sainte-Honorine, Seine-et-Oise, where Christiane completed elementary school. Her mother, originally a dressmaker, then a furrier, the widow of a sailor in the merchant marine, married an artist. She had eleven children, but no more than five were alive at any one time: they all died at an early age of meningitis or convulsions.

"My young brother and I were raised alone. Our mother was working in Paris and came home very late. We had to take care of the food, the fire, the dishes ourselves. Mother often found us asleep at the table with the oil lamp smoking and the fire out. We went to school two kilometers from home. At thirteen, I went to work. After dressmaking, I made fur coats. I married at seventeen, I had a daughter at nineteen, I was divorced at twenty-one. In 1941 I placed my daughter with a nurse in order to join the Resistance."

She was in the FTP, distributing tracts in German to the occupying army and printing *L'Humanité*. She stocked propaganda material, transported it, researched locations—which had to be changed frequently, acted as an intermediary between the printers and distributors. "I got the job of transporting suitcases full of lead for the printer, and I had to make the suitcases look light. . . ." On June 18, 1942, all the printers were arrested. Cécile managed to elude the police, so she moved and changed assignments, providing food coupons to comrades, hiding out in the Paris suburbs.

On July 7, 1942, leaving the Monge metro, she was recognized by one of the inspectors who had followed her the previous month. Bad luck. She was sent to the cells and transferred to Romainville on August 20, 1942.

Auschwitz # 31650

She worked on all the Birkenau detachments (marshes, earthworks, gardening, demolition, wheelbarrows, wood cutting), including the Raisko unit, where she was placed in July 1943. On January 7, 1944, she was one of a small group transferred to Ravensbrück (along with Poupette, Lulu, Carmen, Charlotte, Gilberte, Marie-Jeanne Pennec, and Madeleine Doiret), and was sent from there, on August 9, 1944, to the factories at Beendorf, in the salt mines. Evacuation of the mine, liberation by the Red Cross, repatriation by the Swedes—the same itinerary as Simone Alizon.

She remarried after the return and had two sons. She did what many of the survivors did: started a family so as to feel truly alive, to feel like others, to pretend as though the deportation had not left its mark. Her determination was not enough. Cécile has had several serious depressions. She suffers from debility and osteoporosis, and she is constantly forced to repress the violence that rises up inside her: her sense of injustice makes her sick, the horrors experienced from 1940 to 1945, the colonial wars since then. She was named a candidate in the RIF, but she draws only a soldier's pension.

Marie Mathilde CHAUX, née Sapin

She was from Tain-l'Hermitage and married a salesman from Châlon-sur-Saône. Widowed in 1911, she turned the large house where she was living, owned by the Châlon hospital, into a boardinghouse and earned her living by renting out six or seven rooms.

She was arrested at home, in Châlon-sur-Saône by the Gestapo in November 1942. She had been denounced for stockpiling weapons. These "weapons" turned out to be a service revolver she was keeping as a souvenir, something her son, who had died in 1937, had brought back from World War I. It was later known that she had lodged resisters.

While she was in the prison at Châlon-sur-Saône, her house was completely ransacked.

Madame Chaux arrived at Romainville on December 19, 1942.

Auschwitz # 31824

One morning at roll call, between February 3 and 8, 1943, an SS doctor stopped in front of our ranks. He asked: "Which of you women who are older or ill cannot tolerate roll call?" Marie-Claude was translating. Two raised their hands: Marie Dubois and Line Porcher. Just then our blockova from Block 14, Magda, managed behind the back of the SS to signal to Marie-Claude, who immediately added without changing her voice: "But it would be better not to say so. Lower your hands." Hands were lowered. Then Madame Chaux, who was small and hidden in a back row, stood on tiptoe, raising her hand as high as she could. The doctor was already on his way. She cried: "Me, sir, I'm sixty-seven years old." She was taken to Block 25.

She was born on August 14, 1875.

Marguerite CHAVAROC, née Boucher

Born October 3, 1894. Her husband, Louis Chavaroc, established a flourishing automotive electronics business in Quimper, but both were from modest backgrounds.

From the beginning of the occupation, Louis Chavaroc was an active member of the Johnny network [see *Marie and Simone Alizon*], and his wife backed him. They were both arrested in Quimper by the Gestapo on February 14, 1942.

Marguerite Chavaroc, like the Alizon sisters, was sent from one prison to another: from Rennes to the Santé, from the Santé to Fresnes—always alone in a cell and in isolation—from there to Romainville on November 6, 1942.

Auschwitz # 31796

She died of dysentery at the Birkenau revier in the middle of March 1943.

After resisting all the Gestapo interrogations, after spending nearly a year in prison himself, Louis Chavaroc was deported to Oranienburg-Sachsenhausen on the same train as his wife. Quite ill on his return, he went around to all the offices of the Red Cross and the various ministries to find out what had happened to his wife. He did not want to believe it. Those who had been in other camps never really understood what it was like in Auschwitz, where the average survival period was twenty days. The ministry of prisoners told him that March 12, 1943, was the date of his wife's death, according to the testimony of one of the survivors.

Marie-Louise COLOMBAIN, née Méchain ("Marilou")

Born April 12, 1920, in La Courtine, Creuse, she was raised in Paris, in the nineteenth arrondissement, then in a nearby suburb. Her father was employed at the postal service. She completed her elementary education and became a dressmaker.

In 1938, in Paris, she married Henri Colombain, a tradesman.

A resister from the outset, Henri Colombain was arrested in October 1941 at his home, where there was a mimeograph machine, a typewriter, and paper for tracts. Marilou would have been arrested as well but she was not at home. Warned in time by a neighbor, she moved elsewhere. Around this time, her child died of diphtheria (the hospital had a shortage of serum; there was an epidemic in Germany, and the antidiphtheria serum had been requisitioned by the Germans). Knowing the police were on her trail, she did not go to the funeral. Left alone, she kept on fighting and joined the FTP. A liaison and intelligence agent, she also transported arms and explosives. She was part of the group headed by Maurice Alexandre [see *Jeanne Alexandre*].

She was arrested in Paris on December 16, 1942. The police of the special brigades were waiting for her at the place where she was to meet Suzanne

Lasne [see this name]. Imprisoned in Fresnes, Marilou joined the convoy at Compiègne on the eve of departure.

Auschwitz # 31853

On March 25, 1943, she left Birkenau to work at the Stabsgebäude, a workshop that made uniforms for SS women. They worked there from six in the morning to six in the evening. Roll call lasted only a few minutes. There were showers. You could hope to survive. She was sent back to the revier at Birkenau at the beginning of April because she had dysentery. She subsequently caught typhus and left the revier only in June. The quarantine, which began on August 3, 1943, came none too soon.

Marilou followed the path of most of the survivors and was liberated at Mauthausen on April 22, 1945.

She did not find her husband again. He died at Gusen, one of the most grueling labor camps at Mauthausen; there were scarcely any survivors. Marilou had no way of knowing when he died.

She remarried and had three children, in 1946, 1951, and 1955.

She said: "I don't think I've readapted very well. I'm very happy to have the children. They stop me from thinking too much and force me to be active."

Marguerite CORRINGER, née Helleringer

Born on June 15, 1902, in Paris, in the twentieth arrondissement, she went to elementary school on Rue de la Mare, where she completed her basic education.

A working-class girl, trained in all sorts of tasks without any particular profession, Marguerite always earned her living: as a lady's maid in a mansion on Avenue Montaigne, as the manager of a newspaper kiosk in a suburban train station, as a ticket seller for the national lottery—nothing discouraged her.

In 1928 she married Jean Corringer, an engraver and toolmaker and a militant communist, who participated in the clandestine struggle from 1940 on. She shared his life and his risks, even as she took on tasks of her own, such as putting up posters. She worked as a housekeeper in offices on the Champs-Elysées, where she could steal ink for the mimeographs to print tracts; and in the early mornings when she left for work, she carried with her the first bundles of *L'Humanité* to distribute on the metro.

She was arrested on March 6, 1942, along with her husband, by the special brigades of the French police. From General Intelligence, where she remained until March 10, she was sent to the cells until March 23, to the Santé—in isolation—until August 24, 1942, and from there to Romainville.

She fell ill upon arrival at Birkenau. Soon admitted to the revier—she was not photographed on February 3, 1943—she caught all the camp illnesses, one after the other: dysentery, typhus, abscesses, mastoiditis (she was operated on by an inmate physician), malaria. Inexplicably, she managed to recover and joined the others in quarantine on August 3, 1943. Like them, she was transferred to Ravensbrück on August 2, 1944, to Mauthausen on March 2, 1945, and was liberated on April 22, 1945. She arrived in Paris on April 30, 1945, and the following day she marched in the parade for the May Day celebration.

Today, she is a very sick woman. Since her return, she has undergone a serious operation, suffered from osteoporosis and arthritis, can hardly stand, and must have constant care.

Her husband, Jean Corringer, was executed by firing squad at Mont-Valérien on September 21, 1942. He was in Romainville, where she was permitted to say good-bye.

Renée COSSIN, née Raquet

Born on March 8, 1914, in Amiens, she did not know her father, a Paris fireman killed in World War I. Madame Raquet remained a widow, and raised her only daughter by making ready-to-wear clothing. Renée completed elementary school in Amiens and married at sixteen.

Her husband, a municipal employee in Amiens, was mobilized in 1939, and taken prisoner in June 1940. She was a communist and joined the underground organization in September 1940. In 1940 and 1941 she crossed the demarcation line more than twenty times to make contact between the two zones. These were her first missions. Then she was given responsibility for propaganda efforts among women; at her instigation the women of Picardy addressed petitions to the occupying authorities to demand the addresses of prisoners and the right to send them parcels and news.

On November 11, 1941, Renée Cossin carried to the war monument at Place du Maréchal-Foch in Amiens a sheaf of wheat dedicated to Jean Catelas, communist deputy of the Somme, who had been guillotined the previous September after being sentenced to death by the Special Court. The police were on her trail. She went north, leaving her two children (nine and four years old) with her mother. Petitions, protests, women's actions followed one after the other. The housewives of Pas-de-Calais attacked a train carrying foodstuffs on the way to Germany. Renée was everywhere.

On July 13, 1942, coming to collect tracts for the demonstrations the following day, Renée arrived in Paris and found that the friends' home where she usually stayed was locked. She decided to spend the night in the room of a comrade from Bordeaux. She had the key. What she did not know was that the comrade had been arrested the week before. The police had discovered his identity and his Paris address and were staking the place out. When Renée arrived, inspectors from the special brigades arrested her.

She was interrogated by the French police and by the Gestapo, confronted with the comrade from Bordeaux (who was deported and survived), and imprisoned at Fresnes. She was transferred to Romainville on December 20, 1942.

Auschwitz # 31830

She died in the revier at Birkenau (edema, dysentery) in April 1943.

Her mother, her children, and her husband, who returned from the prisoner of war camp, learned of her death when the survivors returned.

Suzanne COSTENTIN, née Boineau

Born on May 13, 1893, in Deux-Sèvres. She was a schoolteacher and in 1927 married a colleague, Emile Costentin, whom she had met the previous year on a trip to the Soviet Union. They had both been part of a delegation from the CGTU teachers union, in which they were prominent.

Emile Costentin died in 1937 as the result of an illness contracted during World War I. Suzanne, who was teaching at a nursery school in Rouen, henceforth lived alone but was not solitary. She was secretary of the House of Culture, where she started a leather- and metal-working studio, working the materials she crafted with great talent. The House of Culture was closed in 1939, and Suzanne divided her life between her school and her books. She was content at home, on Rue Pouchet, where she owned a fine library.

At the beginning of 1942, a wave of arrests suddenly reduced the ranks of the National Front in the Seine-Inférieure region. Her friends advised Suzanne—who helped them as a relay—to leave her house and go into hiding. She delayed. She was arrested on February 9, 1942, at around eight in the evening: she had come home after visiting a friend, her former teacher at the teachers' college, to whom she had brought a long letter—a tract, in effect—relating the fate of the martyrs of Châteaubriant. She was carrying this letter under her skirt, in her corset.

Three agents from the Gestapo were waiting to take her to the law courts. During the car ride, Suzanne concentrated on tearing the letter into little pieces. The Germans gathered up the pieces and reconstructed the text. When they asked her where this letter had come from, she answered that she'd found it in her mailbox that morning. They made her recite the last words: "Long live the martyrs of Châteaubriant! Long live the Soviet Union!" and so had proof that she was the one who had copied it.

She was kept at the law courts in Rouen until November 1942, then sent to Romainville, where she found her comrades from the Seine-Inférieure: Germaine Pican, Suzanne Roze, Alida Delasalle, Madeleine Dissoubray, and little Guérin.

Auschwitz # 31765

She died at Birkenau at the beginning of March 1943. She had been beaten so badly that her body was bruised all over. Her fingers and big toes were frozen and gangrened, and she could no longer hoist herself up on her tier without the help of her companions. The ends of her fingers were torn where she needed to grip. She suffered all night, and the next day, after roll call, she fell down dead almost as soon as she crossed the threshold of the revier.

She had not given the address of any family member. For someone to contact in case of accident—as the formula went—she had named her housekeeper, who had brought her parcels in Rouen and had sent them to her in Romainville. This woman was called to police headquarters in Rouen in September 1943 and read the following message: "Suzanne Costentin deceased on March 31, 1943, at 6:30 in the morning."

Yvonne Marie COURTILLAT, née Le Maguer

Born May 30, 1911, in Languidic, Morbihan, to a family of three children, later orphaned in World War I. Her father had been an agricultural laborer.

Yvonne was raised in Hennebont, where she went to school. She was a nurse's aid at the hospital in Béziers in 1933, when she married Georges Courtillat, a hospital orderly originally from Vierzon. In 1939, the Courtillats left Béziers for Vierzon, where the husband was employed at the hospital.

Yvonne Courtillat was arrested by the Gestapo in September 1942. Her house, on Rue Grelon, was situated along the Cher River, in the unoccupied part of Vierzon. The town straddled the two zones, with the Cher serving as the demarcation line. The Gestapo seized Yvonne Courtillat just as she set foot on occupied territory after wading across the river to people waiting for her on the other side. Like Madame Bergin [see this name], whose café was situated on the opposite bank, she had been denounced.

Yvonne Courtillat was imprisoned in Vierzon, then in Orléans. She arrived at Romainville on October 31, 1942, along with Madame Bergin.

Auschwitz # 31 . . .

She was among the first to die. No eyewitness report.

Her son, who was eleven in 1942, was raised by the maternal grandmother in Hennebont; her nine-year-old daughter was taken in by the paternal grandfather in Vierzon. Georges Courtillat died of illness several months after his wife's arrest.

At the end of 1950, at the conclusion of investigations undertaken by the mayor's offices of Vierzon, the children learned that their mother had died at Auschwitz. They did not know she had been deported.

Jeanne COUTEAU

Born in Paris in the twelfth arrondissement on July 13, 1901, she was raised in Bagnoles-de-l'Orne, where she completed elementary school.

By the time of the occupation she was in the process of divorcing her husband and was living with Louis Pisetta in Tours.

During the day Jeanne Couteau worked as a cook, Louis Pisetta as a chauffeur. In the evenings, either together or separately, they posted notices and put tracts under doors or in letterboxes. They were communists.

They were arrested on August 4, 1942, at three in the morning, at their home on Rue du Champs-de-Mars in Tours. They had returned from their nightly rounds just before curfew.

Jeanne Couteau left the prison at Tours for Romainville on November 7, 1942.

Auschwitz # 31772

She died of typhus, in the Birkenau revier, at the beginning of April 1943.

Her family learned of her death from Hélène Fournier when the survivors returned.

Louis Pisetta was deported, and died in 1968.

Madeleine DAMOUS, née Demiot

Born on March 17, 1913, in Saint-Aigny, Indre, to a family of two children. Her father was a farmer in Breuil, a district of Saint-Aigny, and she went to elementary school in Mérigny, Indre. After completing her basic education, she helped on the farm until she turned fifteen, then left to work in Paris. In 1930 she married René Damous, a bookkeeper. The Damouses settled in Champigny-sur-Marne.

René Damous was a communist, Madeleine became one, and in 1942 they were both part of the FTP.

They were arrested in Paris on April 1, 1942, by the special brigades. Madeleine Damous was imprisoned in the Santé, held in isolation until September 29, then sent to Romainville—where she could write to her mother—until the departure.

Auschwitz # 31690

She died in the Birkenau revier around March 15, 1943. She had been beaten by a kapo, who held her hands to prevent her from protecting herself. Several days later her face was scarlet and so swollen she couldn't see and had to be led to roll call. After roll call, Germaine Renaudin and Gilberte Tamisé took her to the revier, where she died soon after (of erysipelas). Her mother learned that Madeleine had died when the survivors returned.

René Damous, lieutenant in the FTP, fighter with the National Front from the time of its creation, was shot at Mont-Valérien on October 2, 1943. They had no children.

Vittoria DAUBEUF, née Nenni ("Viva")

She was one of the four daughters of Pietro Nenni, head of the Italian Socialist Party. She was born in Ancona on October 31, 1915. Her father, then a socialist journalist, was mobilized at the time. Viva spent her childhood in Milan, where she attended school until 1928, when Pietro Nenni was forced to go into exile. The family sought refuge in France, and Viva did her secondary studies in Paris.

In 1937, she married a Frenchman, Henri Daubeuf, who, after trying various trades, established himself as a printer. In 1942 he was solicited by the communists to print their underground newspapers and brochures—a very risky enterprise. When he spoke to Viva about it, she didn't hesitate: "My father would do it." She never knew that Daubeuf was being paid for his work.

On June 18, 1942, a number of printers were arrested, Henri Daubeuf among them. Viva should have fled. Everyone advised her to do so. But instead, she went every day to police headquarters, where her husband was being held at the General Intelligence offices. She took him food, drink, and cigarettes. In the course of one of these visits, she was arrested as well.

She was interned in the cells until August 10, 1942, along with her husband and the other printers. On August 10 the men left the cells; no one knew where they were being taken. The women worried. Then they too were transferred to Romainville. The next morning they were awakened by singing. They ran to the windows of the barracks and saw the men on their way out. None of them knew they were to be executed.

While Viva was at Romainville, one of her sisters, also French by marriage, tried to free her. She moved heaven and earth, seeking support from important people who had known their father. One day, Viva was summoned by the fortress commandant, who made the following proposition: if she would renounce her French citizenship, which she had acquired by marriage, she would be sent to Italy. She refused point-blank: "My father would never have done it." If she had accepted, she would have been remitted to the Italian police and imprisoned in Italy. Like her father. Even after several months in Birkenau, she never regretted her decision.

Auschwitz # 31635

On April 26, 1943, despite her determination to stay on her feet and not to go to the revier, where the sick usually died, Viva lined up with the others seeking admission. Her typhus was so violent that she staggered and couldn't see. Yet she resisted. She was supposed to have been released from the revier when an abscess formed on her eyebrow. A woman doctor drained the abscess, which scarred. We were hoping she would join us in the Raisko unit, as she was slated to do, but she had a relapse of typhus. I saw her on July 15, 1943. She seemed well. Her hair, which had been shaved six months before, had grown back in big curls. Someone had gotten her a fine comb; she ran it constantly through her hair and killed the lice, one by one, with her nails, which had grown long since she wasn't working in the fields. I told her that the allies had landed at Nettuno (we learned this from a German newspaper stolen from the pocket of an SS officer at Raisko). "My father will soon go home. How happy he must be!" (In fact, Pietro Nenni, arrested in France, was then in prison in Italy.) Then, in the same voice, she began to tell me that her sister had come to see her, that they were making preparations to send her back to France, that her sister was waiting for her. She was calmly delirious. This was the delirium typical of typhus.

Pietro Nenni learned of Viva's death from the secretary at Saint-Siège, Monsignor Montini (later Pope Paul VI) in 1944. The notification of decease from the camp at Auschwitz was remitted to him in 1956 by Souslov. This notification gave July 16, 1943, as the date of death and influenza as the cause.

Henri Daubeuf was executed by firing squad at Mont-Valérien on August 11, 1942, at the age of thirty. When she saw the men at Auschwitz, Viva said: "Henri died a proper death. Now I envy him."

SIMONE DAVID, née NOYER

Born June 13, 1921, at Evreux. Her father was a station supervisor for the railway. Simone was the elder of two daughters.

Though her parents wanted her to continue her studies, Simone left school after completing her primary education in Evreux and married at seventeen. Her husband, Noël David, wanted to go to the colonies and took correspondence courses with that in mind. They had been married only a year when the war broke out. Noël David was mobilized. Simone returned to her parents' house. Taken prisoner and ill, Noël David was sent home at the beginning of 1941. The Davids rented an apartment in Petit-Quevilly, on the outskirts of Rouen. Noël David still thought of going to the colonies. He was offered a post in Madagascar, where he would be the director of a plantation. The Davids left Petit-Quevilly, stored their things with a relative, and settled into a furnished apartment in Evreux to make preparations: passports, applications, etc. They bought trunks. While waiting to leave, Noël David worked for a real estate agent, for whom Simone also did a little bookkeeping. Simone's parents, who lived nearby, did not suspect their daughter and son-in-law's clandestine activities; they later discovered that the Davids had collected funds for the National Front and distributed propaganda material.

On February 24, 1942, the Davids were invited to dinner with two of Noël's brothers-in-law, Jean Buée and Lefebvre, and a friend. A stranger showed up and seemed to know the password, so they let him in. He was a policeman from Rouen. All the guests were taken to police headquarters. In the course of the search, a packet of tracts hidden under the mattress escaped notice. The next day, Simone's younger sister went to find them and burned them. Simone was released two days later. Her father advised her to flee. She might have gone to stay with friends. But then they would arrest her father and detain her brothers-in-law. Summoned to police headquarters on February 27, she turned herself in.

She was taken to Paris immediately and imprisoned in the cells until April 30, then in the Santé in isolation until August 24, 1942, and finally in Romainville until the departure.

Auschwitz # 31658

She died of typhus in the Birkenau revier at the end of May 1943.

Her godmother, arrested in 1943 and deported to Ravensbrück, met some of the survivors of the convoy there in August 1944. Through them, she learned of Simone's death. She conveyed the news to the parents when she returned to Evreux on May 2, 1945.

Noël David, twenty-nine years old, was shot at Mont-Valérien on September 21, 1942.

Lefebvre—one of the brothers-in-law—was shot at the same time; he was twenty-eight. His wife, summoned to the prefecture to learn that her husband had been executed, went home and committed suicide.

The friend, whose name we could not find, was also shot on September 21, 1942.

Only Jean Buée, the other brother-in-law, was released because he was the father of eight children. But a few weeks later he died in an accident.

Madeleine DECHAVASSINE

Born in 1900, the daughter of a teacher, she was raised in the Ardennes and did a degree in chemical engineering at Nancy. She joined the Communist Party in 1936, following the strikes; she thought that there would be greater opportunities for scientists, and especially for women, under a socialist government.

On August 23, 1939, *L'Humanité* was banned. The Montreuil section of the Communist Party published a first underground issue of the paper shortly thereafter; Madeleine and her comrades took on the responsibility of distributing the edition in Paris-East. The police were alerted and set a trap, which the group managed to evade.

Madeleine worked at a factory as an engineer and continued to distribute underground newspapers until she was arrested in March 1940. She had been denounced. Imprisoned in La Roquette, she was evacuated in June 1940 to the prison at Blois, from which the prisoners were again evacuated a week later, walking in columns along the roads. She managed to escape and reach Toulouse. There she procured false papers and reentered Paris in September 1940.

She made contact with former comrades from the Communist Party and, going entirely underground, took up her job of distribution for the Paris-East region.

A few months later, she coordinated the activities of women in the southern zone of Seine-et-Oise: protests against unemployment and the lack of supplies, which were the first attempts against the occupation.

Soon after, she was asked, as a chemist, to prepare explosives for the FTP (the Dumont, Jean Laffitte, Douillot group), though they had only the meagerest resources at their disposal. The members of her FTP group were nearly all arrested in April and May of 1942. Madeleine Dechavassine eluded the police. Cut off from all her connections, she tried to make contact again. She located Jacqueline Quatremaire [see this name], whom she had known before the war, and was arrested with her on June 17, 1942. She was thus implicated in something she hadn't done.

From the cells she was sent to the fortress at Romainville on August 10, 1942, and remained there until the departure.

She was immediately accepted into the group of chemists who made up the Raisko unit. She left Birkenau on March 21, 1943, first for the *Stabsgebäude*, then for Raisko itself in July 1943. She left Raisko on August 14, 1944, for Ravensbrück; and Ravensbrück on March 2, 1945, for Mauthausen, where she was liberated on April 22, 1945. She retired in 1960, after a serious operation, and lives alone, a rather embittered woman.

Charlotte DECOCK, née Dauriat

Born on August 14, 1911, in Oradour-sur-Vayres, Haute-Vienne, into a family of five children. Her father was a cabinetmaker. She spent her first years in Oradour-sur-Vayres, then her parents went to live in Nogent-sur-Oise, where she attended school until the age of thirteen. She went to work as a metalworker with Brissonneau, in Nogent, and married a fellow worker, a master laminator in the same factory.

In October 1942 Charlotte Decock's husband, arrested for an act of resistance, escaped from Beauvais prison. On October 15 the Gestapo, accompanied by a gendarme from Nogent-sur-Oise, arrested Charlotte at the factory. She was taken to the Royallieu camp (Compiègne) in her blue work clothes. Several days later, two policemen escorted her home to collect some clothing. When he learned of his wife's arrest, her husband also wanted to be taken prisoner. The family dissuaded him, convinced they would not hold a woman. On another occasion, Charlotte Decock had permission to leave to attend a baptism. She returned to the camp when the ceremony was over.

On October 24, 1942, she was transferred to Romainville.

Her children, a ten-year-old son and seven-year-old daughter, were taken in by her sister. Her husband returned to the Maquis [the rural resistance].

Auschwitz # 31756

Charlotte Decock conducted herself at Birkenau with unforgettable high spirits and good humor. In July 1943 she was sent to the unit at Raisko, where she was a cook for the SS. She stole everything she could: a liter of wine, which was shared among twenty-five, eggs, flour, a jar of pickled pork, a spoonful for each woman—but getting rid of the jar by pulverizing it with a rock was not easy. The Raisko group was transferred to Ravensbrück on August 14, 1944, from there to Mauthausen on March 2, 1945. On March 21, 1945, a month before the liberation of the camp, Charlotte Decock was killed in a bombardment at

Amstetten, a switchpoint station near Mauthausen, where the deportees were employed filling in holes from the shellings.

Her family learned of her death from Berthe Falk, who was working near Charlotte Decock that day and was wounded in the same attack.[6]

Alida DELASALLE, née Charbonnier

Born July 23, 1907, in Fécamp, where she grew up and attended elementary school, then became a dressmaker. In 1928 she married Robert Delasalle, a baker.

Before the war, they were both communists. They participated in the resistance networks that formed in 1941 and that constituted the National Front: they acted as liaisons, distributed tracts, and provided supplies to the clandestine struggle. Robert Delasalle donated bread to fighters who had no identity or ration cards.

When they arrested Suzanne Roze [see this name] in Rouen, the police found a letter in her pocket from her mother, Madame Clément. The following day, February 21, 1942, they were at Fécamp: "So you correspond with your daughter, but not through the mails. How, then?" "Through Alida Delasalle," replied Madame Clément.

The police arrested Alida at the corsetmaker's where she worked, and also arrested her husband. Their lodgings were searched to no avail. Tracts were hidden in the corsets at the shop. Alida and her husband denied everything. They were taken to the police commissioner and confronted with Madame Clément, who did not retract her statement.

Alida and Robert Delasalle, along with Madame Clément, were arrested and joined Suzanne Roze and Madeleine Dissoubray in Rouen. They were

---

6. We met Berthe Falk at Raisko. She was # 14148. It was a miracle that she was still alive after eight months at Birkenau. Originally Romanian, she had studied science in Paris and had opened a laboratory for medical analysis on Avenue de Suffren. She had been arrested as a Jew on the night of July 16, 1942, caught in the first roundup of Jews held in the Vél d'Hiv, transported to Pithiviers, and deported from there to Auschwitz on July 30. Around twenty thousand of them. There were hardly any left when we arrived at Birkenau: Berthe was the only woman with a 14,000 number. Our group adopted her; more than one of us owed our life to her. She was not even five feet tall, but she had inexhaustible courage and energy. We never saw her beaten, even in the disciplinary unit where she'd been sent for writing an article on July 14, after the liberation of Paris. Written on the spur of the moment to boost our spirits. She joined us at Ravensbrück in November 1944. We were happy to see her again. She was part of the group that went to Mauthausen and was wounded in the bombing of March 21, 1945. Repatriated while still ill, she healed, recovered all her energy, and reestablished her laboratory, which had been requisitioned. She seemed back afloat when she suddenly fell ill in July 1948. Colon cancer carried her off in two months. She was born August 9, 1911.

all taken to Paris on February 24, 1942, interrogated at police headquarters, then taken to the cells. Alida was sent a few days later to the infirmary at La Roquette because she had a boil on her face that needed attention. When she returned to the cells in April, her companions from Fécamp and Rouen had gone.

On April 30, 1942, she was transported to the Santé, where she was kept in isolation. Interrogated by the Gestapo, she persisted in denying everything. Madame Clément was released and went home.

On August 24, Alida was transferred to Romainville, where she saw her husband again.

Robert Delasalle was shot at Mont-Valérien on September 21, 1942. She said good-bye to him the evening before.

Auschwitz # 31659

She left Birkenau on March 21, 1943, to work at the *Stabsgebäude* with Marilou Colombain.

Alida entered quarantine with the others on August 3, 1943, and followed the same route until the liberation of Mauthausen, April 22, 1945.

She was in the revier at Birkenau five times (for dysentery, typhus, ear infections, surgery for an abscess, a heart attack following beatings). She had great difficulty readjusting. "I can bear life only by fits and starts," she says. Since the return, she has spent months in the hospital: acute pericarditis, nephritis, general rheumatism, a gynecological operation. She has lost all her teeth and is hard of hearing from the ear infections she had in the camp; she suffers from serious intestinal problems and has sclerosis of the lungs. She certainly cannot work. Her nights are troubled by nightmares.

Rachel DENIAU

Born on May 1, 1899, in La Croix-de-Bléré, Indre-et-Loire, where she spent her childhood and attended elementary school. She worked for the post office in Amboise. Her husband was a worker. In 1942 their two children were already grown.

Rachel Deniau was arrested by the Gestapo on September 10, 1942, at her home in Amboise. She had been carrying letters to the southern zone and helping prisoners escape across the demarcation line. She was part of a chain that included Germaine Jaunay (her aunt), Marcelle Laurillou, and Madame Gabb, who were all arrested at the same time and who all died at Auschwitz.

Rachel Deniau's husband was not aware of his wife's activities. He was not arrested.

She left the prison at Tours for Romainville on November 7, 1942.

Auschwitz # 31773

She died in the revier at Birkenau, two days after entering, at the beginning of March 1943.

Her family learned of her death from Hélène Fournier after the return.

Madeleine DISSOUBRAY ("Jacqueline")

Born November 25, 1917, in Sainte-Marguerite-les-Aumale, Seine-Inférieure, she grew up in Aumale and in Rouen. Her father was an agricultural engineer.

She pursued her studies and earned a teaching certificate, but taught for only a short time. In 1941 she left her profession in order to join the Resistance. She participated in the first Special Organization for sabotage [OS] (which would become the FTP) and in the secretariat of the communist section for Rouen.

She was arrested on February 20, 1942, in Rouen, by the special brigades. A city policeman with a pass—one of two halves of a torn postcard, for example—probably found on a comrade arrested shortly before, showed up at the apartment where Jacqueline was living under an assumed name. She was not suspicious. She told him: "Make yourself comfortable, wait for me, I'll be back in a moment. I have an appointment." The false comrade had posted his colleagues outside. Jacqueline and Suzanne Roze were arrested together.

Transferred to Paris, incarcerated in the cells from February 24 to March 23, 1942, then in the Santé—in the disciplinary division, probably because she had tried to escape several times, upon her arrest and during the transfer from Rouen to Paris. Jacqueline Dissoubray arrived at Romainville on August 24, 1942.

Auschwitz # 31660

She left Birkenau for Raisko at the end of February 1943. Jacqueline was not a chemist, but she had enough scientific knowledge for Danielle Casanova to enlist her as a botanist.

Like the other French women in this group, she was transferred to Ravensbrück on August 14, 1944, from there to Mauthausen on March 2, 1945, and was liberated on April 22, 1945.

After the return, she resumed her activities as a militant: at the departmental secretariat of the Union of French Women; at the federal office of the Communist Party for the Seine-Maritime; then in Paris, where she was a teacher with the Union of French Women.

She married, settled in the Paris suburbs, and had two children. She is now [1965] an academic and a vocational guidance counselor.

Her brother was deported and he returned as well. Her father was forced to retire. Her sister was arrested, then released.

Madeleine Dissoubray was named second lieutenant in the FFI [French Forces of the Interior], decorated with the Croix de Guerre and the Medal of the Resistance with rosette.

Madeleine DOIRET

Born on November 2, 1920, in Ivry-sur-Seine, the eldest of five children. Her father left his native Morvan to earn his living in Paris. He had no profession, properly speaking, and found work as a groom. Entering military service in 1911, he was not demobilized until 1919. His memories—of the trenches, the mud, Verdun—left their mark on Madeleine's childhood; she would remember the mud at Birkenau. After the demobilization, he married a girl who sold dairy products in les Halles [the farmers' market]. In 1924 he was working as a groom with Javel La Croix (they delivered sterilized water in horsedrawn carriages) when he met his former commander, who hired him as director of his lime-and-cement factory. The Doirets then built a detached house in Ivry; their children attended school until the age of sixteen.

In September 1938, Madeleine interrupted her studies for her high school diploma to learn stenography. With the declaration of war, however, so many teachers were mobilized that she became a temporary teacher in Yonne until the defeat.

In December 1936, during the Spanish Civil War, Madeleine Doiret had joined the Union of French Girls and become an active militant. In August 1940, returning from her exodus, she joined the Young Communists of Ivry, who were planning acts of resistance. Jean Compagnon (arrested June 18, 1942, shot on August 11, 1942) brought her texts which she typed onto stencils that were printed at night on an electric mimeograph—the first electric machine in the Paris region—in a walled cellar at the Doirets' house. With her sixteen-year-old brother Roger, who carried the bags on his back, she deposited tracts at various collection points in Ivry, where other young people picked them up for distribution. She was thinking of taking another teaching job when she was asked to join the Resistance full-time. She agreed, left the house, and went to live under an assumed name in a little place in the fifteenth arrondissement; she lived alone, breaking ties with family and friends. She typed the first letters, cast as posthumous messages from the men who had been executed in 1941, calling for sabotage and resistance. Once her job was done, she lay down on her bed and wept out of loneliness and boredom. Except for brief and secretive meetings with a few others working in the Resistance, she had no one to talk to.

She was arrested on June 17, 1942, at 10:30 p.m., by five inspectors of the special brigades, who had spent some weeks tailing Jacqueline Quatremaire, one of Madeleine's contacts.[7] She spent two days in the large holding cells at police headquarters, and was then sent to the cells, where she remained until the transfer to Romainville on August 10, 1942.

Auschwitz # 31644

Birkenau, the marshes, the bricks, in the revier with typhus from April 26 until May 15, 1943, then Raisko. She was part of the little group of eight women who were sent from Raisko to Ravensbrück on January 7, 1944. To avoid being conscripted for work units outside the camp (you never knew what kind of work you'd have to do and could be sent to a war factory or another strategic target of allied bombing), she got into the Siemens workshop, thanks to Czech friends involved in recruiting.

Liberated by the Red Cross on April 23, 1945, she was taken to Sweden, where she met the first deportees from the camp at Neuengamme. She asked if they knew her brother, Roger Doiret. A member of the Maquis in Yonne, her brother had been arrested on March 2, 1944, in Bassou, along with a cousin, Serge Sens, who was also a resistance fighter. She knew this from her mother's letters, because the eight women who arrived from Raisko in January 1944 were not "NN" and could receive letters until the Normandy landing. Serge Sens died of exhaustion at the infirmary in Watenstett, a Neuengamme unit, in March 1945. He was twenty-two. Roger Doiret, evacuated from Neuengamme, perished on the *Cap Arkona*, in the harbor at Lübeck, on May 3, 1945.

Madeleine returned. She found her mother, her sisters, and her father, who at the age of fifty-three had joined the Yonne resistance. She went to work as a secretary in December 1945, then married (her husband had been interned as a resister in the camp at Kobiercyn, in Poland), and had a son, Jean-Michel, in 1952. But Madeleine never completely returned. In 1958 she lost her job; her spinal column had been affected and she could no longer type. She missed her work, the social interchange and conversations at the office.

By now [1965], she suffers from the indifference, ignorance, and incomprehension of those who were not deported. Who still thinks of the forty thousand Jewish children of Paris burned at Auschwitz? One hundred and sixty-five from a single elementary school in the fourth arrondissement. She says:

---

7. The five inspectors were: Handsome (an assumed name)—wounded by a mine explosion and lost a leg; Curiner—was at Fresnes in 1945, as well as his colleague Le Leer; Tissot—freed in 1945; Guéniffet—sentenced for life.

"According to my observations of many camp survivors, there are two categories: those who came out and those who are still there. I am still there. On September 24, 1952, when I gave birth, I was not thinking of the joy a child would bring, I kept thinking—for days, months, years—of the women my age who died in the mud without knowing this joy."

Aimée DORIDAT ("Manette"), née Godefroy, and her sister-in-law Olga GODEFROY, née Camus

Born March 14, 1905, in Neuves-Maisons, near Nancy, Manette was the fifth of eleven children (seven of them boys). Their father was foreman of the factory at Neuves-Maisons, where all the sons went to work as they came of age— except for one, Louis, who worked as a peddler. They all married in the region and stayed there.

Two of the Godefroy brothers, Louis and Jean, communists before the war, joined the clandestine struggle (the Lorraine group) at the beginning of the occupation. Manette, who had never been involved in politics, hid in her home what her brothers gave her, whether tracts, grenades, or gasoline. Her husband, a designer at the factory, knew nothing about it.

On June 11, 1942, Louis and Jean were arrested in Nancy. Louis was released soon after, for lack of evidence, they said. Being cautious, he left the region, and his wife, Olga, went with him. Jean Godefroy was executed at La Malpierre (Nancy) on July 29, 1942. But the case was not closed. Once again, the Gestapo went after Louis. In order to catch him, they took all the others. Manette quickly sent him a telegram from the post office across the street from her house. The gendarmes were at Manette's a moment later. They searched the house, found nothing, and took Manette away.

All five men, their wives, and Manette were transported to the fortress at Ecrouves without any interrogation. Receiving Manette's telegram in Chaville, Olga Godefroy, Louis's wife, took the train for Neuves-Maisons. She wanted to know what was happening. Manette's eight-year-old son, informed by a railway worker, came to meet her at the station and told her the news. She should go back the way she came. Instead, she turned herself in to the gendarmerie. There was no arrest warrant for her and they would have let her go, but she insisted on following the others.

Louis had to be warned. Manette's husband, the only one still free, took it upon himself. He phoned Louis and ordered him once and for all to go into hiding. When the gendarmes of Chaville (who had probably picked up his trail through Manette's telegram) appeared at Louis Godefroy's, they said:"Get going. No one's found you." "No," he replied, "Take me away. I don't want my brothers shot on my account."

First imprisoned in the Cherche-Midi in Paris, Louis Godefroy was transferred to Nancy, to the Charles III prison. His sisters-in-law were freed from Ecrouves fifteen days later, his five brothers a week after that.

Remaining in Charles III were Louis Godefroy, his wife, Olga, and Manette Doridat. All three were transported to Romainville by train, October 30, 1942.

Auschwitz # 31766

Olga Godefroy died on February 26, 1943.

The previous evening, sick with dysentery, she had managed to slip into one of the blockhouses to avoid going to work. The block chief discovered her and sent her off with a demolition crew that included Jewish prisoners under the command of a cruel kapo. One blow from this kapo's cudgel and Olga's spinal column was broken. She returned that evening, her head touching her knees. We wondered how she'd managed to walk, even with help. She weakened and died upon arrival at the revier, right in front of Manette, who'd been working there as a cleaning woman for two days.

Three months after her death, her family received a notification from the camp: "Olga Godefroy, née Camus, born in Neuves-Maisons on April 5, 1910, deceased from a renal infection."

Auschwitz # 31767

Aimée Doridat ("Manette") entered the revier on February 24, 1943, as a cleaning woman. One day in July 1943, she broke an ankle: the stepladder she was using to climb onto a truck and fill a bucket with coal collapsed. An open fracture, gangrene. Erna, a Czech who was head of the revier and friendly with the SS doctor, arranged for Manette to be transported to the men's camp, where there was a surgery unit. Manette was entrusted to Polish surgeons, prisoners. They anesthetized her, examined her more carefully, then waited for her to regain consciousness. "We have to cut off your leg above the knee. The gangrene has gone that far," they told her. — "I don't want you to. I'd rather die." — "Don't you have two children?" — "Yes, two." — "They still need their mother. They're waiting for you, even minus one leg." — "Cut." The amputation was performed that day, July 26, 1943, and she was taken back to the revier at Birkenau. Erna, accompanied by the SS doctor, went to see her. "You've been brave," said the doctor, "ask me for anything you'd like." Manette asked for a French companion; she was surrounded by Polish women and had no one to talk to. Betty (Odette Langlois) moved next to her and spent her time killing the lice in Manette's dressing. The wound healed, they found her a pair of crutches (there was everything in the "Canada"), and Manette rejoined the members of the convoy who had gone into quarantine in August 1943. She was transferred to Ravensbrück with them on August 2, 1944; and when most of them were sent to Maut-hausen, on March 2, 1945, Manette, who was working in the *Betrieb* (the Ravensbrück workshop where they made the SS uniforms), remained behind.

Ravensbrück became hellish in the final months. Every day they made selec-tions among the old, the infirm, and the ill. They were sent to the *Jugendlager* ("the camp for young people"). This was a "death camp": the women were left to die without food or water. Manette, caught in the selection, was sent there. The blockova of the *Jugendlager* sent her back to the camp, but she lost her job as seamstress. All day long she wandered in and out of different blockhouses. Let-ting herself be seen on one leg was like asking to die. Marie-Claude was secre-tary for the revier. Every time she got wind of a selection, she warned Manette so she could hide—once under a bed where she got her head stuck in a soup pail and couldn't get out. The dogs passed close by, smelled only the soup, which did not appeal to them, and went away.

Manette was liberated by the Red Cross on April 23, 1945, transported to Sweden, and repatriated by air on June 10, 1945. Manette found her children again, who had been taken in by their grandmother, and her husband, who had not been arrested. Shortly after her return, she learned that her brother Louis, deported to Mauthausen, had died in the Gusen detachment on January 31, 1944. He was forty-four.

Aimée Doridat was one of three survivors of our convoy who was given the Legion of Honor.

Charlotte DOUILLOT, née Merlin, her daughter, Rolande VANDAËLE, and her sister Henriette L'HUILLIER

Charlotte and Henriette Merlin were both born in the twentieth arrondisse-ment in Paris, on Rue Ramponneau, where their mother was a concierge: Charlotte on January 27, 1898, Henriette on September 30, 1903. After leaving elementary school at the age of twelve, they each had to earn a living. Their mother was raising five children by herself. Then Charlotte married Henri Douillot, a machine-tool mechanic who had a workshop in Bondy. She worked with him as a machine cutter—a job in which you can easily cut your fingers, too. When we knew her, the last fingers on her right hand were missing. The Douillots lived in Bondy with Rolande, born on April 18, 1918, the daughter from Charlotte's first marriage.

Henriette married Alphonse L'Huillier, who worked as an undertaker, and she quit her job. The L'Huilliers lived in Paris.

In 1936 Henri Douillot was elected communist city councilor in Bondy. Mobilized in September 1939, he returned in December with an occupational deferment. In February 1940 he was summoned to the police: they wanted him to sign a statement renouncing the Communist Party. He refused. He was arrested, interned at Saint-Benoît-sur-Loire, then at the citadel of Sisteron, from which he escaped in 1941 and joined the FTP.

Clearly, Henri Douillot could not show his face in Bondy. He had to live underground. Rolande, who was married in 1939 during the "phony war," had a room in Paris in the eleventh arrondissement. Rolande's husband was taken prisoner in June 1940. Rolande returned to her mother's in Bondy. The room in Paris was free, so Henri Douillot lived there, hoarding weapons and explosives.

On May 16, 1942, the special brigades, who had been on Douillot's trail for several days, arrested him there.

During that day, his wife, Charlotte, and Rolande, who were coming as usual to bring him supplies and clean laundry, were apprehended by police posted near their building.

At police headquarters, the Douillots were reunited with the L'Huilliers: Henriette, her husband, Alphonse, and their son, Roger, all arrested a few hours earlier. When the Douillots had gone to lunch with the L'Huilliers the previous Thursday, Ascension Day, Henri Douillot was already being followed. Charlotte Douillot and Rolande, Henriette L'Huillier and her son were imprisoned in the cells.

Alphonse L'Huillier was shot at Mont-Valérien on August 11, 1942, without a trial. He was forty-one years old. After his execution, the police released his son, Roger, "because of his age" (seventeen), but not his wife, who was in a cell at the Santé from August 24 until September 29, and transferred from there to Romainville.

Henri Douillot was sentenced to death by a German court on September 30, 1942 (along with Losserand, Carré, and France Bloch-Sérazin), and shot on October 21, 1942, at the shooting range at Issy-les-Moulineaux. He was forty-one years old.

Charlotte Douillot and her daughter arrived at Romainville on October 27, 1942. There they were reunited with Henriette L'Huillier. All three left in the convoy on January 24, 1943.

Auschwitz # 31762

Charlotte Douillot died of dysentery in the revier at Birkenau, March 11, 1943.

Auschwitz # 31688

Henriette L'Huillier died of typhus, May 23 or 24, 1943.

Rolande Vandaële entered the revier with typhus at the end of April 1943, after her mother's death. She saw her aunt die there. She left the revier, scarcely able to stand, went into quarantine on August 3, 1943, and later passed through Ravensbrück and Mauthausen, returning to Paris on April 30, 1945.

She was reunited with her grandmother, still working as a concierge on Rue Ramponneau. The old lady had learned of her daughter Charlotte's death from a notification of decease from Auschwitz dated August 7, 1943, but had received nothing for Henriette. Rolande did not dare tell her that Henriette had died as well. It took years for Madame Merlin to understand what had happened. She died in 1949.

Rolande's husband returned from captivity in May 1945. The two young people, who had been married in November 1939, had spent only twenty-three days together—he was on leave for a time during the "phony war"—when they were separated. An auxiliary with the PTT before the war, Vandaële was hired back again as a mailman. The Vandaëles settled in the Douillots' detached house in Bondy, with grandfather Douillot.

Responsible for her two grandparents and further debilitated after the birth of a son in 1946, Rolande nonetheless went back to work as a pattern maker and cutter for ladies' coats and suits. She stopped working only after having a serious operation. In 1964 she finally obtained an identity card as a political deportee and was officially recognized as disabled. She has a pension of 330 francs per month, but now she never leaves her little house. Her husband does the shopping, brings back groceries and other supplies. Not that she is physically incapable of coming and going, but she is afraid to go out, afraid of being alone in the street, and uses all sorts of pretexts to avoid crossing her threshold. It's as if Rolande, like Yolande Gili and many of the returnees, used up in a few months at Birkenau all their resources of energy, all the vitality meant to last a lifetime. She is alive, but her will to live is broken.

Germaine DRAPRON, née Lagarde

Born on January 1, 1903, in Sireuil, Charente; her father died when she was still a small child. She would remain an only daughter. Her mother remarried a railway worker, a communist, who was interned in Algeria during the war.

Germaine married another railway worker, Gaston Drapron, in 1929.

They were arrested on September 21, 1942, at their home in Saintes. A railway employee, a friend of Germaine's stepfather, came to live with them and brought a suitcase he intended to leave in their keeping. The man was being followed; the suitcase contained tracts for the National Front.

Germaine Drapron was imprisoned in La Rochelle until the end of October 1942, then in Angoulême, and transferred to Romainville on November 18, 1942.

Auschwitz # 31808

Germaine Drapron had exanthematic typhus, participated in all the work details at Birkenau (the marshes, the bricks, the sand, etc.), benefited from the quarantine on August 3, 1943, and was transferred to Ravensbrück on August 2, 1944, and from there to Mauthausen on March 2, 1945. She was liberated on April 22, 1945.

She returned to Saintes and was united with her daughter, who had been fourteen at the time of her parents' arrest and taken in by a grandmother. Germaine's house, situated near the train station, had been bombed. Her husband returned from Oranienburg shortly after she did. They resumed their peaceful life.

Named soldier second-class in the RIF.

Marie DUBOIS, née Corot

Born on February 27, 1890, in Beaune, Côte d'Or. Her father was a stonecutter in Dijon. Orphaned early, she was handed over to public assistance.

She took a job near Paris several years after leaving elementary school, working as a cook and waitress in a Levallois restaurant. She married Lucien Dubois, a road worker; in 1936 the couple bought a café in Saint-Denis, 4 Route d'Aubervilliers (now Rue Marie-Dubois).

In 1942 Lucien Dubois was a prisoner of war. Marie Dubois managed the café alone; a sister-in-law sometimes came to help her. This sister-in-law was intrigued by the comings and goings in the café, by the errands that took Marie Dubois away from the café without saying where she was going, hiding something under her apron. The café was a meeting place for resisters, a mail drop.

Marie Dubois was arrested by the Gestapo at the end of September 1942 (public rumor accused a neighbor of denouncing her). She was doing her washing. "Just one question." She followed the Germans without removing her apron. They interrogated her in Rue des Saussaies, and immediately sent her to the fortress at Romainville, where she remained until the departure. On the eve of departure, January 21, 1943, Lucien Dubois, freed from the prisoner-of-war camp under the troop relief of January 15, 1943, came to the fortress. They refused to let him see his wife.

Auschwitz # 31693

Marie Dubois died in Block 25 on February 10, 1943.

She had raised her hand the morning that the SS doctor asked the women who could not bear roll call to identify themselves. When Marie Dubois raised her hand, Marie-Elisa, who was no more aware of Block 25 than the rest of us—we'd been at Birkenau only a couple of weeks—but was suspicious, tried to stop her: "Stay with us. You don't know where they're going to take you. Stay . . ." —"Oh, you know, now or two weeks from now . . ." She left the ranks.

At the end of 1943, Lucien Dubois was summoned to Rue des Saussaies. An interpreter told him that Marie Dubois's death, occurring on February 10, 1943, "resulted from an attack of uremia."

Aurélie, called "Marie-Louise," DUCROS, née Dudon ("Mama Loulou")

Born March 11, 1902, in Villenave-d'Ornon, Gironde, where her parents were truck farmers and where she was raised. After elementary school, she learned pottery glazing.

She married Joseph Ducros, a lead and zinc craftsman. They had four children: François, who was twenty when his mother was arrested; Marie, who was seventeen; Paulette, eleven years old; and Arlette, a baby of fourteen months. The two younger children were taken in by Joseph Ducros's brother and later returned to the house, which was kept by their big sister Marie.

Joseph Ducros was part of the FTP; he stored gunpowder and grenades at their home and participated in acts of sabotage. His wife supported him and sheltered resisters.

In July 1942 Joseph Ducros felt threatened and left for Oloron (Basses-Pyrénées) with their oldest son, François. He did not think they would arrest his wife.

But on July 9, 1942, Marie-Louise Ducros was arrested at home (along with Marie, who would be released) by Poinsot's police, accompanied by the Gestapo.

Marie-Louise Ducros was imprisoned in the Bourdet barracks in Bordeaux and transferred to Romainville on October 14, 1942.

Auschwitz # 31746

She died on February 28, 1943, of dysentery, after a few days in the revier.

In 1943 the mayor's office of Villenave-d'Ornon, informed of her death by the German authorities, sent a notice to the house. Marie conveyed the information to her father and brother, who were in prison. They had been arrested in Oloron on August 17, 1942.

Joseph Ducros, deported to Mauthausen, returned; the oldest son, François, deported with his father, returned as well. Their health was seriously affected. Marie-Louise Ducros was named corporal in the RIF. Military medal.

Charlotte DUDACH, née Delbo

One Sunday in September 1941, in Buenos Aires, I sat down on a bench in a square to read the most recent issue of *La Razon*. I read the news from France first, and learned that André Woog had been guillotined in Paris. Our friend Woog, a young architect and a communist, had been arrested in April 1941 by the French police in a room where he was lodging under an assumed name and had stored anti-Nazi tracts. I had known of his arrest before leaving France in May 1941. I had not known that he might be guillotined, since this was not legally possible; he was sentenced to death by the special court created in August 1941 by Pétain for trying terrorists. This was retroactive justice. I ran to the *Alvéar*, where I found Louis Jouvet.*

"What's happened?" Jouvet said to me, still in his bathrobe. "Calm down."

"Monsieur Jouvet, I'm going home. I must go home right away."

"Because you think everyone in France can't get along without you? You think your husband will be happy to see you again? He's much better off without you. The resisters don't need any responsibilities. For a soldier, a wife is just a worry."

"I must go home. I can't stand being safe while others are guillotined. I won't be able to look anyone in the eye."

Louis Jouvet, my boss for four years, had taken me along as his assistant on his tour of South America; he tried everything to dissuade me. He refused to give back my passport, he claimed there was no ship. I harassed him so much, he finally relented. I left the troupe in Rio de Janeiro, where I embarked on a Brazilian ship bound for Lisbon. There were three passengers on board. Jouvet wept as he said good-bye: "Try not to get caught. Silly girl, are you really leaving? Stay, stay, you're rushing into the lion's den." I arrived in France on November 15, 1941.

Georges was waiting for me in Pau. We went to Paris by different routes: I had a pass to cross the demarcation line; he went by back roads through the Tours region.

In Paris, we rented a studio under an assumed name and lived "in the shadows." I stayed at home; he went out several times a day. He would always tell

---

*Louis Jouvet was a well-known theatrical impresario. Charlotte Delbo was his assistant and was on tour in South America with his theatrical company when the Germans occupied France in 1940. (Trans.)

me: "I'll return at such and such a time." I did not know where he was going. Half an hour after the appointed time, my stomach would knot up. This anguish seemed to last forever, when finally I would hear his footsteps—he's coming home again, this time. He brought work home: there were texts to type, clean copies to make of articles that needed to be set for the printer. I listened to Radio London and the broadcasts from Moscow, and I took notes which I transcribed. Nearly the whole floor was taken up with documents, printing plates, one issue of *Lettres françaises* (whose editor-in-chief was Jacques Decour[8]) ready for the printer. Typing with a blanket around my knees—the winter of 1941–42 was exceptionally cold—cooking, running errands, writing, waiting. We never went out together. That way, only one of us could be recognized at a time.

When five police from the special brigades barged into our place on March 2, 1942, at noon, they threw themselves on Georges and handcuffed him, and were surprised to see me. I was too preoccupied with our guest, whom we'd sent to the bathroom before opening the door, to think about what was happening to me. When one of the policemen returned from the bathroom saying, "Nothing there," my heart beat with violent joy. The boy had gone out through the window—we were on the second floor—and had hidden in the apartment below. I learned his name only when I returned: Pierre Villon.

Georges was shot on May 23, 1942, at Mont-Valérien. I said good-bye to him that morning at the Santé. Two sergeants took me to him. He was twenty-eight years old.

On August 24, 1942, I left the Santé for Romainville, where I became acquainted with the women who would share my bunk at Birkenau: Viva, Yvonne Blech, Yvonne Picard, Lulu, Cécile, Carmen, then Madeleine Doiret and Poupette.

Auschwitz # 31661

A good number, since it can still be read on my left arm. Except for the fact that I did not go to the revier at Birkenau when I had typhus, the events of my incarceration were much the same as they were for Madeleine Doiret.

Born on August 10, 1913, in Vigneux-sur-Seine, Seine-et-Oise. Eldest of four children. Father, civil engineering riveter.

I joined the Young Communists in 1932, met Georges Dudach in 1934.

My youngest brother, aged eighteen, FFI member in Lattre's forces, was killed crossing the Rhine on April 9, 1945. I learned this when I returned on

---

8. Writer and German teacher Daniel Decourdemanche, known as Jacques Decour, was arrested on February 17, 1942, and shot at Mont-Valérien on May 30, 1942.

June 23, 1945, and I felt my will power abandon me. I have had to summon it back often since then.

Named sergeant major in the RIF.

ELISABETH DUPEYRON, née Dufour ("Babet")

Born on August 25, 1914, in Lormont, in greater Bordeaux, where she completed elementary school. Her father was a driver for the Grands Moulins of Bordeaux. The family had five children.

In 1942, Elisabeth and her husband, who was a layout carpenter in an aviation factory, were active members of the Resistance.

They were arrested on July 28, 1942, at the Guillons' [see this name] in the Charente, where they had gone to collect weapons for distribution to the first groups of the FTP.

Elisabeth was imprisoned in the Boudet barracks at Bordeaux until October 14, 1942, and transferred from there to Romainville.

Her husband was shot at Souge on September 21, 1942.

Her children, nine and a half and four and a half years old, were taken in by one of her sisters.

Auschwitz # 31731

Elisabeth Dupeyron died on November 15, 1943. She had been in quarantine with the others since the previous August 3. There were not many deaths during the quarantine. Exempt from work crews and roll calls, somewhat better fed thanks to the parcels they received, the women who had survived the six months at Birkenau came back to life. Elisabeth contracted typhus. No sick persons were allowed in quarantine: they were sent back to the Birkenau revier or to worse. "She had such a lump in her throat that she couldn't swallow. When they carried her to the gas chamber, she was still alive," said one of her companions.

Her relatives did not receive a notification of decease. On her return, Félicienne Bierge informed the children of their mother's death.

MARIE-JEANNE, CALLED "MARIANNE," DUPONT ("LILI")

Alias "Nelly Nelson": posing as an Englishwoman though without identity papers, she was arrested under this name on August 2, 1941, in Douai.

She was born in Douai on March 11, 1921, to a family of seven children. She was orphaned early and raised by the Sisters of Misericord; she had hardly any education and did not even complete elementary school.

At the Santé, where she was imprisoned on August 3, 1941, she tried to commit suicide by breaking and attempting to swallow the fragments of her lightbulb. She arrived at Romainville on October 1, 1942.

Auschwitz # 31703

She is one of the forty-nine survivors of the convoy. She was repatriated from Mauthausen on April 30, 1945.

She was married in 1947, had two children, is not in good health, and does not seem very happy.

CHARLOTTE CLÉMENCE HENRIETTE DUPUIS
("MAURICETTE")

Born on February 6, 1894, in Champvallon, Yonne, she was the eldest of three children. Her parents were farmers in Champvallon, and, after completing elementary school, she worked on the farm, which she eventually took over with her brother Charles, who was also unmarried.

In 1942, she and her brother joined the FTP. They stored tracts brought by some comrades and collected by others for distribution. Then they kept a weapons-and-munitions cache for the Resistance in Paris and sheltered fighters who came looking for arms.

Charlotte Dupuis and her brother were arrested on August 19, 1942, in Champvallon, by four inspectors from the Paris mobile brigade, four inspectors from the Dijon brigade, and Inspector Grégoire from the Yonne police. They were interrogated in Paris by French inspectors in Rue Bassano and imprisoned in the Santé on August 24, 1942.

On October 20, 1942, they saw each other again at Romainville, but in the meantime Charlotte Dupuis had done a stint in Fresnes.

Neither of them was tried. Charles Dupuis was deported to Mauthausen, Charlotte to Auschwitz.

Auschwitz # 31751

Charlotte Dupuis died of dysentery in the revier on March 8, 1943.

On his return from Mauthausen, Charles Dupuis made a stopover in Switzerland. There he met the returnees from the convoy. He learned of his sister's death from Marilou Colombain. No official notification was sent to Champvallon.

Named sergeant on March 25, 1947. Military medal.

Citation from the army awarded the volunteer Dupuis, Charlotte:

> *Resister from the first, animated by the purest patriotic spirit. From 1941 in direct contact with the national staff officer of the FTP, she completed dangerous liaison missions and kept an arsenal of weapons and munitions retrieved from the defeat of 1940.*
>
> *Arrested by the Germans on August 19, 1942, at Champvallon, Yonne, maintained a heroic attitude facing her judges, revealing nothing about her organization.*
>
> *Deported to Auschwitz, she died at this camp in 1943.*
>
> *The present citation includes the award of the Croix de Guerre with purple star.*
>
> *By general order of the 7th military region on March 28, 1947.*
>
> — *The general commander of the 7th military region.*

Noémie DURAND, née Lesterp, and her sister, Rachel FERNANDEZ

Noémie, born on July 2, 1889, in the Haute-Vienne, was raised in La Rochelle, where her sister, Rachel, was born on January 8, 1895. Both girls left elementary school very early (Rachel before finishing) and apprenticed as dressmakers. Their father was a mason, their mother worked as a domestic.

After her marriage, Noémie stopped working. Her husband was a mechanic and an officer in the navy, and earned a good living. The Durands were communists. Noémie had begun her militant activities during the Spanish Civil War, and these increased during the occupation, especially after the arrest of her husband, who as secretary of the Union of Naval Officers was executed on October 24, 1941.

In 1942 Noémie was a representative of the National Front on the regional level, arranging liaisons for the FTP throughout the Charente and printing tracts and underground newspapers.

Her sister Rachel married a café waiter, who left her a widow in 1936. She worked in a large men's store in La Rochelle. Madame Lesterp, their mother, aged seventy-two and living with Noémie, was seriously ill. Rachel had come to visit her. The police were there when their brother arrived: he was coming for news of his mother. They were all arrested. The mother was released at the end of ten days. She died, insane, the following year. The brother—who had already been interned in Gurs in 1940—was interned in the fortress at Hâ. The house was requisitioned by the Gestapo to lodge a German woman.

Noémie and her sister were interrogated the day of their arrest at the Lafond prison in La Rochelle, then imprisoned at Hâ and sent to Romainville on October 14, 1942.

Auschwitz # 31727

Noémie Durand died on February 22, 1943. She always had very swollen legs and could walk only with the help of friends. She was caught in "the race" on February 10, 1943, thrown into Block 25, and from there taken to the gas chamber in the same truck as Annette Epaud.

Auschwitz # 31723

Rachel Fernandez died of dysentery in the revier at Birkenau, March 1, 1943.

Their family received a notification of decease on June 8, 1945, when the ministry of prisoners was given the list of the deceased established by the survivors on their return.

Simone EIFFES

Born in May 1920 in Paris, she was twenty in 1940 and working as a dressmaker when she made the acquaintance of a young man whose flight from Vichy had led, like hers, to Cognac.

Simone had always given her parents cause for concern: she liked to have fun, she liked to please the boys, and she did. Georges Feldmann, this young man, was a communist who hurried back to Paris to make contact with his party and undertake whatever job they might ask him to do in the struggle against the Germans. He went back in July, and Simone went with him. In November 1940, pursued after distributing tracts in the seventh arrondissement, he hid out with Simone, who had a room on Rue Myrrha in the eighteenth. That was where they found him. Simone was arrested along with him. This was 1940, and justice still made distinctions: she was sentenced to three months in prison, and once her punishment was over, she left La Roquette. She was not personally involved in any communist activity. As for Georges Feldmann, he was sentenced to death and executed.

In October 1941 a comrade of Feldmann's met Simone by chance at the Barbès Uniprix. What had become of her? She had been working for the past two years for a tailor in Sentier; she was his mistress and had become pregnant.

She was happy to discover this friend of Georges Feldmann; she wanted to know the latest news and to visit the Grunenbergers, who lived on Rue de la Goutte-d'Or. Feldmann's young communist comrades were all now in the Special Organization (combat groups that led the first armed attacks against the occupiers). They did not want her hanging around; it was too dangerous. Yet she paid another visit to the Grunenbergers. After spending the evening with them, she gave birth to a little girl at the Tenon hospital. They did not see her again for some time.

By March 1942—she had parked the baby with a wet nurse—she resumed her visits to her neighbors. Because they trusted her, they occasionally asked her to shelter various men in the group, who were always being followed and rarely spent the night in the same place twice. On May 8, 1942, the Grunenbergers told her not to come any more, or even to walk in front of their building. They were definite about this, without offering any explanation. Simone was probably excited by the adventures of all these young people, coming and going and always armed, and did not realize the gravity of their struggle; she did not take the warning seriously. On May 13, 1942, carrying a beautiful strawberry tart, she went to Rue de la Goutte-d'Or. Strangers opened the door. Following an attack that had taken place against a hotel of "gray mice" [informers] in Place Montholon, the Grunenbergers had not come home. The police staked out the apartment. A classic mousetrap. Simone Sampaix, coming to ask after a comrade whom she hadn't heard from in several days (he had been arrested on May 9, after the attack), showed up as well. The two Simones, who did not know each other, would stay together for one year.

Simone Eiffes was sent to the cells on May 13, 1942, until the following October 27, then to Romainville.

Auschwitz # 31764

She died of typhus in May 1943. She was twenty-two years old.

Her daughter—the baby born on November 10, 1941—was raised by Simone's parents, who were informed of their daughter's death only on the survivors' return. They never told their granddaughter. When the girl turned thirteen she finally learned that her "mother and father" were really her grandparents, and that her "godfather," the kind gentleman with a family of his own who sometimes brought her toys and delicacies, was really her father. Once the girl knew the truth, he never saw her again.

YVONNE EMORINE, née LACHAUME

Born on December 17, 1912, in Montceau-les-Mines. Her father was a miner in the Blanzy coal mines. Yvonne, an only child, lost her mother at the age of six, around the time she started school. A grandmother took care of her. After elementary school, she became a dressmaker and in 1936 married Antoine Emorine, a mediator at the Blanzy mines, a militant union man, and a communist.

In 1941, Yvonne and her husband joined the National Front. They moved away from Montceau-les-Mines, leaving their four-year-old daughter behind, and were given responsibility for organizing groups in the Charente and the Bordeaux region. Each of them had his own sector. They rarely saw each other.

Antoine Emorine was arrested by the special brigades on December 12, 1941, at the home of Marthe Meynard, in Angoulême. After the arrests in this region, Yvonne had changed assignments, so it was only several weeks later that she learned her husband had been caught.

She was arrested herself in Paris on February 15, 1942, after the police had tailed André Pican [see *Germaine Pican*], her principal contact. After several days at General Intelligence, she spent time in the cells until March 23, 1942, in the Santé in isolation until August 24, and in Romainville until the departure.

Auschwitz # 31662

She died in the Birkenau revier on February 26, 1943.

Antoine Emorine died at the Santé on April 1, 1942. The Germans said he had hanged himself. Rumor has it that he was really tortured to death on Rue des Saussaies; a fellow inmate saw him when he returned from interrogation, lying inert on a litter borne by two guards. He was in no state to hang himself.

People learned of Yvonne Emorine's death from the BBC in 1943. One of the survivors of the convoy, in quarantine at the time, must have mentioned it in a letter to her parents, who conveyed the information to London.

Little Monique Emorine was taken in by a brother of Antoine's and his wife, Jeannette, who raised her as their own.

ANNE-MARIE EPAUD, née MACHEFEUX ("ANNETTE")

Born on November 14, 1900, in La Rochelle, where she kept a café, "At the Sign of the Porpoise." Her husband was a chief mechanic with the merchant marine.

Her father was a sailor. She had two brothers who were metallurgists, another who was a sailor and died at sea, and two sisters. These women were arrested along with her and kept at the Hâ fortress for around ten days.

During the Resistance, Annette lodged many resistance members who had gone underground, and her café served as a meeting place for those responsible for interregional contacts. In addition, she had responsibility locally for tracts and underground newspapers.

Denounced by Vincent [see *Marguerite Valina*], who used to stay at her place to meet some of the FTP leaders, she was arrested in her café on July 28, 1942.

Her husband was arrested on August 8, 1942, and interned at the camp in Mérignac until August 22, 1944.

She stayed for one day in the Lafond prison, in La Rochelle, and was transferred on July 19 to Hâ, where she remained until October 14, 1942, then to Romainville.

Auschwitz # 31 . . .

Caught giving water to a woman begging for a drink at the window of Block 25, she was thrown in there herself. She was taken to be gassed on February 22, 1943, on a truck piled with the dead and the dying. Noémie Durand was with her. They sang "la Marseillaise." We were at evening roll call and saw them leave. Annette cried: "Danielle, take care of my son." Her son was fifteen years old.

GABRIELLE ETHIS, née PAPILLON, AND HER NIECE HENRIETTE PIZZOLI

Gabrielle Ethis, born on January 16, 1896, was the wife of Marcel Ethis, who had a foundry in Romainville; she helped him in his business. Before the war they were Communist Party sympathizers. German communists who had fled Germany when Hitler came to power found shelter with them. They had no children of their own but adopted a little Spanish girl, orphaned in the Spanish Civil War.

Henriette Pizzoli—born on March 5, 1920, a cardboard maker by trade—whose husband was a prisoner of war, took as her lover a neighborhood garage mechanic, a married man in his forties. She tried to break it off, but the infuriated lover threatened to kill her. Henriette was afraid. She filed a complaint. The commissioner of Romainville had been tipped off that this garage mechanic was trading on the black market, so he opened an inquest, perhaps just to discourage the man. During the inquest, he discovered that Henriette had profited from her lover's black market activities, and had taken supplies to her aunt and uncle, the Ethises. Since the Ethises were well known for their political views, the Gestapo took over the case. A productive case at that, as it turned out: the Ethises were hiding Louis Thorez and Le Gall (a communist city council member before the war), who had just escaped from the camp at Royallieu, in Compiègne.

On July 10, 1942, the Gestapo arrested Marcel and Gabrielle Ethis, Louis Thorez, Le Gall, the garage mechanic, and Henriette Pizzoli.

Marcel Ethis, Louis Thorez, and Le Gall were shot at Mont-Valérien on August 11, 1942, the garage mechanic later.

Henriette Pizzoli arrived at Romainville on July 22, her aunt on August 7, and they left together for Auschwitz.

Auschwitz # 31625

Gabrielle Ethis was the first of our convoy to be registered at Auschwitz. She died almost right away. We never heard her reproach her niece, even once.

Auschwitz # 31626

Henriette Pizzoli died of typhus after a long stay in the revier at the beginning of June 1943. She left a daughter, born on May 29, 1939, who was raised by her grandparents.

Lucienne FERRE ("Annie")

Born on October 11, 1922, in Ville-d'Avray, Seine-et-Oise, she was raised in Rochefort, where her father was a railway worker. After completing elementary school, she became a hairdresser, but we do not know if she practiced her trade before her marriage. Indeed, she married very young. In 1942 her husband was a prisoner of war.

Before the war she had joined the Union of French Girls, and at the beginning of 1942 Renée Michaux, who had known her in Rochefort, entrusted Gilberte Tamisé with recruiting her. Gilberte, returning from her mission, observed that Lucienne seemed very young and unstable. Renée Michaux, who was only twenty-two herself, did not share this judgment, and Lucienne became Annie.

Annie was arrested in July 1942 in Bordeaux. From Hâ she was transferred to Romainville on October 14, 1942. The Bordeaux branch of the Resistance accused her of denouncing a large number of her comrades.

Auschwitz # 31722

She died on March 5, 1943. She had entered the infirmary because she was suffering from frostbite of the feet. Before dying, she said to Hélène Bolleau: "Well, I only got what I deserved."

Marie Marcelle FERRY ("Mitzy")

Born on March 6, 1918, in Igney, Vosges, the youngest of five children. A poor family—the father was a glazier, the mother a cleaning woman. They handed the baby girl over to the Saint-Genest orphanage, which she left at thirteen to earn a living. She worked cleaning other people's houses here and there, moving from one town to another.

At the end of 1940, she was a waitress in a restaurant in Moulin, Allier, called "la Madeleine," on Rue des Garceaux. One of the restaurant's customers, a man who went by the single name of Robert, asked her first to perform a few small favors: give a parcel to someone who would introduce himself by a certain name, etc. Then he hired her, or rather used her, to bring prisoners of war across the demarcation line, Jews who were seeking refuge in the free zone.

Mitzy was denounced by a man named Marcel and arrested by the Gestapo in September 1941. Imprisoned in Moulin for three months—alone in a cell, chained by the ankles—she endured five interrogations and beatings. She was transferred to a prison in Dijon in December 1941, and to the fort at Romainville on December 19, 1942.

Auschwitz # 31816

She survived the first six months at Birkenau and profited from the quarantine on August 3, 1943. After two months, she was sent back to the revier with typhus, recovered, and was transferred to Ravensbrück on August 2, 1944.

She was liberated at Mauthausen on April 22, 1945.

She has since settled in the Midi. She has a grown son who is doing his apprenticeship. She leads a very quiet life because she is always tired. An unfortunate injection in the spinal column left her weakened. She has undergone several abdominal surgeries and endless attacks of boils. But she is satisfied: she has a kind husband and an easy life.

Yvette FEUILLET

Born on January 25, 1920, in Paris. At the age of ten, she lost her father, who was a baker. Left alone to raise Yvette and her older sister, the mother worked at temporary cooking jobs. Yvette was in a hurry to earn a living. She completed school at fourteen and became an apprentice in an electric lamp factory on Rue Sedaine, near the Bastille. She was a glassblower, working in suffocating heat in front of ovens with heavy doors that she had to maneuver several times a day. In June 1936 the factory was on strike. Yvette, who was a union member, was elected as a representative of her workshop and conducted herself in a spirited fashion. She joined the Union of French Girls, established in 1937, and again gave of herself unstintingly, devoting all her free time.

When resistance to the occupation crystalized, Yvette took part. At the age of twenty, she led the life of the "illegals": false papers, address unknown, no fixed residence. As a liaison agent for the clandestine central committee of the University [chapter of the] National Front (Politzer, etc.), she was arrested on March 2, 1942, imprisoned in the cells until March 23, in the Santé in isolation until August 24, 1942, in Romainville until the departure.

Auschwitz # 31663

In April she was forced to enter the revier: chilblains on her ankles were infected, making deep wounds, which nonetheless healed. Then she contracted typhus; she died on July 8, 1943.

There was no official notification from the camp. In January or February 1944, someone, informed by a letter from one of us, told her sister Henriette of Yvette's death.

Marie-Thérèse FLEURY, née Naudin

Born July 21, 1907, in Paris. Her parents had come from the Cher before World War I. Her father had first worked on the tramways, then for the postal service. He was a mailman in the fifteenth arrondissement.

After elementary school, Marie-Thérèse went to the secondary school on Rue des Volontaires, then entered the postal service as an apprentice. She was soon hired as a regular employee. She became a union member and was elected to the executive commission of the United Postal Federation, then was named adjunct federal treasurer. She also joined the Union of Women against the War and Fascism. Her life as a militant and her personal life completely overlapped: she married a colleague, Emmanuel Fleury, elected as a communist city council member for the twentieth arrondissement in 1936 and reelected repeatedly thereafter.

From the beginning of the occupation, Marie-Thérèse participated in setting up a resistance organization within the PTT (an intelligence service in liaison with the FTP).

She was arrested in October 1941 by the Gestapo and incarcerated in the Santé. Her whole group was tried by a German war council on June 18, 1942. Like Josée Alonso (who rejoined the group of post office employees), Marie-Thérèse Fleury was acquitted but not freed: she was interned at Romainville on August 1, 1942.

Auschwitz # 31839

Emmanuel Fleury, by then living clandestinely, received a telegram from Auschwitz on April 20, 1943: "Marie-Thérèse Fleury deceased on April 16, 1943, myocardial deficiency, at the Auschwitz hospital." In fact, the telegram was addressed to Marie-Thérèse's parents (she could not have given her husband's address, as he had none), but the postal workers had quickly communicated with Emmanuel Fleury and had transmitted the telegram to London as well. Before the end of April 1943, the BBC announced in a French-language broadcast that the wife of Emmanuel Fleury, communist city councilor, had died at Auschwitz.

A tract was distributed in Paris. One day in May 1943, people filed silently past the Fleurys' house, some with flowers.

Marie-Thérèse had left behind an eight-year-old daughter, Denise, who was first entrusted to her grandparents in Paris and then sent to the Cher when it became known that the Germans were threatening to take the children of re-sisters hostage.

Rosa-Michelle FLOC'H ("Rosie")

Born on September 15, 1925, in Saint-Aubin-le-Vertueux, Eure, the fifth of six children. She was the youngest girl in the convoy, and we changed her name to Rosie. Her father, a railway worker on the state system, worked at the Mont-parnasse station. In 1940 her mother took the two youngest children and fled to her native region, Le Relecq-Kerhuon, near Brest.

Rosie left school after her elementary education and stayed home to help her mother. In the afternoons she would often go for a stroll through the streets of Brest.

On December 8, 1942, Rosie went out after finishing the lunch dishes; her mother never saw her again.

She arrived at Romainville all alone. She seemed like a little girl. At night she would wake up sobbing, calling for her mother, crying: "Papa, run, they're going to catch you!" Josée used her influence as head of the camp to put her with Simone Sampaix so she could have a friend her own age.

The girl told us that on December 8 she was caught writing on the wall of a school in Brest. She was making "V"s and changing "Vive les Allemands" into "Vive les Anglais" when a sergeant passed by. He took her to headquarters in Brest, and from there she was sent to Romainville by train some days later, es-corted by a single policeman. Before they reached the fort, he left her alone on the streets of Romainville, telling her: "Wait for me, I'll be back." She waited. Finding her where he'd left her, he gave her candy and took her to the prison. He'd given her a chance to escape, but she hadn't understood.

Auschwitz # 31854

She died in the Birkenau infirmary at the beginning of March 1943. Her mother was notified by the Relecq-Kerhuon mayor's office long after the end of the war.

Hélène FOURNIER, née Pellault

Born December 23, 1904, in Cussay, Indre-et-Loire, where her father was a blacksmith and where she attended school. Her father, a socialist and a free thinker, had a great influence on her: he was an upright and uncompromising secularist. Stipulating in his will that he wanted a civil burial with his coffin draped in a red flag, he inspired both fear and respect in this somewhat reactionary village in the Tours region.

During the occupation, Hélène Fournier wanted to do something. She did not belong to any party and was looking for a Resistance group to work with. She spoke to socialist friends who were part of the Libé-Nord network in Tours, and they got her involved.

Hélène and her husband ran a grocery business. They were well-known and respected, and dealt with many people. They took advantage of the possibilities offered by their shop to pass on orders from the Resistance and to influence opinion against the occupiers. They collected funds and supplies to help the families of prisoners and of those who had been executed. They gave asylum to escaped prisoners.

Hélène Fournier was arrested on October 29, 1942, by two undercover agents of the Gestapo. Her husband, as usual at that hour, was out gathering supplies. He was not arrested. On the way from her shop to the prison in Tours, she was beaten. Why? What did they want her to confess? She had been denounced by the daughter of a woman who was buying groceries from the Fourniers to make parcels for her son, a prisoner of war.[9]

Imprisoned in Tours until November 7, 1942, Hélène Fournier arrived at Romainville along with the whole group of Touraine natives.

Auschwitz # 31793

Birkenau: fields, marshes, demolitions, carts, bricks, felling trees, with two breaks (for typhus, entering the revier on April 28, 1943). She took part in the external work crews until June 1943, and for the last month she was the only Frenchwoman. The other women from the convoy were either at Raisko or in the revier, ill or disabled. She was at the end of her tether. Finally in June 1943, thanks to Marie-Claude, she went to work in the revier as a cleaning woman. There she had friends she could talk to and no roll call to endure; if there had been no quarantine on August 3, 1943, however, she wouldn't have made it. She was so thin she thought she saw herself in all the photographs of deportees taken when the camps were liberated. Her thigh bones were fifteen centimeters apart. Thanks to the food parcels she received from home, she regained her strength: "I would curl my fingers into my palms and feel my flesh filling out again."

She followed the group's itinerary: transferred to Ravensbrück on August 1944, from there to Mauthausen on March 2, 1945. She returned to Tours on

---

9. The girl was arrested by the FFI after the liberation, sentenced to ten years of hard labor, and freed after five years for good behavior.

May 1, 1945. Her husband and her daughter, who had been fifteen when she left, were waiting for her. After a period of rest and recuperation, she returned to her business. And for a long time she collected the wilted lettuce and cabbage leaves that fell from the crates.

The only survivor of twenty women from the Tours region (seventeen persons from Tours were arrested when she was, and two others were already in Romainville), she had the task of notifying the families, telling them how their mothers and daughters had died, and what Birkenau had been like. "That was my duty. I was lucky enough to come back." She has now [in 1965] retired, has settled in a pretty house in Tours, and divides her life between her married daughter and her grandson, her husband, who has always treated her with the utmost tenderness, and her many efforts to serve the memory of her comrades.

Named a corporal in the RIF, she received the Legion of Honor in March 1966.

Marcelle FUGLESANG

In July 1914, Jean Fuglesang, a Norwegian living in Paris, where he had an import business, took his wife and four children (Marcelle at eleven was the eldest) to vacation in Norway as he did every year. The war prevented their return to France. Mr. Fuglesang took a new position in Oslo and decided to stay; but Marcelle wanted to finish her studies in Paris. She probably identified more with her French mother, whose nationality she would claim several years later—not without difficulty, for she was born in Oslo on February 21, 1903.

Marcelle Fuglesang returned to Paris in 1920. She studied nursing, social work, and child welfare. She loved France and adopted its manners, ideas, and religion: she converted to Catholicism and became quite religious.

In 1939 she joined the army as a nurse. When the Narvik expedition set off, she thought that her knowledge of Norwegian would be useful and joined an advanced surgical unit that arrived at Narvik just as the expeditionary force was packing its bags. After many hardships, Marcelle Fuglesang crossed Sweden, reentered France, and asked for a new job. The National Relief agency was looking for a social worker to head its operations in Charleville. No one wanted to go there. Communications were intermittent (this was the beginning of 1940), and the zone was dangerous. Marcelle Fuglesang put her pack on her back and reached the Ardennes.

There was a great deal to do in Charleville, supervising social work with the impoverished families of prisoners of war. But easing their hardship was not enough for Marcelle Fuglesang. She despised the Germans and wanted to do more. Her love of France made her a fervent if incautious patriot. When she passed Germans in the streets, she was openly defiant. The chance to do more presented itself when Paul Royaux[10] created a network to help escaped prisoners. Charleville became a link in a chain that began in the prisoner-of-war camps, a way station on the road to Besançon and Switzerland. English and French escapees who came to Charleville were taken in by the National Relief Agency directed by Marcelle Fuglesang and housed in the rest center, where they were provided with identity papers, clothing, food, a train ticket to Besançon, and a password for the person who would help them cross the border into Switzerland.

The Germans soon suspected the existence of this system. They slipped one of their own men among the escapees. Passing himself off as an Englishman, this man showed up in Charleville. Marcelle Fuglesang, who knew English, questioned him. He must have played his role well, since he was given papers and provisions like the others and continued on his way.

Soon after, on October 28, 1942, Marcelle Fuglesang was summoned to command headquarters. She went without hesitation and with the insolence characteristic of her attitude toward the Germans. The false Englishman was there. Marcelle Fuglesang took everything on herself. She could not, however, save Léa Lambert, the cook at the rest center, or Anna Jacquat.

Imprisoned in Charleville until November 10, 1942, in Saint-Quentin until December 19, 1942, and in Romainville until the departure.

Auschwitz # 31826

Arriving in Birkenau, she told Marie-Claude: "If they want to make us work, we'll refuse. They can't force us to work—we're protected by the Geneva Conventions." Dear Fuglesang.

She died at the beginning of March 1943. Marie-Jeanne Bauer was working as a nurse in the revier when Marcelle was there. She called to Marie-Jeanne. Depleted by dysentery, she was lucid and not feverish. She said: "It's over. I've lost my faith. There's nothing to it." And Marie-Jeanne, the communist, the unbeliever, answered her: "Yes, Marcelle, there is. Now, you must have faith."

Marcelle's parents in Norway learned of her death through a cousin in Paris who had contacted the survivors on their return.

Croix de Guerre. Medal of the Resistance. Legion of Honor.

---

10. Paul Royaux, who had become a commander in the RIF, was caught in another circumstance and shot at Lille in June 1944.

Marie GABB, née Thomas

Born on March 24, 1891, in Amboise.

Along with her husband, a worker in the lime ovens at Amboise, on the way to Tours, she and her two brothers—the Thomas brothers—were passing letters to the unoccupied zone. They belonged to a network. Which one? No one is left to tell us. They are all dead, and no one in the Resistance ever knew the real names of their comrades. Marcelle Laurillou, Germaine Jaunay, and Rachel Deniau were part of the same organization. They were all denounced and arrested during the summer of 1942.

Madame Gabb was imprisoned in Tours and transferred to Romainville on November 7, 1942.

Auschwitz # 31 . . .

She died, exhausted by the journey, the very day she arrived at Birkenau, January 27, 1942.

Her husband and her two brothers died in the deportation. She had no children.

Madeleine GALESLOOT, née Van Hyfte

Born on May 17, 1908, to a Belgian farm couple who had three children and eventually settled in Bassevelde, where Madeleine lived from 1912 until her marriage. She left school early and was hired out as a servant.

In 1937 she married Pierre Galesloot, a Dutch typographer living in Belgium, and settled with her husband in Forest (Brussels).

Wanted for their activity in the Resistance, Pierre and Madeleine Galesloot came to Paris in 1942, not to seek refuge but to continue the struggle. They must have made immediate contact with the underground printing presses of the National Front: they were arrested by the special brigades along with the National Front printers on June 18, 1942, in a hotel where they were staying, at 17 Rue Claude-Bernard, in the fifth arrondissement.

Madeleine Galesloot went from the cells to Romainville on August 10, 1942, and from Romainville to Compiègne and Auschwitz.

Auschwitz # 31642

She died in March 1943 of dysentery.

Her parents learned of her death from survivors of the convoy in November 1945.

Pierre Galesloot was shot at Mont-Valérien on August 11, 1942. He was thirty-three years old.

Yvonne Renée Lucie GALLOIS

Born on April 25, 1921, in Sorel-Moussel, Eure-et-Loir, to a family of four children. Her father was an agricultural day laborer, her mother a domestic at the sanatorium in Dreux. Yvonne Gallois went to elementary school first in Sorel-Moussel, then in Muzy, and began to earn a living after completing her primary education.

In 1942 she was a cook in Paris, in the twentieth arrondissement, a job with no room provided and the board so stingy that her mother had to send her supplies. She kept company with a young man, Marc Laine, who was in an FTP combat group. At the beginning of September 1942, he took part in an attack at the Porte d'Orléans. A man was killed. *Paris-Soir* related the event as if it were a crime. Yvonne Gallois wrote to her mother: "This wasn't an ordinary event. I'll explain later." Marc Laine was not caught on the spot; he managed to flee—without being seen, he thought—but the Gestapo came to arrest him at his home on September 16. He was shot on November 24. Yvonne Gallois was arrested at the same time. She was consigned to the cells until January 23, 1943, and the next day took the train at Compiègne.

Auschwitz # 31849

No one witnessed her death.

After the war, the Veterans Ministry informed her family that she had died at Auschwitz on May 25, 1943. This is unlikely, for if she had lived with us at Birkenau from January 27 until May 25, we would have gotten to know her and someone would have remembered her.

Suzanne GASCARD, née Leblond

Born on September 29, 1901, the eldest of three children, she was raised in Rueil-Malmaison, where her father was a mason. She left school in July 1914 after completing her elementary education. Her mother died as a result of illness, her father was mobilized. Suzanne took her mother's place with the two younger children, and she kept house for them until her marriage in 1921.

The couple settled in Pacy-sur-Eure, where her husband was a truck driver. A daughter was born in 1924. In order to help with the household expenses, Suzanne, who had never worked outside the home, became wet nurse to a baby whose mother stopped visiting in 1929 and simply disappeared. The Gascards found themselves with one more child.

Husband and wife were Communist Party sympathizers. They went to meetings, read *L'Humanité*, and this was the extent of their activities. But after June 1940 they wanted to act.

On November 9, 1941, the gendarmes of Pacy-sur-Eure, accompanied by the special commissioner from Evreux, paid a visit to the Gascards. They brought an arrest warrant. Tracts had been distributed in preparation for a demonstration on November 11, 1941 [the anniversary of the World War I armistice]. Suzanne had been denounced by a neighbor who had seen her going back and forth to the station to drop off or pick up a suitcase. This denunciation was enough. And indeed, the neighbor had guessed the truth.

That day Suzanne was home alone with the children. Her husband was in transit. While the police were searching—and found nothing—the daughter, who was eighteen, quickly sent a message to her father not to come home.

Suzanne Gascard was interrogated at police headquarters in Pacy-sur-Eure, where she was kept for two days; then she was transferred to Evreux for two more days, and afterward to Bonne-Nouvelle prison in Rouen.

On November 26, 1941, she was sentenced to one year in prison by the special court in Rouen. She completed her punishment in Bonne-Nouvelle (the following year she could tell Claudine Guerin that she met her mother, Lucie Guérin, there). On November 20, 1942, after serving her sentence, Suzanne Gascard was not released but sent instead to Romainville.

Auschwitz # 31811

She died in the revier of dysentery at the end of February 1943.

On July 5, 1943, two regional policemen—one of them spoke French—arrived on bicycles at the mayoral offices in Pacy-sur-Eure. They were looking for Mireille Gascard and hadn't found her at home. At her place of work, the shop foreman called, "Mireille Gascard." The girl left her post and went to the office. "Your mother died on February 26, 1943, in the hospital at Auschwitz. From the flu," said the one who spoke French. They held out their hands, and she, nonplussed, let them take hers. Suzanne's husband lived in hiding for some time. He was not harassed.

Suzanne Gascard was named a sergeant in the RIF. She was posthumously given the military medal, the Croix de Guerre with palm leaf, and the Medal of the Resistance.

Laure GATET

Born on July 19, 1913. Her father was an inspector of education in the Dordogne. She did her secondary studies at the lycée in Périgueux, her university studies at Bordeaux. She did a doctorate in pharmacology, then a doctorate of science in 1940, and became assistant to Professor Genevois at Bordeaux.

Laure Gatet was a serious Catholic, a believer in justice, and a patriot. She was in the Notre-Dame Society, later the Castille network, transporting supplies and collecting information so cleverly that her aunt, with whom she was living in Bordeaux, and her colleagues at the laboratory were unaware of her activities. Nonetheless, she was caught. What had she done to put the police on her trail? No one knows. At 5 a.m. on the morning of June 10, 1942, three policemen (one French and two German) came to arrest her at her aunt's. They searched the house and found nothing.

Laure Gatet was first imprisoned in the Boudet barracks, then at the Hâ fortress in Bordeaux, where she was held for eight days; she was transferred to the Santé until October 15, 1942, then to Fresnes. She arrived at Romainville on January 15, 1943, one week before the departure. The women at the Santé who had heard Laure's voice reciting the prayer for the dead for those leaving in the convoy finally saw her face: it was clear and fervent, like her voice.

Auschwitz # 31833

She died at Birkenau around February 15, 1943.

She had dysentery from the time we arrived. She was depleted in a few days and entered the revier, but she was sent back because she had no fever. With dysentery, in fact, the temperature is rather lower than normal. One evening, Laure Gatet returned with us from work. She died the next morning at roll call.

No official notice. After our return, Hélène Solomon told Madame Genevois of Laure's death.

Named a second lieutenant in the RIF. Croix de Guerre. Military medal. Legion of Honor. She was not even thirty years old.

Raymonde GEORGES, née Le Margueresse

Born on January 18, 1917. She was a militant in the Communist Youth and embraced life with enthusiasm, even exaltation. For her, love and courage for the struggle were intertwined: love for her husband, Daniel Georges, a young communist whom she had married in 1939, and the struggle for freedom.

She had been arrested a first time at the beginning of 1940, during the "phony war," for being a communist. In June 1940, the prison at La Roquette was subsumed by the prison at Blois, from which, soon after, the female inmates were sent out on the roads in the general exodus. Raymonde Georges escaped during the march and took her place in the ranks of the fighters at the beginning of the occupation.

In 1941, she was in the OS and then in the FTP. Her tasks were numerous: transporting weapons, supplying partisans, acting as liaison between Colonel Fabien (who was her brother-in-law) and the young people who were already forming an underground force in the forest of Fontainebleau.

One day she was getting into a train at Avon when her knapsack came open. Her things fell out, including a revolver. French travelers alerted the police. Raymonde tried to escape, hid out in the toilets of the train car, and was caught. This was August 11, 1942.

She arrived at Romainville on October 21, 1942.

Auschwitz # 31 . . .

She entered the revier at the beginning of March 1943 and died there soon after. Dysentery. She held out as long as she could.

She had managed to keep her engagement ring. Before entering the revier, she confided it to Madeleine Doiret, who shared the same bunk: "Give it to Danielle if I don't come back." When Madeleine Doiret went to the revier in her turn, she passed the ring on to Danielle. At Danielle's death, all the rings and wedding bands she had in her keeping were lost.

Raymonde Georges was named a sergeant in the RIF. She was twenty-six years old.

Sophie GIGAND, née Richet,
and her daughter Andrée

Born on April 17, 1897, in Beaurevoir, Aisne, Sophie Richet, the only daughter of farmers, was raised in Ressons-le-Long and married Alphonse Gigand, a carpenter in Saint-Bandry, near Amblény. In 1942 they lived there with their four children, two sons and two daughters.

The father, the mother, and the two oldest children—Andrée, born March 4, 1921, and her sixteen-year-old brother Jean—were affiliated with a group of the FTP. They were entrusted with weapons which they stored in Saint-Bandry, in a quarry with a well-hidden entrance. Jean oiled and polished the weapons and they all distributed tracts.

In October 1942, one of their group, Norbert Maurice, was arrested. They were afraid of being discovered by the police—the boy may have been tailed as he was coming home—and left their house to hide out some distance away, making sure to survey the neighborhood. At the end of a week, thinking there was nothing more to fear, they cautiously returned home at nightfall on October 22, 1942.

That night the Gestapo broke in and took the father, the mother, Andrée, and Jean, leaving the two younger children alone in the house. They stayed there several days, somehow managing to eat. Then an aunt learned what had happened and came to get them.

After one night in the barracks at Soissons, the Gigands were imprisoned in Saint-Quentin and interrogated by the Gestapo. On January 15, 1943, father and son were transferred to the Royallieu camp at Compiègne, mother and daughter to Romainville.

Auschwitz # 31844

Sophie Gigand was caught in "the race" on February 10 and died in Block 25.

Auschwitz # 31845

Andrée Gigand also died at the beginning.

Arriving at Romainville only ten days before the departure, they had no time to make friends. They disappeared into a crowd, the crowd of women who died almost immediately, amidst others dazed and paralyzed by fear.

Alphonse Gigand, interned at Royallieu for nine months, was deported to Oranienburg at the end of 1943. He learned that his son had been there before him.

Jean left for Oranienburg by the same train we took. From Oranienburg he was almost immediately sent to join a work crew in the Heinkel factories, then transferred to Buchenwald.

The SS evacuated Buchenwald in April 1945. The inmates marched toward the east for twenty-seven days. Those who survived the long march arrived in Bohemia-Moravia, where the Russians liberated them and turned them over to the Americans at Pilsen. Jean Gigand was repatriated by air on March 29, 1945. He was nineteen years old.

At the end of 1945, the Gigands learned through the Red Cross that Sophie and Andrée Gigand had died in Auschwitz.

YOLANDE GILI, née PICA,
AND HER SISTER, AURORE

They were born in Fontoy, in the Moselle—Yolande on March 7, 1922, Aurore on May 2, 1923—where their parents, Italian immigrants, had settled after World War I. (Many Italians had come at this time to work in the factories and mines of the Longwy-Briey basin.) When war broke out in 1939, the population of this region, which was slated to become a theater of operations, was evacuated to the Gironde.

The whole family settled in Vayres. Yolande married a "local," Armand Gili. Their baby was born at the beginning of 1941. Armand Gili saw his son only rarely, during furtive visits—he had abandoned his job as head bookkeeper to fight in the first groups of the FTP. Yolande made contacts, as he instructed her, and gathered intelligence.

By order of the Resistance, which had expressly chosen her because she looked like a naive Madonna by Fra Angelico, nineteen-year-old Aurore got herself hired by the Germans. She worked in the kitchens. While filching supplies for the partisans, she tried to discover the location of the occupiers' weapons cache. After months of observation, she learned that the weapons were stored in Bordeaux. She asked for a transfer ("the town would be livelier for a young woman like her; she was bored here, out in the country"). In Bordeaux she was an office worker. She managed to procure stamped passes that allowed resisters to travel from the northern zone into the southern zone, and at last obtained information on the weapons cache. The FTP, in an operation whose details remain obscure because none of the participants is left, managed to steal the weapons and hide them. But not for long. A traitor fingered the hideout to the police. Aurore and Yolande were arrested on August 30, 1942, in Vayres. Their father and mother were as well. Yolande's baby, eighteen months old, was given by the police to a neighbor.

One of them was in the Boudet barracks, the other in the fortress at Hâ until October 14, 1942; then via Romainville, the two sisters departed together for Auschwitz.

Auschwitz # 31742

Aurore Pica died in Birkenau on April 28, 1943, of thirst. She dragged herself to the marshes as long as she could. Finally, she couldn't stay on her feet anymore and entered the revier. Her lips were split all over.

Auschwitz # 31743

Yolande Gili left Auschwitz on August 2, 1944, with the group saved by the quarantine; she arrived in Ravensbrück on August 4. There she found her mother, Céleste Pica. Mother and daughter dared not speak or look at each other. The mother had to tell her daughter that her father, Attilio Pica, had been shot on October 2, 1943, at Mont-Valérien, at the age of fifty-three; Yolande had to tell her mother of Aurore's death.

Yolande was liberated at Mauthausen on April 22, 1945. She returned to Bordeaux and was reunited with her son, whom the neighbors had kept for three years. Then she went to the Lyon region to find her husband's grave. Armand Gili, commander in the FTP, had been killed in combat on June 8, 1944.

Céleste Pica returned from Ravensbrück. Until her death in 1968, she lived near her eldest daughter, who remained in Longwy, the only other member of the family who was spared.

Since her return, Yolande has remarried. She has not had another child. She doesn't work. For several years, she has been very ill and often bedridden. She cannot do the housework without help. She lives in the country, twenty-five kilometers from Bordeaux, and does not go out. Sometimes she plans on going to town, but when the time comes, she is not up to making the effort or doing anything at all. She stays home alone all day, waiting for her husband, who returns at around eight in the evening. Or she goes to visit her neighbor. Her husband is very kind, her house pleasant. After visiting her, I felt she had no wish to live differently.

Angèle Marcelle, called "Renée," GIRARD

Born on December 11, 1894. We know very little about her, only that she did not like her first name, Angèle, and called herself Renée; that she was a book-keeper, then a secretary, and finally, in 1936, parliamentary secretary to Prosper Moquet, a communist deputy; that she also worked on *Regards*, the illustrated monthly published by the Communist Party during the Popular Front. Did she have a personal life, a private life? Her activity as a militant communist consumed her.

In 1942 she was an agent of the National Front; she had no salaried employment and was available to the Resistance twenty-four hours a day.

She was arrested on June 18, 1942, in Paris, at 166 Avenue de Clichy, where she was living alone in a little apartment; in fact, she had vacated it several months earlier after noticing that the building was watched. She'd gone back that day to pick up a change of underwear; the special brigades were waiting for her. She was imprisoned in the cells from June 20 to August 10, 1942, then sent to Romainville until the departure.

Auschwitz # 31632

She died in the Birkenau revier at the end of April 1943. "I saw her die, sitting up, her eyes open, her gray hair very straight," said Rolande Vandaële, who entered the revier at that time.

Renée Girard, orphan, unmarried, only daughter, was all alone in the world. She had asked the women who managed to return to notify the comrades in her cell, in the seventeenth arrondissement.

As of 1964, no one has registered her death with the state, and although her apartment is occupied by other tenants, the rent notices are still in her name.

Germaine Emma GIRARD

Born on January 30, 1904, in Saint-Cloud. Her father was a tailor, her mother did ironing. She lived in the eleventh arrondissement. She arrived in Romainville at the beginning of October 1942.

Auschwitz # 31 . . .

We have not found her photograph and know nothing about her except that she died in the revier in March 1943. We have had difficulty identifying her because of the other Girard, Renée, and we almost forgot to include her on our list.

Fernande Laurent shared her bunk. After the return, she took it upon herself to convey the news of Germaine's death to a relative living on Rue Basfroi, in the eleventh. This relative died a few years ago.

Marcelle GOURMELON ("Paulette")

Born on June 30, 1924, in Paris, she was the eldest of four children in a family living in a row house in Arpajon. Her father was a bookkeeper who died in 1941.

Paulette left school in Arpajon after completing her elementary education. She did not do an apprenticeship—she was fifteen years old when war was declared.

In 1942 she joined the FTP and got a job in the kitchens of the camp at Montdésir, a Luftwaffe base near Arpajon. The FTP group was preparing to blow up the planes on the ground. Paulette, then eighteen, had to be the main agent, since she worked at the camp and was able to come and go freely. She stored weapons and explosives in her parents' house (in a hiding place beneath the floor). Her mother knew about it.

Paulette Gourmelon was arrested on August 27, 1942, by the special brigades of the French police, in Neuilly-Plaisance, at the same time as Pierre Benoît, a medical student and one of the heads of the FTP group that would be shot in 1943. The action was to have taken place a few days later. On August 31, 1942, Paulette's mother was also arrested in her home. The weapons had been moved. Madame Gourmelon feigned surprise. In vain.

Mother and daughter were interrogated at the General Intelligence offices of police headquarters in Paris, sent to the cells, sent from there to the Santé, then to Fresnes, and at last to Romainville, where they arrived on October 21, 1942.

Paulette left Romainville for Compiègne on January 23, 1943, while her mother remained in the fortress.

Auschwitz # 31753

Having entered the revier in March 1943 (dysentery), Paulette died of typhus in July 1943. She must have been the only one of the group in this part of the revier, since in July 1943 there were only about thirty of us left at Birkenau. No one witnessed her death. She was nineteen years old.

Madame Gourmelon was freed from Romainville on July 18, 1943, the official registration date of her daughter's death. She did not learn about it, however, until the survivors' return.

Franciska GOUTAYER ("Cica")

We knew her as "Cica," and she figured under this name on the list of the convoy's dead until we began our research.

She was born in La Guillermie, Allier, on April 19, 1900, but was a long-time resident of Tours, where she lived at 33 Rue Bernard-Palissy in a small, decrepit boardinghouse at the end of an alley. Madame Bibault was one of her neighbors.

She was arrested one evening returning from work (she was a waitress at the Restaurant Parisien, near the station). She used to leave her key in a crevice in the wall near the door, so that whoever arrived home first—she or her husband—would take it. That evening, the key was not in its place, but instead of her husband she found two Germans from the Gestapo inside. They had known where to find the key because Madame Bibault had shown them the hiding place.

And why had her neighbor denounced her? For a tract that Franciska had found under her door. The truth is, however, that she was helping fugitives to cross the demarcation line, as we learned from one of her fellow workers.

At Romainville, where she was transferred from the prison at Tours on November 7, 1942, Franciska—now Cica—got down to work making the fire, sweeping the cell, cooking the beans and noodles her comrades received and shared together. Madame Bibault was excluded from the community. Cica knew who had denounced her and the informer could never justify herself.

Auschwitz # 31780

Cica died in the revier at Birkenau at the beginning of April 1943. She had bunked with two other women, one of whom had an arm rotting with gangrene. Hélène Fournier went to see Cica: "Don't stay here. Leave. Don't stay next to that arm or you'll get gangrene too."—"I'd like to die now," she answered.

We did not find her son, who was fifteen years old in 1942 and somewhat sickly.

Franciska Goutayer's husband, also arrested, did not come back from the deportation.

Jeanne Claire GRANDPERRET, née Bergöend

Born on July 1, 1896, in Morez, Jura, to a family of five children. The father was an enameler, the mother a homemaker. Jeanne went to school in Morez and completed middle school, then learned the craft of painting on enamel. She married Roger Grandperret, a spectacle maker. These were the crafts of Morez.

In 1942 the Grandperrets, who lived in Paris, did not formally belong to any resistance organization. They received "friends" (English aviators fallen in France, officers, etc.) sent to them by one of Roger Grandperret's brothers, a member of the combat group, and helped them get to England.

On October 15, 1942, as the Grandperrets were coming home for lunch, two Gestapo agents in civilian dress showed up and searched the place. No guests happened to be there that day. The Grandperrets were taken to Rue des Saussaies for questioning. Jeanne was sent to Fresnes and then transferred to Romainville on November 2, 1942.

Auschwitz # 31 . . .

Jeanne Grandperret died in the revier at Birkenau on March 1, 1943, from a fever. Marie-Jeanne Pennec was with her.

Her family received a death notice from the camp, dated May 10, 1943: "Jeanne Grandperret passed away on March 1, 1943, at 10:45 a.m. on Kasernenstrasse, in Auschwitz."

Claudine GUERIN

Born on May 1, 1925, in Gruchet-la-Valasse, in the Seine-Inférieure, where her parents were teachers. She did her studies in Trouville and Rouen, completing her first baccalaureate. In October 1941, she became a boarding student at the lycée Victor-Duruy in Paris.

Her mother, Lucie Guérin, was regional head of the Popular Relief. Sentenced to eight years of hard labor for her activities against the occupation armies, she was imprisoned in Rennes. Claudine, who had been a regular participant in the Resistance in the Seine-Inférieure since 1940 (acting as liaison, transporting underground newspapers like *La Vérité* and *L'Avenir normand*), did not abandon the cause after her mother's arrest. She transmitted information from Paris to resisters in the Rouen region.

She was arrested on February 17, 1942, at the lycée. The special brigades came looking for her after finding a letter she had written to André Pican [see *Germaine Pican*], a Norman friend of long standing, addressed to Marie-Louise Jourdan [see this name], Claudine's Paris contact.

While under observation at police headquarters, Claudine developed ear infections. She was hospitalized at Claude-Bernard, and when she was cured she rejoined the other members of the group at the Santé. She was in isolation for six months. On May 1, her companions celebrated her seventeenth birthday by singing into the air vents. On August 24, 1942, she was transferred to Romainville, already swollen with prisoner's edema from the hunger they had suffered at the Santé.

Auschwitz # 31664

She did not live to her eighteenth birthday.

She died of typhus on April 25, 1943.

Her mother, imprisoned at Rennes, was deported to Ravensbrück in 1944. There she met Germaine Pican, who had arrived from Auschwitz on August 4, 1944, and told her of her daughter's death.

Aminthe GUILLON
and her daughter-in-law, Yvette GUILLON,
née Sardet

Aminthe Guillon was born in Violettes-Sainte-Sévère, Charente, on June 7, 1884, where her parents were farmers. She also married a farmer, Prosper Guillon, and she and her husband took over her parents' land.

In 1942 their three children, two boys and a girl, were already grown. Pierre was a prisoner of war. Jean had married Yvette, born on May 11, 1911, in Vignes, a district of Thors, Charente-Maritime. The young couple settled at the farm in Violettes.

The Guillons were communists, members of the FTP from the beginning. The fighters needed weapons. In Jonzac, there were old quarries, sometimes a thousand meters deep, that were used for growing mushrooms. The Germans used them as an arsenal, the second most important in all of France (holding the equivalent of 1,100 truckloads of munitions), to supply the Normandy front and the Atlantic coast.

Beginning in 1942, there were two hundred resisters among the conscripted workers in this underground arsenal. They were provided with false identity cards by Jonzac's mayor. The organization was very effective: quantities of arms left the quarry every day and were dispersed to the surrounding farms. All the farms of the Charente region had their weapons caches. Marcel Blateau, an electrician, hid some in a transformer. On July 27, 1942, Elisabeth Dupeyron and her husband arrived at les Violettes, looking for weapons for the FTP of Bordeaux.

That day, two men posing as pig dealers asked in a neighboring village how to find the Guillons' farm, where they had heard there were animals for sale. They headed for les Violettes but never arrived. They spent the night in a wooded area between the road and the farm; traces of their hide-out—a number of cigarette butts—were found later. On July 28, between 4 and 5 o'clock in the morning, a neighbor leaving for work at the dairy passed a company of Germans (two hundred men) in trucks. They were moving toward the farm. The farm was surrounded. Prosper Guillon and his wife, Jean Guillon and Yvette, Elisabeth Dupeyron and her husband were arrested. The Germans found some weapons, though fortunately just a few. By design these caches were not significant. The next day a neighbor went to les Violettes to look after the abandoned animals. The men (Prosper and Jean Guillon, Dupeyron) had been taken directly to Hâ, in Bordeaux. The women, first interned in the prison at Cognac, were then sent to the Boudet barracks.

The next day their son Pierre, who had escaped from Germany, arrived in the region. At Balan, a village along the way, he was warned to go no further. The farm was under constant surveillance. He went off to the Vaucluse and rejoined the friend he'd escaped with, at whose home he had spent several days before arriving in Charente.

Aminthe and Yvette Guillon left Bordeaux for Romainville on October 14, 1942.

Auschwitz # 31729

Aminthe Guillon was caught in "the race" on February 10, 1943, and died in Block 25. The official notification says February 26, 1943.

Auschwitz # 31730

Yvette Guillon died on March 16, 1943. She had entered the revier with frozen feet and died of gangrene.

The Guillons' farm was bought by a friend and neighbor, who erected a monument. Every year he bottles his best wine for the commemorative ceremony. People come from all over the region to pay homage to the Guillons.

The monument at the roadside reads:

> *Honor to the martyrs of the Resistance*
> *1940–1944*
> *members of the French Communist Party*
> *arrested July 28, 1942, victims of fascist barbarism:*

Guillon, Prosper, executed at Bordeaux, September 21, 1942
Guillon, Jean, executed at Bordeaux, September 21, 1942
Guillon, Aminthe, murdered at Auschwitz, February 26, 1943
Guillon, Yvette, murdered at Auschwitz, March 16, 1943

JEANNE GUYOT, née Guivarch

Born on September 28, 1913, in Argenteuil, Seine, she became a war orphan in August 1914. Her mother remarried, to her husband's brother, a minor civil servant.

Jeanne went first to the public elementary school, then to the parish school of Argenteuil, where she completed her basic education. She married and had two children: a boy in 1934, a girl in 1935.

Her husband had a small printing press in Argenteuil. At the beginning of 1942 he took an order from some new customers to print tracts in German for the soldiers of the occupying army.

On June 18, 1942, Jeanne Guyot and her husband went to work as usual; inspectors from the special brigades were waiting for them. The husband did not try to deny anything. He took everything on himself, hoping that his wife, who had been neither politically active nor politically interested, and who knew nothing about this clandestine work, would be released. In vain. Jeanne Guyot was sent to the cells until August 10, 1942, and was then transferred to Romainville.

Her husband was one of the group of printers executed by firing squad on August 11, 1942.

Auschwitz # 31631

She died at Birkenau. No one remembered the details of her death. Jeanne Guyot was friends with Marguerite Houdart, who died as well.

Jeanne Guyot's mother, who raised the children, did not learn of her daughter's death until the survivors' return.

ADRIENNE HARDENBERG, née Coston ("LINOTTE")

Born on September 23, 1906, in Saint-Quentin, her mother's home town, she was raised in Paris, where she attended elementary school until the age of thirteen.

Her father, who started out as an asphalt worker, was mobilized in 1914 and, after the demobilization, rose to become a supervisor of public works.

After Adrienne left school, she apprenticed in a ladies' dressmaking shop and became a cutter. In 1927 she married Pierre Hardenberg, a photoengraver; the couple settled in Bagneux. A daughter was born in 1929.

When the war broke out, Pierre Hardenberg, originally an Italian who had done military service in neither Italy nor France, was considered a deserter by the Italians and a foreigner by the French. His boss discharged him. His wife, who had given up her job when their child was born, had to go back to work.

At the beginning of 1940 she was arrested as a "defeatist"—as the communists were called. After a fruitless search of the house and a twelve-hour interrogation at Rue des Saussaies, to which her ten-year-old daughter was subjected as well, she was released for lack of evidence.

The Hardenbergs moved to the thirteenth arrondissement. To be free to devote themselves to their task, they sent their child to the country. Pierre Hardenberg now joined the Communist Party. In Rue Mouffetard, in a painting studio transformed into a printing plant, he worked as a photoengraver for the underground edition of *L'Humanité*. Because of his activities, Adrienne was ordered to do nothing.

On June 18, 1942, Pierre Hardenberg was arrested at home by the special brigades. The police waited for Adrienne to return from the market.

After a week at Intelligence headquarters, Adrienne Hardenberg was transferred to the cells, then to Romainville on August 10, 1942.

Pierre Hardenberg was shot at Mont-Valérien on August 11, 1942.

Auschwitz # 31 . . .

Her father received a notification from the camp at Auschwitz on June 25, 1943: "Adrienne Hardenberg died at the hospital at Auschwitz of a stomach ulcer on February 22, 1943."

She must have died very quickly indeed, for none of the convoy survivors remembered how she died.

She was named an adjutant in the RIF.

In 1942 the people with whom little Yolande Hardenberg was boarding told her the unvarnished truth, that her parents were arrested and taken by the Germans. The little girl fell ill (with jaundice) and when she recuperated, she returned to her grandfather's house. After some time, she went to live briefly with her paternal grandmother in Arcueil, and then to stay with her aunt (her mother's sister) in Gennevilliers. The secondary schools were closed because of bombardments, so her aunt sent her to the Pigier school to take a secretarial course. She finished her secondary studies after the war, but she was an unstable, secretive girl. She always seemed unhappy. At twenty-one, she decided to leave her family and live alone on her salary. She was a secretary.

In 1953 she was found dead at home following an abortion. It was learned that six months before she had secretly had another baby who had been placed with a wet nurse.

HÉLÈNE HASCOËT

Born on November 10, 1910, in Concarneau, Finistère, one of three children. Her father was a cabinetmaker who died in 1940. Her mother is still a dressmaker in Concarneau.

After learning the trade from her mother, she came to settle in Paris, where she opened a dressmaking studio on Boulevard Raspail. She had an exclusive clientele.

In 1942 her Jewish friends had to go into hiding. She gave them asylum.[11] Was she denounced? Or had she put herself in danger by going to Nazi headquarters to try to free a Jewish friend? No one knows. Arrested first in mid-October 1942 for questioning, she was released that evening. Eight days later, at nine in the morning, the bell rang. "Thinking it was the seamstresses arriving for work, I opened the door," her brother said. It was two agents from the Gestapo, who took Hélène to Rue des Saussaies. For a week no one knew where she was. She was at Romainville from October 22 until the departure.

Auschwitz # 31 . . .

Died in the revier at Birkenau on March 9, 1943.

She had dysentery and lesions black with infection on the insides of her thighs and suffered from dehydration.

A *stubova*[12] had beaten and insulted her, treating her as if she were a syphilitic while constantly pounding her with blows.

Afterward, Marie-Jeanne Bauer, an SS doctor, administered euthanasia with a shot in the arm.

Her parents did not learn of her death until the survivors' return.

---

11. Dora, a young Jewish woman who took refuge with Hélène Hascoët, was deported to Auschwitz by a convoy that arrived on February 16, 1943. She died soon after.

12. German-Polish amalgam. A block was divided into four sections, *Stube* in German. The *stubova* was the head of the *Stube*.

Adélaïde, called "Heidi," HAUTVAL

Born January 1, 1906, in Hohwald, the Rhine basin, where her father was a pastor. The youngest of seven children, she did her medical degree in Strasbourg, then worked in neuropsychiatric institutes and hospitals until her arrest.

In April 1942, on her way to the southern zone on private business, she was arrested by feldgendarmes while crossing the demarcation line at Vierzon. She was imprisoned in Bourges with Jews who had also been caught at the line or in the roundups. Heidi Hautval, who spoke German, protested against the way they were treated. "Very well," said the Germans, "since you defend the Jews, you will share their fate." She was sent to the camp at Pithiviers, a collection point for Jews slated for deportation. They lived in ghastly conditions. At first, Heidi Hautval was mistrusted by her fellow prisoners. The Germans pinned a yellow star on her chest with a band saying: "Friend of the Jews." From Pithiviers she was sent to Beaune-la-Rolande. The same sort of place, also full of Jews. Every day there were departures (we still don't know whether they were headed for the gas chambers at Auschwitz).

In November 1942 Heidi Hautval was taken to the prison at Orléans—the star and band were removed—then transferred to Romainville on November 17, 1942.

Auschwitz # 31802

Heidi was not immediately identified as a physician. She was put in Block 14 for the initial quarantine, but after five or six days she went to work as a doctor at the revier. She was assigned to Block 22, where she cared for German prisoners. In April 1943 she was sent as a doctor to Block 10 of the main camp (Auschwitz). This was the block for medical experiments, such as the sterilization of women by injection with caustic substances. When the organ was sufficiently burned, it was surgically excised. An SS Doctor Wirtz also claimed to do research on cancer. Heidi Hautval refused to enter the operating room or help the surgeons. SS Doctor Röder, head of Block 10, acquiesced and allowed her to care for the post-operative patients. Dr. Röder was a curious fellow, probably grateful not to be at the front. He said: "We're not responsible. We're just instruments."

When Dr. Röder left Block 10, his successor ordered Dr. Hautval to be present in the operating room. She refused. As punishment, she was sent back to Birkenau, where she no longer knew anyone. This was in August 1943, and after April nearly the whole camp population had been replaced. Some thirty-five Frenchwomen remaining at Birkenau from the convoy were in quarantine, in a separate block. The others were at Raisko.

On the evening of August 16, 1943, Orli, the inmate administrator of the revier, told Heidi she'd heard that Dr. Hautval was to be among those executed the following day. She advised: "You must give in." "No," Heidi said. So Orli made arrangements: "Take this, lie down there and don't move." She gave Heidi a sleeping pill and directed her to a bed in the revier. When Heidi woke, the danger was past. She never quite knew what had happened; perhaps they'd identified her as already dead. But what about the number tattooed on her arm? Well, so many corpses were mangled by rats, who weren't fussy about tattoos. And besides, the SS doctor in charge of examining the dead was very fond of Heidi Hautval and may have been willing to turn a blind eye.

Indeed, Heidi Hautval had been in frequent contact with this doctor during her time in Block 10; the executions took place under her windows, and she saw hundreds of them. This SS doctor was connected to the camp's Institute for Hygiene, another research institute that prepared mediums for cultures; Heidi had seen him many times coming and going with cadavers. When the bodies were returned, however, entire parts were missing—backsides, hips. Then the *Sonderkommando*, the death detail, would come to take the bodies to the crematorium.

When Heidi Hautval woke up, Orli had arranged everything. Instead of joining the convoy survivors who were then in quarantine, she went to work again as a doctor at Birkenau. In this way, she was free to nurse her comrades like Paulette Prunières (Pépée), for instance, who had pleurisy in September 1943.

In November of that year, Heidi Hautval caught typhus. It was a long illness. She resumed her job only in February or March 1944.

On August 2, 1944, she was transferred to Ravensbrück with the others. At the end of 1944 she was sent as a doctor to the camp at Watenstett, a munitions factory. But after three weeks the Ravensbrück administration realized that she was "NN" [the category of prisoners forbidden to work outside the camp or to be transported elsewhere] and consequently should not have left Ravensbrück in the first place. She was brought back and once again worked as a doctor in the revier.

After the liberation of Ravensbrück on April 30, 1945, she stayed on with Marie-Claude Vaillant-Couturier to care for the ill who could not be transported. She was repatriated only on June 25, 1945, with the last French patients.

Because she was not part of any organization or resistance network, Heidi Hautval had trouble getting a resistance deportee card. She was decorated with the Legion of Honor in December 1945 for her devotion to her comrades in the camps of Auschwitz and Ravensbrück.

Marthe, called "Violette," HEBRARD, née Guay

Born on October 15, 1911, in Paris, in the twelfth arrondissement, but raised in Montreuil. Her father was a metallurgist (later a police agent), her mother worked as a seamstress in the fur business. They were a family of militant communists.

After completing elementary school, Violette learned data processing and worked at Crédit Lyonnais and then at La Concorde insurance company until 1942. Married to a communist, Hébrard, she joined him in the clandestine struggle at the beginning of the occupation.

In 1942 they printed the underground edition of *L'Humanité* at a press on Rue des Thermopiles (in the fourteenth arrondissement) and lived on Rue Cadet (in the ninth), where they were strangers to the neighborhood. An inadequate precaution: they were both arrested on October 15, 1942, at the press.

Violette Hébrard spent six weeks in the cells, a week in Fresnes, and was transferred to Romainville in the middle of December 1942.

Auschwitz # 31 . . .

She died in April 1943 in the revier at Birkenau. No witness.

Her husband, deported to Germany by the same train on January 24, 1943, died of exhaustion during the evacuation of Oranienburg.

Violette's parents did not learn of her death until the survivors' return. They obtained a civil pension.

Lucette Suzanne HERBASSIER, née Magui

Born on December 6, 1914, in Tours, where she was raised, completed elementary school, and married. Her husband was a housepainter; she kept a small bar and snack shop on Rue de la Paix in Tours.

She was arrested on August 4, 1942, at home. She had been denounced by neighbors who had seen people coming to her house with suitcases and others leaving with the same bags. In fact, these contained underground newspapers and tracts printed by the National Front. Her husband and her nine-year-old son were also arrested. The child was brought back to the neighborhood the next day by the police, the husband was released after eight days. He claimed to know nothing. That was true. He was then taken by the STO [Obligatory Work Service] but escaped from Germany after eighteen months. He denied having any involvement in resistance activities.

Lucette Herbassier was imprisoned in Tours until November 7, 1942, and transferred from there to Romainville.

She died at the end of March 1943.

She was sent to the revier with dysentery. The next day, at work, she had a hemorrhage, returned to the revier, and never left.

Her family learned of her death from Hélène Fournier, after the return.

JEANNE, CALLED "JANINE," HERSCHTEL

Janine was a bleached blonde with hints of red in her hair, who had offered her gold watch studded with diamonds to a female SS officer in exchange for sparing her hair (the SS officer took the watch, plus several rings, and Janine's hair was cut anyway). Once she stole Alida's shoes because she had received only two socks for the same foot; the two women nearly came to blows. This was all we knew about her until 1964.

We found her name and date of birth—November 5, 1911—and a distant relative, who could give us no information on the circumstances of her arrest.

She belonged to a Jewish family of the commercial middle class. She lost her mother at an early age and traveled with her father, who had contracted tuberculosis, to various sanatoria in Switzerland. After her father's death, she went to England to complete her studies at a convent school. In 1939 she left for the United States, where she was supposed to marry, but the plans fell through. She returned to France on the eve of the war. During the occupation, provided with a certificate of baptism, she did not admit to being Jewish or wear the star. She had settled in a studio in the sixteenth arrondissement, where no one knew her. She was probably denounced (but not as a Jew, or she would not have been part of our convoy) and arrested just as she was preparing to depart. Indeed, she arrived at Romainville on January 15, 1943, with her luggage carefully packed: these were not the bags of a woman who had simply grabbed whatever she could. Her sister, who may have known something more, is now dead. Her family did not know the exact date of her arrest or even that she had been deported. More than twenty years later, we told them about the transport and the fact that Janine had died at Auschwitz in the middle of February 1943.

JEANNE HERVE

Born on June 11, 1900, in Marzer, Côtes-du-Nord, the youngest of six children, to a family living in poverty on a little tenant farm. Her father died in 1905, the mother five years later. The lease was broken, the tools and flocks sold at auction, and the children dispersed. Jeanne was taken in by an aunt, who withdrew her from school when she was thirteen and placed her in a job in the district. At eighteen, she left Guingamp, where she was a domestic, to work in Paris as a housemaid. In 1926 she married, divorced two years later, and worked at a variety of jobs: as a waitress at numerous restaurants, at the canteen of Houbigant perfumes, at the buffet in the Gare de Rouen (1928), as an usher at the Colonial Exposition (1931), as a housekeeper, etc. She always felt displaced, had no friends, and held a grudge against everyone. When she drank, which happened frequently, she was spiteful.

During the occupation, her spitefulness became dangerous. Without rhyme or reason, Jeanne Hervé denounced Jews and people she accused of dealing on the black market. One day in October 1942, her neighbors on the fourth floor were having a party to celebrate their anniversary. Jeanne Hervé was convinced she would be invited. She wasn't. Out of spite, she ran to the nearest police station—in the third arrondissement—and accused the people on the fourth floor of singing the "Internationale." Her windows were on the first floor and faced the courtyard like theirs, so she could have heard. Shortly afterward, everyone—accused and accuser—were summoned to the police station. The accused showed up, the accuser did not. The police officer came to question her, talked to others in the building, and made her face the people from the fourth floor. Jeanne Hervé was confused and admitted that she had lied. The neighbors went back to their apartment, but the policeman, probably figuring that her misdemeanors should be brought to a halt, arrested her and the Gestapo took over.

Jean Hervé was imprisoned in Romainville on October 30, 1942. Her mania was incurable: one day she wrote the commandant of the fortress to denounce one of the women in her cell as a Jew. Josée Alonso, serving as liaison between the prisoners and the camp administration, intercepted the letter.

Auschwitz # 31768

Jeanne Hervé died around February 15. An acute nephritis killed her in two days.

Her only relative, an older sister, did not know she had been deported. The two sisters had fallen out. At the Liberation, in September 1944, this sister learned from the concierge and Jeanne Hervé's neighbors that she had been arrested, and learned from us, twenty years later, the place and circumstances of her death.

Marguerite Joséphine HOUDART, née Houdelaine

Born on April 3, 1904, in Verdun to a family with three children. She was given at an early age to an aunt, who raised her in Draveil, Seine-et-Oise. There she completed elementary school.

She learned paper manufacturing, and in 1930, in Paris, she married Robert Houdart, a printer, who had a small press in the eleventh arrondissement. With the occupation, the press slackened its pace; it had done mostly advertising work, and there is hardly any need for advertising when everything is scarce and in demand. In January 1942 Marguerite Houdart had the chance to make a profit selling a stock of paper—this was the period of the black market. She got a taste for it and led her husband into similar activities; as printers, they had the right to large rations of paper, which they resold to discreet strangers.

Marguerite Houdart and her husband were arrested at their place early on Thursday morning, June 18, 1942, by the special brigades, who sealed off their apartment and workshop. The police had caught the buyers of the paper, who turned out to be communists supplying the underground presses. Marguerite Houdart and her husband denied they had acted for political motives. Indeed, they were people who held no political opinions.

In the cells, husband and wife joined the other printers arrested that day. Marguerite Houdart was transferred to Romainville on August 10, 1942. Robert Houdart was executed at Mont-Valérien on August 11, 1942. He was thirty-seven years old.

On September 3, 1942—probably because there was evidence that the Houdarts were not members of a resistance organization—Marguerite Houdart was summoned to command headquarters at Romainville: she was free to go.

But she protested: "How do you expect me to go home? There are seals on my door. Remove the seals." This was too complicated for a military man. The commandant sent her back to her cell, and that was how she left for Auschwitz with the others.

Auschwitz # 31 . . .

She died around May 10, 1943. Madeleine Doiret saw her in the blockhouse for typhus patients during the disinfection on May 1, 1943. She was not terribly thin. Then someone saw her lying on a pile of cadavers, all of one side eaten by rats.

Her daughter, who was fourteen in 1942, did not learn of her mother's death until the survivors' return.

JEANNE HUMBERT, NÉE LARCHER

Born on February 12, 1915, the only daughter of an electrician in Blénod-les-Toul, where she was born and completed elementary school.

She learned dressmaking, married, and worked at her profession; her husband, who had returned from military service with tuberculosis, could not work.

On November 4, 1942, probably following a denunciation, the Gestapo descended on the Humberts to interrogate the husband. When they learned he was on a full military pension, the police went into an adjoining room and questioned his wife. They took her away; she did not return.

In fact, Humbert had participated in several sabotage operations on the railroad tracks and his wife had transported weapons.

Jeanne Humbert left behind two children, aged three and five years, who were taken in by the two grandmothers when their father was subsequently arrested and interned in a camp in France, where he was held for five months.

Jeanne Humbert was imprisoned in Charles III, in Nancy, from November 4 to 21, 1942, then in Romainville until the departure.

Auschwitz # 31 . . .

She died at the end of March 1943.

On a demolition crew one day she was beaten so badly by an SS officer that she had to be carried back to the camp. She was already weakened by dysentery. The next day she entered the revier. There was a selection, and she was sent to the gas chamber. Manette Doridat was a nurse in the revier where Jean Humbert lay dying. On her return in 1945, Manette went to inform the family of her death.

Her husband obtained a card identifying her as a political deportee.

Anna JACQUAT, née Karpen

Born on May 24, 1894, in Gilsdorfberg, in the district of Bettendorf (the grand duchy of Luxembourg), the youngest of seven children. Her father worked in a local brickyard. In 1914 the family was scattered by the war. Anna came to Paris and worked in a restaurant in Argenteuil. At a meeting of natives from the Ardennes living in Paris, she met Jacquat, who had just been demobilized. They married in 1919 and returned to the east.

In 1942 Anna Jacquat became part of the chain organized by Paul Royaux [see *Marcelle Fuglesang*] and was involved in supplying provisions to escaped prisoners, which her business allowed her to do without being noticed: she and her husband ran a café-restaurant near the train station in Charleville.

On October 28, 1942, the Gestapo summoned Monsieur Jacquat and arrested him. For several days they searched the Jacquats' home but found nothing.

On October 30, 1942, Anna was arrested. Probably because questioning had revealed that only the wife was part of the organization, the husband was released on November 3, 1942. He returned home where his children, a fourteen-year-old daughter and a son of sixteen, were waiting for him.

Anna Jacquat was imprisoned in Charleville until November 10, 1942, in Saint-Quentin until December 19, 1942, and at Romainville until the departure.

Auschwitz # 31827

In March 1943 Monsieur Jacquat was summoned to the Gestapo, where he learned that his wife had died at Auschwitz of stomach trouble. He was so overwhelmed that he did not understand the word "Auschwitz" as it was pronounced by his German informant—he heard something like "Austria"—and when he got home he did not even know the exact date of death, though he must have been told.

It was not until the end of the war that the children understood. On their mother's behalf, they received the medal of French gratitude and a certificate of thanks from General de Gaulle, confirmation in the RIF, and a resistance internee card, although Madame Jacquat was a deportee; but until we made contact with them to do this book, they had no proof that their mother had been deported, since her death had been reported to them verbally.

GERMAINE JAUNAY, née Mouze

Born on October 12, 1898, in Francueil, called "La Bergerie," in Indre-et-Loire. Her mother died nine months after her birth. She was taken in by neighbors for some years, but then her older brother Jean, nine years her senior, took her into his house. Her father remarried, and when Germaine was eleven years old, her stepmother withdrew her from school and placed her at a farm.

She married and had four children; the eldest was fifteen in 1942. Her husband, a truck driver, was brutal and gave her no money; she did day work at various farms to raise her children.

During the occupation, she helped resisters cross the demarcation line—she lived at the border between the two zones.

She was arrested on September 10, 1942, by the Gestapo of Amboise, along with her niece Rachel Deniau [see this name], a postal worker in Amboise who was part of the same resistance chain. The organization had been denounced. By whom? We don't know. Germaine Jaunay's husband was not questioned.

She arrived in Romainville with the group from the Tours region on November 7, 1942. Her comrades nicknamed her "Philosopher" because she was always even-tempered.

Auschwitz # 31782

She died in the revier at Birkenau on April 5, 1943.

To Hélène Fournier, who tried to boost her morale, she said: "Why go back? To be beaten?" She had never been happy. She simply let herself die.

Her children learned of her death from Hélène Fournier after the return.

Marie-Louise JOURDAN, née Bonnot

Born on February 27, 1899. Her husband was a printer. She kept a dry cleaning and dye shop in Paris, in the eighteenth arrondissement.

Germaine Pican and Lucie Guérin met her first in Châteauneuf-Val-de-Bergis, in the Nièvre, during the exodus of June 1940.

In October 1942, when Lucie Guérin put her daughter Claudine in the lycée Victor-Duruy as a boarding student, Marie-Louise Jourdan was the friend who acted *in loco parentis* for Claudine Guérin. When Germaine Pican came to Paris to meet her husband, André, who was involved in the clandestine struggle, Marie-Louise Jourdan offered her place for their meetings. Marie-Louise Jourdan had very little interest in politics, but she readily volunteered such services.

On February 15, 1942, André Pican was arrested at his home in Paris. He had been followed for several days. The police had seen him go to the Jourdans'. They went there immediately and found Germaine Pican, who had just arrived from the provinces to see her husband.

Germaine Pican was arrested, as well as Marie-Louise, Raoul Jourdan, and their eleven-year-old son. These last two would be released after preliminary questioning. Two days later, during a search of the dye shop, the police found a letter that Claudine Guérin had entrusted to Marie-Louise Jourdan to forward to André Pican. They went to look for Claudine Guérin at the lycée and confronted her with André Pican. She claimed not to know him. Marie-Louise Jourdan insisted: "Come on, Claudine, you know André Pican very well."

Marie-Louise Jourdan was in the cells until March 23, 1942, then in isolation in the Santé until August 24, 1942, and then transferred to Romainville until the departure.

Auschwitz # 31665

She died of typhus in April 1943. Like Claudine Guérin.

Suzanne Renée JUHEM

Born on October 2, 1912, in Geneva, though she was not Swiss. Her father, a PLM employee at the Gare de Lyon in Paris, was originally from l'Ain and her mother from Loir-et-Cher. She was raised in Paris in the twelfth arrondissement, completed elementary school, and became a dressmaker.

She was arrested on May 8, 1942, at her home in Vitry-sur-Seine by the French police, and arrived at Romainville on October 27, 1942, coming from the cells where she had shared a cell with Marie-Elisa Nordmann.

What was her story? We learned an incomplete version of it only recently. In the autumn of 1940, she and her friend, Jean C., freely decided to go work in Germany and left for Nuremberg. What work? We don't know: until then, Renée Juhem, who was living with Jean C. in Vitry, had worked in the dressmaking studio of a Parisian department store. Several months after arriving in Germany, Jean C. fell seriously ill. He was sent back to France. Renée did not want to stay in Nuremberg alone. As it was impossible to break her contract, she fled. Caught en route, she was imprisoned in Nuremberg. She did her prison term, went back to work, and escaped again. This time, she succeeded. She went through Switzerland and stopped on the way home with a cousin in Bourg. Then she reached Loir-et-Cher, where she stayed with her father. Thinking that after a few weeks the Germans would stop looking for her, she went home to Vitry-sur-Seine. Jean C. was not there. He had gone to the Toulouse region. Rumor has it that he was a militant in the ranks of the Communist Party, though we could not verify this. How and why was Renée arrested? The police must have searched her place and found tracts in Russian. She was sent to the camp at Miguères, then to Orléans, and was transferred from there to the cells, where she found herself with the group that included Antoinette Besseyre, Yvonne Carré, and Louisette Losserand. She did not seem to be an opportunist.

Auschwitz # 31759

She died of dysentery between March 11 and 15, 1943, in the revier.

Her family was notified of her death in 1948 by the mayor's offices of Vitry-sur-Seine.

Irina KARCHEWSKA, née Byczeck

Born on December 5, 1899, in Gzichow, Poland, she had emigrated to France with her husband in 1924 or 1925; they kept a restaurant-grocery featuring Polish specialties at 20 Rue Charlemagne, in Paris.

Irina and her husband were arrested by the Gestapo on July 15, 1942, at their home, where they'd been hiding Poles trying to get to London; they had been denounced.

After the Santé and Fresnes, Irina Karchewska arrived at Romainville on September 30, 1942.

Despite her age and infirmity (she was lame), she held on until April 30, 1943, when she died of dysentery.

EMILIA, CALLED "LÉA," KERISIT, NÉE BALITEAU

Born on July 30, 1895, in Jaunay-Clan, Vienne, where she completed elementary school and later earned her nursing degree.

Her husband was a cabinetmaker. At the time of their arrest, they were living at 135 Rue Colbert in Tours, and had three boys: René, twenty-two; Marcel, twenty; and Jean, eighteen.

Léa Kerisit was arrested on September 23, 1942, in front of the Tours cathedral, as she was leaving work at the Saint-Gatien hospital. She was wearing her nurse's uniform. She had been denounced by Werner Hermann, a Gestapo "mole" who had passed himself off as an escaped prisoner of war attempting to reach the unoccupied zone; he exposed the whole chain, in which Germaine Maurice was also involved.

From the prison in Tours Léa Kerisit was transferred to Romainville on November 7, 1942.

Auschwitz # 31783

Soon after our arrival, on February 24, she was taken into the revier as a nurse, in the German block. Most of the German inmates were common criminals. They made the law in the camp. Léa Kerisit was her patients' scapegoat. She was beaten more than once because she refused lesbian advances. When she was sick with typhus, in April 1943, one of her torturers bludgeoned her to death.

Léa's family learned of her death from Hélène Fournier after the return.

KAROLINA KONEFAL
AND ANNA NIZINSKA

Karolina was born on October 25, 1920, and Anna on November 7, 1917, in Warsaw. They arrived from Poland, no one knows how, knowing not a word of French. They were dressed like peasants with kerchiefs on their heads, huge, colored shawls wrapped around their shoulders—more like bedspreads than shawls—and long, garish skirts. For luggage, they had only a white string bag to which they were very attached and an alarm clock to which they were even more attached, though they didn't know how to set it and it rang at all hours in the cell at Romainville.

Why had they been imprisoned in Romainville on October 2, 1942? Perhaps—though this is only conjecture—they were hoping to join compatriots in Paris. They had an address that corresponded to someone in the Monika network: they arrived on the same day as Félicia Rostkowska and Eugénie Korzeniowska.

Auschwitz # 31707

Karolina was thrown by an SS officer into the stream where she was trying to take a drink. Beaten and soaked (this was in March 1943 and it was cold), she died a few days later.

Auschwitz # 31702

Anna Nizinska died around the same date, March 1943. No one can say precisely when or how.

Eugénie KORZENIOWSKA

Born on November 11, 1901, in Poland. She was raised in Lublin. Her father, a railway employee, was a socialist. He had taken part in the revolution of 1905 and been deported to Siberia.

Eugénie had come to France in 1931, hired as a teacher by the Polish board of inspectors, at the Polish embassy in France, to work at a school near Saint-Etienne for the children of Polish miners.

Her colleagues lost track of her during the war. She was probably affiliated with the Monika network (she was connected to the Brabanders). We do not know the circumstances of her arrest, but perhaps she was detained at the same time as the Brabanders, since she arrived at Romainville on October 2, 1942.

Auschwitz # 31700

She was not at Birkenau for long. We think she was caught in "the race" on February 10, 1943, and put in Block 25, for she was disabled: she had bad hip problems and walked with a serious limp.

Marguerite Maria KOTLEREWSKY, née Urgon

Born on February 15, 1903, the only daughter of Auvergne natives who had left their land in 1900. Marguerite left the convent school at seventeen, and through her father got a job as a secretary at *Paris-France*.

In 1923 Marguerite Urgon met Nathan Kotlerewsky and married him. The family from Auvergne was indignant. As a Russian émigré sixteen years older than Marguerite, Kotlerewsky must have led a wild life, and he had owned a Russian nightclub during the Roaring Twenties. Furthermore, he was a Jew. Only Marguerite's father did not break with his daughter, who was very happy with her foreign husband. Kotlerewsky successively had a shoe repair shop in Belleville, a shoe store, and a knitting business in the third arrondissement. They lived on Rue Saint-Martin and had three children: Gisèle, Léon, and Jacqueline. They paid no attention to religion.

In 1942, when the "racial" laws went into effect, Marguerite was fearful. She looked for a priest who would be willing to issue predated certificates of baptism for her husband and children. She could find no one. In Blois—in the unoccupied zone, where she had convinced her husband to follow her—a Protestant minister baptized the whole family and predated their certificates to 1937. She was somewhat reassured.

Nathan Kotlerewsky did not want to stay in Blois. What could they do in the Auvergne? Besides, what was there to fear? Should he wear the star? He wore it. This was the rule. But he liked to go out in the evening, and there was an eight o'clock curfew for Jews. At eight o'clock, he unpinned his star and stayed in the cafés. He even frequented the Café de la Paix, which was off-limits to Jews. Every evening his wife and children trembled for him. The roundups of Jews began.

Nathan Kotlerewsky left Russia in 1911 because Jews had been mistreated there. As a child, he had seen pogroms. So he had left to join an uncle in Lyon, where he had worked for a while as a shoemaker; then he had come to Paris and sent for his ten brothers and sisters and his mother. He should have been less trusting. But what the hell, France was not czarist Russia. In July 1942, two of Nathan's brothers were caught in a roundup. Marguerite begged her husband to leave. He finally agreed and departed on August 2, 1942. Marguerite calmed down and stayed in Paris with her children.

On September 26, 1942, a Saturday, the doorbell rang: the Gestapo. They had come specifically to arrest Madame Kotlerewsky. Why? She had done nothing, was doing nothing, did not belong to any of the resistance movements. She was dumbfounded. —"A Frenchwoman has denounced you as a communist and a Russian agent," said the Germans. This was clearly a misunderstanding, a mistake. The police ordered the two older children—Gisèle, nineteen, and Léon, seventeen—to present themselves at Avenue Foch on the following Tuesday, September 29, sealed the apartment, and took their mother away. Gisèle and Léon ran to neighbors. The neighbors advised them to flee, to go into hiding, and they proposed hideouts. The children wanted to talk it over with their grandfather. The following day, on Sunday, they went to Perreux to see Monsieur Urgon, who was keeping their little nine-year-old sister, Jacqueline. The grandfather didn't know what to advise them. The children decided to go to Avenue Foch: they would explain to the Gestapo, there must be some mistake. They would defend their mother.

The grandfather waited for them, in vain. Then he went to Avenue Foch to find out what had happened. There, a Frenchman working in the offices whispered to him that he would free his daughter and grandchildren for 150,000 francs. The grandfather brought the money: his life savings.

Marguerite Kotlerewsky arrived at Romainville on November 21, 1942. She did not tell us where she'd been since her arrest on September 26. Her daughter Gisèle joined her. Her son Léon followed. He was in the men's section.

During this time, the youngest child, Jacqueline, was in Perreux, under surveillance: the Gestapo were visiting every fifteen days. When the grandfather knew that Marguerite had been deported, he took the girl to the Auvergne to join her father. The Germans sacked the house in Perreux.

Marguerite Kotlerewsky left with us on January 24, 1943. She threw notes from the train car with her father's address. The notes arrived. She said that she was in good spirits, that she would hold on. She had left her two children, Gisèle and Léon, in Romainville, probably reassured. They were clearly innocent.

Auschwitz # 31814

On February 16, 1943, twenty days after our entrance into Birkenau, we saw the young Jews arrive from Romainville. The others had been gassed when they disembarked. They had left Romainville on February 11, and had gone by way of Drancy. Among them was Gisèle. She was in a Jewish block, while we were with the Poles in a block for "Aryans." That evening, risking a beating, she left her block and came to see her mother. And Léon? What had become of him? "He left with us," said Gisèle, "but I didn't see him again after Drancy." They both wept and Gisèle, who had been so sweet, became resentful. She said: "Why am I Jewish? Why? And look at me now. . . ." Shaved, dirty, dressed in a khaki overall, a mechanic's overall that was too tight to be buttoned. (The Jews did not have striped uniforms. They wore civilian clothing, strange odds and ends, marked on the back with red paint.) "Look at me now." Marguerite Kotlerewsky lost heart. She stopped eating. She stopped sleeping. She let herself die.

Marguerite Kotlerewsky died on February 26, 1943, ten days after her daughter's arrival. Gisèle had her nose crushed and her eye half gouged out by a whipping administered by Taube [13] one evening as she was leaving her block to

---

13. Taube was the SS officer in charge of the women's camp. We did not see his name among the Auschwitz SS condemned twenty years ago at Nuremburg.

visit her mother. Alida managed to get a little water to wash her swollen face, but Gisèle died a few days later.

When the deportees returned, little Jacqueline and her father searched everywhere, running from one office to another. At least one of the three would return. Gisèle was strong. Léon, too. Mama was very brave.

Long after the war, the Red Cross informed them that Marguerite Kotlerewsky had died at Auschwitz in June 1943. They could not believe that she'd given up so soon. About Gisèle and Léon, nothing. Disappeared.

The old uncle whom Nathan Kotlerewsky had joined in Lyon in 1911, Nathan's two brothers, his two sisters and their husbands, and a nephew and a niece around the same age as Gisèle and Léon: all were taken in the roundups and sent to Auschwitz. Only the niece returned.

Lina KUHN (or KUHNE)

She belonged to the Johnny network, like the Alizon sisters [see *Marie Alizon*], but they did not know her. She was arrested by the Gestapo in February or March 1942. She arrived at Romainville at the beginning of November 1942, after going through the Santé and Fresnes. She had lived in Paris with her friend Roger Mirande, who was also a member of the Johnny network and who was arrested at the same time. He, too, was deported and died in the deportation. Neither of them was known to have any family.

Auschwitz # 31795

One evening, Lina came to see me in my bunk and whispered in my ear: "Listen, I have a secret to tell you." She wanted to take me to the back of the blockhouse to talk. A scuffle separated us. The next day she entered the revier. I'll never know.

Lina Kuhn died at the beginning of March 1943. She was between thirty-five and forty years old.

Georgette LACABANNE, née Réau

Born on August 20, 1910, in Bordeaux, where she was raised and attended the Cazemajor elementary school. Her father was an ironmonger. Georgette became a dressmaker, and she married a pipefitter.

They had two children: a nine-year-old daughter and a son of eighteen months at the time of their mother's arrest. The children were first taken in by their paternal grandmother, then separated: the girl went to live with an uncle, the boy with the maternal grandmother.

Georgette was arrested on July 7, 1942, at home in Bègles, Gironde. She was sheltering resisters. One of them, Dancla, had taken refuge with Yvonne Noutari [see this name], who had just been arrested, and he was taken at the same time. He was executed by firing squad in Souge, on September 21, 1942.

The husband signed up as a volunteer worker in Germany, hoping that his wife would be freed.

Georgette Lacabanne was imprisoned at Hâ until October 14, 1942, then at Romainville until the departure.

Auschwitz # 31717

She died in Birkenau on March 8, 1943.

Her husband—now deceased—was notified of his wife's death by the mayor's offices of Bègles.

Madeleine LAFFITTE, née Guitton ("Michèle")

Born on October 15, 1914, in Longeron, Maine-et-Loire, the second of five children. Her father was a self-employed mechanic, her mother a home-maker. After completing elementary school, Madeleine went to work in a spinning mill.

Life was not easy in this part of the country, where a girl had to walk six kilometers to go to the rare dance—and would get a beating from her father when she came home. At the age of eighteen, Madeleine left to go to Paris. She married Jean Laffitte, a pastry chef and Communist Party militant.

In 1942 Madeleine Laffitte, who had joined the Resistance at the end of December 1940, was a liaison agent for the National Front. She was arrested on February 23, 1942, at the home of Félix Cadras, 119 Boulevard Davout, in Paris, where she was delivering secret correspondence. Cadras had been arrested the evening before, and the police of the special brigades had staked out his apartment. As a member of the central committee of the Communist Party, he was shot on May 30, 1943.

Madeleine was in the cells until March 23, 1942, in the Santé (in isolation, in the German section) until August 24, 1942, and in Romainville until the departure.

Auschwitz # 31666

She died of dysentery at the end of November 1943, while she was with the others in the quarantine block, when the worst was over and there was a chance to survive.

For weeks her companions had hidden her so she wouldn't be sent back to the revier at Birkenau (no sick prisoners were allowed in quarantine). Fernande

Laurent took care of her, in particular collecting her diarrhetic stools in a box to prevent the blockova from suspecting anything. Madeleine was discovered, however, and sent to the revier, where she died.

At this period, she had already written home (we were allowed one letter per month, beginning in July 1943), and her mother was sending her parcels. One parcel was returned, stamped: "Return to sender." This is how the family learned of her death.

She was named a sergeant in the RIF.

Her husband, Jean Laffitte, was arrested on May 14, 1942, and deported. At Mauthausen, he met survivors of our convoy who told him of his wife's death.

A sister of Madeleine Laffitte's, who had taken Madeleine's place in Jean Laffitte's group, was arrested at the same time he was; she was in various internment camps in France until the Liberation.

A brother, conscripted for the STO, died in Germany on April 14, 1944.

A cousin, Albert Piffeteau, arrested in June 1944 and deported in July 1944 in one of the last convoys, died in a camp on May 6, 1945.

Gisèle LAGUESSE, née Iung

Born on January 29, 1915, in Poitiers, she was raised in Levallois, where she went to elementary school. Afterward, she attended a commercial school on Rue de Naples, in Paris, and obtained her secretarial degree. Her father was a railroad engineer at the Gare Saint-Lazare.

On June 18, 1938, she married Paul Laguesse, a teacher, who had been one of the first secretaries of the French Communist Party in the Twenties. In 1942 Gisèle and Paul Laguesse, involved in the clandestine struggle since August 1940, were sheltering representatives of the National Front, acting as liaisons between the National Front leadership and its regional representatives, transmitting to the leadership the transcripts of broadcasts from Radio London, and printing tracts.

Arrested on the morning of March 2, 1942, by the special brigades in their home in Saint-Maur, where Pierre Villon, national secretary of the movement, managed to escape by jumping from the second floor to the garden, Gisèle and Paul Laguesse were taken to General Intelligence headquarters, where they spent one week. They were in the same large holding cell, sleeping on the floor, and the police threw Paul Laguesse back into this cell after his interrogation; he was unconscious, black and blue, and disfigured.

Gisèle Laguesse was transferred: to the cells from March 10 to March 23; then to the Santé—in isolation, in the German section—until August 24, 1942; and to Romainville until the departure.

She died in the Birkenau revier on March 11, 1943. She had entered several days earlier, exhausted by dysentery. Because she had soiled her cot, she was beaten by one of the revier *stubovas*. She died the following day. She told Louise Magadur, her neighbor: "Louise, I'm going to die. But you'll return; take a good look at everything that happens here so you can tell about it. Don't forget anything." The morning of her death, Gisèle dragged herself to Louise's bed; she wanted to tell her something else, but Louise was so ill she didn't wake up, and Gisèle died there, next to her bed. When Louise finally awoke, Gisèle was on a pile of corpses to be taken to the crematorium. Her entire face had been eaten by rats.

Her sister-in-law, Germaine Laguesse, learned of Gisèle's death when she arrived at Ravensbrück on January 10, 1944, from the survivors of the convoy who had arrived from Raisko (Auschwitz) on January 8. Germaine was sent on to Mauthausen and returned after the Liberation in very poor health; she died in 1975.

Paul Laguesse was shot on September 21, 1942. He was taken from Romainville, where Gisèle said good-bye to him.

Léa LAMBERT, née Durbecq

Born on April 9, 1892, in Rocroi, Ardennes, she was raised in Hiraumont, a hamlet of Rocroi, and completed her elementary education.

In 1942 she was both cook and housekeeper for the National Relief rest center for the Ardennes, in Charleville, where Marcelle Fuglesang [see this name] was chief welfare officer. When prisoners escaping from Germany stopped in Charleville, they were sheltered and given papers and food supplies at the center, as was the imposter who exposed them.

Léa Lambert was arrested along with Marcelle Fuglesang on October 28, 1942. Like Fuglesang, she was in Saint-Quentin prison from November 10 to December 19, and in Romainville from December 9 until the departure.

Auschwitz # 31821

She died soon after our arrival.

In the middle of March 1943, Monsieur Lambert was summoned to Gestapo headquarters in Charleville; he was told that his wife had died in . . . (a word that sounded like "ish") of stomach problems, on March 1, 1943. Knowing that his wife had been with Madame Jacquat, he hurried to speak with Monsieur Jacquat, who had just returned from command headquarters, where he had been told that his wife, too, had died in . . . (again, a word like "ish") and of stomach problems. Emile Lambert, an impulsive, powerfully built man, a livestock dealer with a loud voice, gave vent to his anger and cursed the Germans. He was arrested and deported to Dachau. He died there in December 1944.

Thérèse LAMBOY, née Gady

Born on July 25, 1918.

She arrived in Romainville on November 15, 1942. No one knew where she came from. She had a baby staying with a wet nurse, and she was making a teddy bear for him out of bits of fabric.

We don't know why she was arrested; perhaps it was never mentioned.

Auschwitz # 31800

One of the forty-nine survivors. She was repatriated from Mauthausen on April 30, 1945. Simone Loche met her once, many years ago, on Rue de Malte, in Paris. We don't know what happened to her.

Fabienne LANDY

Born on April 27, 1921, in Villefranche-sur-Cher, Loire-et-Cher, where she spent the first ten years of her life. Then her father, who was a railway worker, was transferred to Tours, where she completed elementary school. She was a stenographer.

A Communist Party sympathizer before the war, in 1942 she was a member of the National Front and worked typing tracts. She was arrested at her parents' home, in Saint-Pierre-des-Corps, on July 23, 1942: a comrade in her group had buckled under torture.

She was transferred from the prison at Tours to Romainville on November 7, 1942.

Auschwitz # 31784

She died on February 25, 1943. She had entered the Birkenau revier with diarrhea, though it was not very serious. At first she had a little blister on each hip; these blisters became enormous. Hélène Solomon, a nurse at the revier, thought she was having an allergic reaction to the straw mattress on which she had to lie naked. Hélène found her a pair of trousers to protect her from contact with this mattress, and the blisters diminished. The chief SS doctor came to inspect the patients. He diagnosed a rare disease, which he mentioned to Doctor Hautval, but there is no proof that this diagnosis was correct. Fabienne was sent to the revier at the men's camp, where the SS doctor gave her an intra-cardiac injection of formol.

Fabienne Landy's family learned of her death from Hélène Fournier on the return.

Lucienne LANGLOIS ("Betty")

Born on May 23, 1914, in Montet, in Allier, she was raised in Paris, where her father was a craftsman. After completing middle school, she did two years at a teachers' training college, but changed courses to become an administrative secretary.

She joined the Resistance at the beginning of the occupation, and in 1941 she was a liaison agent for the national committee of the FTP.

She was arrested by the special brigades on March 2, 1942, in Paris, in a room she had rented under an assumed name. She had been caught in the trap set for the Politzer group [see *Marie Politzer*].

After a week at General Intelligence headquarters, she was in the cells until March 23, 1942; in the Santé, where she was in isolation, until August 24, 1942; and then in Romainville.

Auschwitz # 31668

She entered the revier as a nurse on February 24, 1943. She had typhus from April to May 1943, went back to her nursing work, and through the favor of the chief SS physician was assigned to Manette after Manette's leg was amputated. Betty rejoined her companions from the convoy, who were sent to quarantine on August 3, 1943, and left with them for Ravensbrück on August 2, 1944. She was not sent to Mauthausen because she was ill; she was liberated from Ravensbrück by the Red Cross and taken to Sweden on April 23, 1945. She re-turned to Paris on June 23, 1945.

Several years after her return, she married and had a son. Betty returned to work and now leads quite an active life, but she tires easily. She is sometimes overcome by crushing fatigue, even if she hasn't had a particularly hard day.

She was named a sergeant in the RIF.

Berthe LAPEYRADE, née Lescure, and her sister-in-law, Charlotte LESCURE, née Zanker

Berthe, born on April 26, 1895, in Passage, Lot-et-Garonne, attended elemen-tary school in Cenon until the age of eleven, then worked in a restaurant in

Bacalan, Bordeaux, where Jean Lapeyrade, an adjuster at the Bacalan workshops, frequently lunched. They were married in 1917.

Charlotte, born on May 31, 1902, in Saint-Paul, Gironde, went to school in the same village. Then her parents settled in Cenon, on the outskirts of Bordeaux. Living on the same street was Berthe's brother Henri Lescure, a worker in a Bordeaux factory. Charlotte and Henri Lescure were married in 1921. They lived in Floirac.

The Lescures were storing propaganda material for the National Front, making contacts, and sheltering resisters. They would send them on to the Lapeyrades, who gave them a warm welcome.

Jean and Berthe Lapeyrade were arrested first on July 25, 1942, by Poinsot's police, at their home in Bordeaux. The relationship between the Lapeyrades and the Lescures was obvious. A moment later, the same police officers arrested Charlotte Lescure at her home in Floirac. Her husband, Henri Lescure, was at work. Summoned to the commissioner's office, he went (fearing for his wife and his son, then aged nineteen) and was instantly arrested.

Berthe and Charlotte were imprisoned in the Boudet barracks and transferred to Romainville on October 14, 1942.

Auschwitz # 31721

Berthe Lapeyrade died in March 1943, in the afternoon, in the marshes. Charlotte Delbo, Viva, Lulu, and Carmen brought her body back to the camp for the evening roll call.[14]

Her friends said she died on February 21, but this must be a mistake since we didn't go to work in the marshes before the beginning of March, when they had finally thawed.

In May 1943 the mayor's offices in Bordeaux received a notification of decease from Auschwitz and informed the family.

Jean Lapeyrade had been executed by firing squad in Souge on September 21, 1942.

Auschwitz # 31733

Charlotte Lescure died on March 22, 1943. She was caught in "the race" on February 10, but her comrades managed to pull her out of the group of women selected for gassing. Saved this time. On the night of March 21, she was sick and groaning with pain. The blockova, armed with a cudgel, beat Charlotte to death. In the morning, she did not get up for roll call; she had died in her bunk.

Henri Lescure, her husband, died in the deportation on July 6, 1944.

---

14. See Charlotte Delbo, "None of Us Will Return" [in *Auschwitz and After* (New Haven: Yale University Press, 1995), 79].

Suzanne LASNE ("Josette")

Born on January 20, 1924, in Paris. She lost her mother at the age of nine. Her father was an electrician in Paris, in the twelfth arrondissement. She completed middle school at the Sophie-Germain school, then worked as an assistant bookkeeper while studying to become a certified accountant.

She became involved in the Resistance when Louise Magadur [see this name], whose hairdressing salon was in the neighborhood, asked her to shelter a militant in a room adjoining the apartment Suzanne shared with her father. This militant, Moïse Blois, persuaded Suzanne to join his FTP group. When Louise Magadur was arrested on March 9, 1942, Suzanne prudently left her father's house and went to stay in a room used for munitions storage by the FTP. A young FTP member, Raymond Lambert, was lodging there as well.

On December 14, 1942, Suzanne Lasne was apprehended by the police of the special brigades, who had come to arrest Raymond Lambert on his return home (they had been tailing him for several days; he was deported to Mauthausen and eventually returned). Suzanne had no time to escape. Raymond Lambert could not warn her, though he heard her coming: the police had gagged him. Suzanne had a piece of paper in her pocket with notes on her meetings for the next few days. They were quite legible. She intended to transcribe these notes into code once she got home. This is how Jeanne and Maurice Alexandre, Marie-Louise Colombain, and Angèle Mercier were taken by the police.

Suzanne's father was interrogated but cleared when he testified that his daughter no longer lived with him, and he was not informed of her current activities.

Suzanne Lasne was imprisoned in Fresnes until January 23, 1943. She joined the convoy at Compiègne on the eve of departure.

Auschwitz # 31 . . .

She died in the Birkenau revier on March 14, 1943.

From the day of her arrest she was consumed with remorse. Yet neither Jeanne Alexandre nor Angèle Mercier nor Marilou ever reproached her. She was nineteen years old. She stopped sleeping the day she was arrested.

Fernande LAURENT, née Liéval

Born on December 31, 1902, in Nantes, to a family of eighteen children. Her father was a railroad mechanic; after a work-related accident, he was retrained with a pension and then worked in a sawmill. The family was very poor. The children attended elementary school. Fernande went to work at the age of twelve but managed to learn shoemaking. In 1919, at the age of seventeen, she married a man who worked in construction and they had three children, born in 1921, 1922, and 1924.

One morning, on June 11, 1942, Fernande Laurent, who was living in a second-floor apartment at 16 Rue Saint-Jacques in Nantes, came downstairs for water from the faucet on the ground floor. She was making breakfast for her children, who were about to leave for work. At the bottom of the stairs, she saw—rather dimly, since the corridor was poorly lit—a German soldier holding a revolver. He said in flawless French: "I'm wounded. Help me." "Put down your weapon," she said. "And get out of here. There's a commissariat just down the street." The man staggered off. She went back upstairs. Then she went out to the market. This soldier, the neighbor's nephew, was involved in the LVF [Legion of French Volunteers against Bolshevism]. That was why he was wearing a German uniform. Evidently, he'd been wounded by a resister on leaving his aunt's apartment. His sister, Germaine Chevalier, was known in the neighborhood for her relations with the Germans. Later that morning, when Fernande Laurent was busy with her housework—the activities in the street had quieted down—Germaine Chevalier came up and accused her, cursing and shouting: "They won't allow this to happen, I'll ask for thirty hostages!"

The next morning, June 12, 1942, six men from the Gestapo searched Fernande Laurent's home and found nothing, since no one in the family was involved in any kind of subversive activity. Nonetheless, they took Fernande off to command headquarters, then to La Fayette prison. Twice the Gestapo confronted her with young Chevalier, who was wounded in the thigh but would recover, and who claimed he didn't know her. The Gestapo arrested thirty-nine people fingered by Germaine Chevalier—her revenge on the people who condemned her behavior. Nine of these hostages—children and the mothers of young children—were released. The thirty men and women remaining under arrest were all deported to different camps. Fernande Laurent was transferred to Paris on October 14, 1942, interned in the fort at Romainville, and sent in the convoy. Of these thirty hostages, only eight would return.

Auschwitz # 31748

Birkenau, quarantine, Ravensbrück, Mauthausen, where she was liberated by the Red Cross on April 22, 1945. Neither her husband nor her children were bothered.

After coming home, she filed a complaint against Germaine Chevalier and her brother. The police found them hiding out in a convent in the Pyrénées. Chevalier was sentenced to five years in prison and ten years' local banishment.

Germaine Chevalier, condemned to life imprisonment, died several years later at the central prison in Rennes.

After the return, Fernande Laurent found the building where she had lived destroyed, razed in the explosion of a nearby bridge. Her husband was living with friends, the children elsewhere. She managed to requisition an apartment and settled in as well as she could. But she was in a very poor state. She had seven attacks of spitting blood. She spent two years in Switzerland in a sanitorium, courtesy of the Swiss, where there were a number of places reserved for seriously ill deportees.

Now? Heart trouble, infectious bronchitis, a damaged circulatory system. She's had many attacks of phlebitis and can hardly walk. Since she played no part in the Resistance and was arrested for nothing, the government figured she could live on nothing. Her identity card as a political deportee, totally disabled, entitles her to a pension of 330 francs per month [in 1965]. Clearly, she cannot work. Her husband, who died in 1962, left her a pension of 160 francs per trimester.[15]

Marcelle LAURILLOU, née Mardelle

Born on November 19, 1914, in Perrusson, Indre-et-Loire, where her father had a big construction business. She completed middle school there and eventually married a veterinarian from Tours.

In 1941, her husband, who was in a resistance organization, was arrested. Released, he resumed his place in the clandestine struggle but came home at night. Marcelle Laurillou left her house in Tours and took her two children, six and eight, to live with her parents in Amboise. There she became part of a chain that helped resisters on the run across the demarcation line. This chain was entirely destroyed, denounced by the Email woman—a Frenchwoman and Gestapo agent who was executed by firing squad after the Liberation.

Marcelle Laurillou was arrested on September 10, 1942, by Gestapo agents. She was incarcerated in the Michelet prison in Tours until November 7, 1942, and transferred from there to Romainville.

Auschwitz # 31 . . .

She died of dysentery around April 20, 1943. She told her comrades from Tours: "We won't get out of here. They'll never let us out alive with these numbers on our arms."

Her family was notified of her death by the mayor's offices in Amboise.

---

15. Fernande Laurent died on November 23, 1965, in the hospital in Nancy.

Louise, called "Anaïse," LAVIGNE, née Amand ("Nayette")

Born on March 17, 1904, in Iteuil, Vienne, she was raised in Poitiers. She left school early because her family, which included eight children, was extremely poor. The father, first a day laborer in Iteuil (he did road work without being a highway repairman, that is, without drawing a guaranteed salary), later killed livestock in the slaughterhouse in Poitiers. Nayette worked in a factory making clogs.

Her brother, René Amand, left school at ten and a half. He was a railroad worker and a member of the Communist Party. He was the first representative of the National Front in Poitiers.

In 1933 Nayette married an electrician, Marcel Lavigne. They joined the Communist Party during the war. When René Amand was arrested in June 1941, Marcel Lavigne said: "We must take over." He and Nayette took over the leadership of the National Front in Poitiers. They helped imprisoned resisters escape from the camp at Rouille.

On March 25, 1942, a man showed up at the Lavignes'. He wanted to get to the unoccupied zone and knew that the Lavignes would take him across the demarcation line. But the password he used was outdated. To stall for time, Nayette told him that her husband was not there. The man went away. That evening, when Marcel Lavigne returned to the house, he was followed by the police. He was arrested, and Nayette with him. The man was a mole.

Nayette was taken to Paris after spending three days in prison in Poitiers. She spent some time in the cells, and was then kept in isolation in the Santé until August 24, 1942. From there she was sent to Romainville.

Auschwitz # 31669

She died around March 25, 1943. "She'd gone crazy working in the woods. An SS officer beat her with a revolver and her companions carried her to the camp that evening for roll call," said Hélène Bolleau and Alida Delasalle. "I saw her enter the revier, her eyes rolled to the back of her head," said Simone Loche. How can we know exactly what happened?

The police headquarters in Vienne received an official notification from the camp. Perhaps this notification was transmitted to Madame Lavigne, Nayette's mother-in-law.

The returnees told the family that Nayette had died of typhus.

Marcel Lavigne was executed at Mont-Valérien on September 21, 1942. He was thirty-two years old.

René Amand, Nayette's brother, was deported to Auschwitz where he died on November 11, 1942. Alphonse Rousseau, an uncle on the Lavigne side, also died at Auschwitz.

Nayette's two daughters, aged six and one in 1942, were raised by their grandmother Lavigne, who held a grudge against her daughter-in-law, accusing her of luring her son Marcel into the Resistance and to his death.

Lucienne LEBRETON

Born on February 26, 1905, in Paris, in the thirteenth arrondissement. Her father was employed by the gas company. Raised in Paris, she was married for the first time in 1924, divorced, and married again in 1930, this time to Fernand Ginestet, whom she divorced on May 11, 1939. She was a cashier with the Paris bus system until 1939, then worked as a concierge at 9 Rue de la Collégiale, in the fifth arrondissement. (The plaque on this building is engraved with the name of Lucienne Ginestet.)

She was arrested at the end of September 1942 by a German policeman and a French gendarme at the bistro across from the café where she had her coffee every morning. She'd been denounced as a communist by one of her tenants.

In Romainville from September 29, 1942, until the departure.

Auschwitz # 31 . . .

Died at Birkenau at the end of March 1943, in the revier. The Veterans Ministry says April 30, 1943, but this is not right. We could not locate any relative.

Angèle, called "Danièle," LEDUC, née Denonne

Born on April 28, 1891, in Roubaix, to a Belgian father and Dutch mother. She left the elementary school in Roubaix at the age of twelve, then worked as an operator in the factory where her father and her younger sister worked. Eventually, she became a dressmaker.

She married in 1920 and left dressmaking to work as the cashier at her husband's butcher shop in Paris—a large shop with five or six clerks. Business was bad. Confident of her powers, Danièle Leduc set herself up as a palm reader in her very bourgeois apartment on Boulevard Malesherbes.

In 1942 the Leducs, who had left Paris in the general exodus, were living in Saint-Brieuc. Danièle Leduc listened to Radio London and did not conceal the fact; on the contrary, she spread the news in the neighborhood. Was she denounced? One evening, a self-styled Englishman arrived asking for asylum. They took him in, cheered him up, and encouraged him with the latest communiqués from London. The next morning, December 11, when Danièle awoke, the Englishman was gone, and the Gestapo arrived. Her husband had already left to walk the dog. When he returned to the house, his wife was gone.

After several days in prison at Rennes, Danièle Leduc was sent to Romainville—around mid-December 1942—and left with us from there.

Auschwitz # 31841

She died at the end of February, beginning of March 1943, in the revier at Birkenau. From edema. Her legs were so swollen she couldn't walk.

Her husband and her niece—whom she'd raised and treated like a daughter—learned of her death on the survivors' return.

MARCELLE LEMASSON, NÉE BÉZIAU

Born in Saintes on November 28, 1909, she lost her father, a locomotive engineer, when she was fifteen. He'd been ill for some time, and Marcelle had to earn her living very early, without the benefit of an apprenticeship. She worked as a saleswoman.

In 1926 she married Alexandre Lemasson, a railroad worker. In Saintes, where they had always lived, they were both known as communists.

Marcelle Lemasson was arrested at her home on Rue Pont-Amillon, on March 27, 1942, by the special brigades of Bordeaux. Octave Rabaté [16] had just arrived. He was carrying identity cards for the members of the clandestine organization in Charente. He had probably been tailed all the way from Paris. Alexandre Lemasson managed to escape by jumping out the window facing the garden.

While the police searched the house, Madeleine Normand [see this name], waiting in a nearby square for Marcelle Lemasson to bring identity cards for herself and her husband, grew impatient and came to see what was holding things up. She too was arrested.

Marcelle Lemasson was taken to Paris on April 1, 1942, and stayed in the cells until April 29. From there she was sent to the Santé—in isolation, in the German section—and transferred to Romainville on August 24, 1942.

---

16. A militant in the CGT before the war, then a local leader responsible for special groups of the FTP in the Charente after 1941, Rabaté was deported to Mauthausen in March 1943. He was repatriated at the end of April 1945. He died in July 1964 after a long illness.

Birkenau, typhus, quarantine, Ravensbrück, finally Mauthausen, where she might have met her husband, who had reached Landes when he fled on March 27, 1942, and had been arrested in Souston on August 29, 1942.

The couple found each other again at their home in Saintes, in May 1945. Alexandre Lemasson had survived the Gusen work crew (at Mauthausen).

Their first child, a rather sickly little boy, was born on October 29, 1946. Like all those who came back, Marcelle Lemasson had serious back trouble; she has a bad heart and has to live a very restricted life.

Elisabeth Marcelle Marthe LE PORT

Born on April 9, 1919, in Lorient, she was raised in Saint-Symphorien, near Tours. Her father was a railroad worker.

She did her secondary studies and entered the teaching profession.

She was a "communist," a word that frightened her parents. In 1942 she held a position of local leadership in the National Front. She was arrested by the Gestapo while teaching her class at the elementary school in Saint-Christophe-sur-le-Nais.

Doctors had ordered a rest cure in the country for a young sixteen-year-old girl named Nicole, who was sent to the Tours region by her parents. Behind in her studies, this Nicole asked Elisabeth to give her private lessons. Elisabeth settled her in her own office to do homework. Elisabeth should have been more careful and not kept the stencils she was typing up for tracts in her desk drawer. Nicole denounced her.

After Elisabeth's arrest, Nicole left to work in Germany as a volunteer, and she was repatriated in 1945 using Elisabeth Le Port's name.

Imprisoned in Tours, Elisabeth was transferred to Romainville on November 7, 1942.

Auschwitz # 31 . . .

In March 1943, depleted by dysentery, she could hardly stand. Her comrades had to support her and hid her under the greenhouses where they worked because she hadn't even the strength to create the illusion that she was repotting plants. She ate nothing but toast and drank only hot water. Her friends threw bread into the fire lit by the SS to warm themselves, and sometimes managed to warm a pail of water. One morning when she awoke, Elisabeth couldn't find her boots. They had been stolen during the night. Hélène Fournier filched some wooden clogs from the dung heap, cleaned them with snow, scraping them with a stone. Elisabeth was shod for roll call, but she couldn't leave for work. "If you knew," she said, "how they beat me in Tours, in the prison, to make me denounce the others. They promised to free me if I talked. I have no regrets. If I had my mom, a bowl of milk, and my bed, I'd be saved."

She died in the revier on March 14, 1943.

In June 1943 her parents were summoned to command headquarters in Tours to learn that their daughter had died of pleurisy. At the same time, they were handed an official notification of decease from Auschwitz dated May 14, 1943.

Marguerite LERMITE, née Joubert

Marguerite from Nantes . . . : that's all we knew about her. She was born on February 25, 1910, in Vallet, Loire-Inférieure, one of three children. She studied for her teaching credentials at the teachers' college in Nantes from 1926 to 1929, interrupting her studies to stay in the sanatorium at Sainte-Feyre between 1927 and 1929. Her father was an insurance employee.

She married a colleague, André Lermite. One son was born in 1939. Husband and wife were communists. During the "phony war," they helped publish and distribute writings to influence public opinion; when the occupation began, they distributed tracts explaining the Nazi's politics and the Pétain government's collusion with the Germans.

André Lermite was arrested by the French police on July 11, 1941. He was deported from Compiègne on July 6, 1942. He died at Auschwitz on November 15, 1942. According to the testimony of his comrades, he was probably gassed. His wife did not know of his fate when she herself arrived at Auschwitz on January 27, 1943.

Marguerite Lermite was arrested on September 5, 1942, in Boulay, in the Mouzeil district, Loire-Inférieure, where she was spending the vacation with her son and her in-laws. She had hoped to go into hiding, but she became ill. Bedridden and feverish, she couldn't implement her plans. French police came in the night and drove her away in their car. The grandparents told the little boy, who was three years old, that his mother had gone to the hospital.

She was hospitalized in Nantes, interned in La Roche-sur-Yon, in Fontenay-le-Comte, then in Romainville, where she arrived on January 15, 1943, a week before the departure.

Auschwitz # 31 . . .

She died at the end of February 1943. No witness.

On April 28, 1943, the police headquarters of the Loire-Inférieure, notified by the occupation authorities, informed the superintendent of schools in Nantes that Marguerite Lermite had died on March 18, 1943, of acute enteritis.

Marie LESAGE

Born on January 13, 1898, in Doville, Manche, to a family of eight children. Her parents had a small farm. Marie Lesage never went to school and did not even know how to read. During the war, her brother was a prisoner in Germany, and she dictated her letters for him to her maid. Before the war, she was a communist sympathizer; during the occupation, she hid fighters from the National Front. She was put in contact with this organization through her brother-in-law, Pierre (Paul) Vastel, who was the guard at the Equeurdreville cemetery and printed tracts on a mimeograph hidden in a tomb.

On February 18, 1942, word was sent of the impending visit of one of the leaders from Paris. A comrade from Cherbourg was going to meet him at the station (each man had a piece of the password: "Cher"—"Bourg") and take him to Marie's place; she was running a café on Rue Gambetta in Equeurdreville, on the outskirts of Cherbourg. This comrade from Paris turned out to be a policeman.

Transferred to Paris for interrogation at General Intelligence headquarters, Marie Lesage was kept in the cells until March 23, 1942; then imprisoned in the Santé, in isolation, until August 24, 1942; and interned in Romainville until the departure.

Auschwitz # 31671

She was photographed on February 3, 1943, but died a few days later, probably during the first week of February.

Her parents learned of her death from the survivors of the convoy.

Arrested on August 14, 1942, her brother-in-law Paul Vastel was executed by firing squad at Saint-Lô in October 1942.

Sophie LICHT, née Schaub

Born on June 11, 1905, in Welferdingen, Moselle, she went to school in Uckange and then in Thionville. Her father had a good position with the Eastern Railroad. She married a manufacturer from Thionville, Edgard E. Licht, and had a daughter, Denise, in 1932 and a son, Jean-Paul, in 1938.

In May 1940 Thionville was evacuated. The Lichts took refuge in Onzain, in the Loir-et-Cher.

They were arrested on October 10, 1942, at their home in Onzain, by local gendarmes acting, they said, on orders from the occupation authorities of Orléans. Why did they suddenly come looking for Sophie Licht, her husband, who was a Jew, their two children, and Edgard Licht's parents, who lived with them? No one is left to tell us. People spoke of "contacts with the BBC" without being more specific.

Sophie Licht was interned for three days in prison at Blois, and put in isolation in the Orléans prison from October 13 to November 13, 1942; she was then transferred to Romainville. She didn't know what had happened to her family.

Auschwitz # 31803

She endured the marshes and roll calls for three months. Since she knew German, she was sometimes excused from work to stay with the kapo and translate orders for her comrades.

She died of typhus in the revier at the beginning of April 1943. A niece, the only survivor of the family, learned of Sophie Licht's death through the Auschwitz Association some time in the summer of 1945.

Her husband, Edgard Licht, left Drancy on September 2, 1943. Arriving at Auschwitz, he was registered at Birkenau. From there he was transferred to Sachsenhausen, then to Buchenwald. He was shot in Ohrdruf on April 3, 1945, by an SS who decided that he was in no condition to walk when the camp was evacuated.

The children, Denise, aged ten, and Jean-Paul, aged four, also left Drancy for Auschwitz on September 3, 1943. They were gassed as soon as they stepped off the train. As were the parents of Edgard Licht.

Yvonne Rose LLUCIA

Born on October 3, 1910, in Oran, interned in the fortress at Romainville on October 1, 1942, died at Auschwitz in March 1943. That's all we know about her.

We found her mother and went to see her.

"We'd like to speak to you about your daughter, Yvonne."

"You're not bringing me bad news, are you?"

"It's about a book on the convoy that left on January 24, 1943, which your daughter was on...."

"But my daughter is not dead."

"Then you've had news from her?"

"No. But I know. I have a gift."

We arranged a meeting in the hopes of finding out what Yvonne Llucia had done, why she'd been arrested, and the circumstances of her arrest. The evening before the meeting, we received the following letter:

Madame,

I would be obliged if you wouldn't trouble yourself about next Thursday, as we arranged, on the subject of my dear daughter, Yvonne Llucia, deportee.

I want to keep my hope alive, and to reopen the wound I carry in my heart is too painful for me.

Please excuse me, Madame, and accept my best regards.

Simone LOCHE, née Fougère

Born on October 27, 1913, in Saint-Sulpice des Landes, Loire-Inférieure, where she was raised and completed elementary school. Her parents were in business. Simone worked in an office and married a taxi driver, secretary of the drivers' union of the CGT in Paris.

They were both involved in the clandestine struggle from the beginning of the occupation. Simone Loche was arrested on March 6, 1942, by police of the special brigades, who took her to the restaurant where she worked as a waitress, a favorite resisters' haunt. They'd found her address on a comrade arrested earlier and subsequently executed. The police wanted Simone to tell them the whereabouts of her husband, who was fighting in the southern zone, and she naturally refused to talk.

After several days at General Intelligence headquarters, she did time in the cells until April 30, 1942; went on to the Santé, in isolation, until August 24, 1942; and was transferred to Romainville until the departure.

Auschwitz # 31672

She entered the revier as a cleaning woman on February 24, 1943. She had dysentery and exanthematic typhus, but managed to survive and to benefit from the quarantine on August 3, 1943.

At Ravensbrück, where she arrived on August 4, 1944, she worked in the revier, then fell gravely ill and spent the rest of her time in the camps being nursed with enormous devotion and few resources by inmates and medical staff. When Ravensbrück was liberated, a Soviet doctor operated on her under emergency conditions. She was repatriated to Paris by plane on June 25, 1945, and was hospitalized for many months in Créteil.

She was reunited with her husband, who had never abandoned the clandestine struggle and had not been arrested; and her son, who was four when she was deported and had been taken in by a grandmother. Her family nursed her, supported her, comforted her. She regained her taste for life, but she has remained in precarious health and must ration her strength. She is under constant medical supervision.

Named soldier second-class in the RIF.

Alice LOEB

Born on February 2, 1891. She lived in the thirteenth arrondissement in Paris, where she was an active communist after August 1940. Arrested on October 13, 1942, imprisoned in Fresnes, she arrived in Romainville on December 20, 1942.

Auschwitz # 31829

As a chemist (someone remembered her working in a pharmacy in the twentieth arrondissement, on Rue Sorbier), she was chosen for the Raisko project. While waiting for the detachment to form, she worked in the Birkenau clothing warehouse (*Effecktenkammer*), like Marie-Elisa Nordmann and Madeleine Dechavassine. A selection took place at work on February 20, 1943. The SS doctor entered the barracks: everyone stood up, everyone barefoot, skirts lifted high. Swollen legs—death. Alice Loeb, who had already been undermined by dysentery, was nearly caught, managed to escape, but died the next evening after roll call.

Louise Marie LOQUET, née Le Du

Born on April 30, 1900, in Plouray, Morbihan, she was orphaned at the age of eight, along with three brothers. They were all that remained of a family of thirteen children. She was the one who kept house. She had barely three years of schooling, just enough to learn to read and write while she made lace to pay for her pinafore. The pinafore was obligatory. Her older brother, aged twelve, was the only breadwinner. He worked for the village blacksmith, who had taken over from his father. The children managed as best they could, earning a few sous here and there, living alone in their cottage.

At the age of twenty, Louise came to Paris. She took a factory job as a solderer on battery accumulators. The working girls had eyebrows and hair eaten away by the acid. In 1927 she married Lucien Loquet, an electrical worker. He was a member of the Communist Party, and she joined too. A daughter was born in 1928. Louise Loquet left the factory and operated a machine, stitching bindings for a printing shop.

Louise and her husband immediately took their place in the ranks of combatants during the occupation. They had a typewriter at home. Louise composed tracts. Her daughter proofed them for spelling mistakes.

On November 30, 1942, Louise Loquet did not return home. Father and daughter immediately understood what had happened. Two days later, the Gestapo searched the apartment and found nothing. The Germans said that Louise Loquet was arrested at Place Clichy, where she was distributing tracts. Lucien Loquet was arrested but released the same evening, thanks to a good alibi. He and his daughter visited the prisons to try to discover Louise's whereabouts until a card, dated December 20, 1942, informed them that she was in the fortress at Romainville.

Auschwitz # 31828

We do not know the date of Louise Loquet's death. It must have been near the beginning. She suffered from large varicose veins and certainly couldn't have endured roll calls for long.

Her family had no news. Not even a note thrown from the train, nothing. After April 1945, the daughter, then seventeen, went to all the collection points for the returning deportees: the Lutétia Hotel, the train stations, Bourget. Then to all the offices of the ministries, the Red Cross, the associations of deportees, showing a photograph of her mother. She learned where her mother had died only at the end of December 1946, from Marie-Claude Vaillant-Couturier, who happened to be at the Auschwitz Association offices one day when she was making inquiries.

No Witness

The families of our companions who died at Birkenau, especially their sons and daughters, were wounded a second time when we, the survivors, could not tell them how these women died. They expected an eyewitness report or, better, last words. And we could not meet their expectations. How could we explain to them that if some were dying, the others were exhausted, ill, barely lucid? That in this large group of two hundred and thirty, we knew each other best in small groups—the eight who slept on the same tier—and that these small groups were formed before the departure, according to affinities often determined by age. Women over forty kept to themselves even at Romainville, where the turmoil and levity of the young women often made them impatient. And the majority of the survivors were younger than thirty-eight years old. Small groups made up of older women were entirely wiped out. No one returned to bear witness.

Yvonne LORIOU

Born on June 15, 1905, in Saint-Jean-de-Liversay, Charente-Maritime, to a family of three children that settled in Paris in 1919. Her father was a construction worker.

Yvonne Loriou completed elementary school, then took a commercial course in Paris to become a secretary.

The three children lived with their mother, who became a widow in 1928. It was a very close family. In 1942 her older brother was a prisoner of war in Germany, the younger in the free zone. Yvonne was employed at la France Mutualiste, 44 Avenue de Villiers, in Paris. This company was sympathetic to the Resistance, no doubt moving Yvonne to send letters to her brother in Germany, typewritten on onionskin paper and concealed in parcels, relating anything that might bolster the courage and hopes of the prisoner and his comrades — reports of Radio London, the Resistance, etc. The parcels were searched, a letter was discovered.

On October 20, 1942, the Gestapo arrived at Madame Loriou's, Avenue du Général-Michel-Bizot, in the twelfth arrondissement, to arrest Yvonne, who was at work. The mother was forced under threat to give the office address. One of the men guarded the mother and searched the apartment while the others went to Avenue de Villiers. They found Yvonne's private copies of the letters.

Yvonne was taken to Rue des Saussaies and interrogated, imprisoned in Fresnes until December 18, 1942, then transferred to Romainville, where she remained until the departure.

Auschwitz # 31835

She died on March 8, 1943, in the Birkenau revier, of erysipelas, according to Marie-Jeanne Pennec.

Her family learned of her death from Marie-Jeanne Pennec at the end of 1945.

Louise LOSSERAND, née Marie ("Louisette")

Born on February 23, 1904, in Paris, in the eleventh arrondissement, the second of seven children in a family that moved to Montreuil after the floods of 1910. The father was a copper caster.

Louisette went to school for a short time in Montreuil, but in June 1914 the schools were requisitioned by the army, which used them as barracks or surgical operating theaters.

Louisette worked sewing fur garments, and in 1922 she married a furrier,

Raymond Losserand. He was a militant communist and became, in 1937, a city councilor for the fourteenth arrondissement in Paris.

In 1942, Raymond Losserand was a commander in the FTP. He was tailed by the police and arrested on May 16, 1942, at his secret lodgings in Paris, where the special brigades arrived at four in the morning. This was a productive day for them: they caught the entire Douillot-Losserand group.

Louisette was arrested along with her husband.

She went to the cells (a stay interrupted by two weeks at the infirmary in Fresnes), and left for Romainville on October 27, 1942.

Auschwitz # 31757

Birkenau and all the usual work details: marshes, sand, bricks, gardens—a month in the revier for typhus, then quarantine—the sewing workshop. Ravensbrück from August 4, 1944, until March 2, 1945; Mauthausen from March 5 until April 22, when the camp was liberated. Repatriated by the Red Cross via Switzerland.

Raymond Losserand was executed on October 21, 1942, at the shooting range in Issy-les-Moulineaux.

Louisette had great difficulty readapting. She cannot work. She did remarry. Since she was arrested along with her husband, whose risks she shared, she was not given a resistance deportee card but rather a political one. She was named a soldier second-class in the RIF.

Louise MAGADUR

Born on April 21, 1899, in Pont-Croix, Finistère, the fourth of six children born to a Breton family going back at least two centuries. Her father was a miller and worked a small farm attached to the mill.

After completing elementary school in Pont-Croix, she learned dressmaking. She came to Paris in 1924, did a variety of jobs to earn a living, and saved to pay for beauty school.

In 1942 she ran a small beauty parlor in the twelfth arrondissement. She had been a Communist Party militant before the war and was a member of the National Front. She sheltered militants; served as a letter drop; helped to disguise hunted resisters by dying their hair, beards, and eyebrows; distributed tracts (at the fair in Trône, for example); arranged parcels for prisoners of war and mutual aid for families of prisoners whose wives demonstrated on Rue de Lille, in front of the German embassy, for the right to news of their loved ones.

She was arrested at home on March 9, 1942, by the French police of the special brigades after the arrest of Chassefière, a militant for whom she served as witness when he had applied for an identity card two years earlier. (Chassefière would be executed on September 21, 1942.) She denied it; at her house the police found tracts ready for distribution.

After several days at General Intelligence, she was put in the cells until April 30; then in the Santé, in isolation, until August 24, 1942; and in Romainville until the departure.

Auschwitz # 31673

One evening returning from the marshes, she broke ranks to gather water from the stream. The SS pushed her into the water, rolled her around in it, then set the dog on her. The bite on her leg formed a huge abscess that became infected. She had to enter the revier in March 1943. The abscess healed, but Louise caught typhus; finally, she was able to rejoin her comrades in quarantine on August 3, 1943.

She followed the itinerary of the other returnees: to Ravensbrück on August 4, 1944; to Mauthausen on March 5, 1945, where she was liberated on April 22, 1945.

Since then? She has had great difficulty readapting. Still, she had to earn a living, and six months after her return, she reopened her beauty parlor, finally hiring another worker so she could reduce her work to part-time. She could not stand on her feet all day: her wounded leg never entirely recovered its strength. She retired in 1961. The nightmares and anguish have never stopped. She is the oldest of the survivors, the only one born before 1900.

Named a corporal in the RIF.

Suzanne MAILLARD, née Potet

Born on April 1, 1894, in Hamelet, near Corbie, in the Somme, where her parents were hosiers. She had two brothers and a sister. She went to school in Hamelet and completed her basic education.

In 1921 she married Henri Maillard, a cabinetmaker from Pas-de-Calais and her senior by eleven years. The Maillards then settled in Gagny, where their son was born on June 17, 1930.

All three were arrested at their home, 3 Rue Guerbette in Gagny, on June 18, 1942, by the special brigades, who barged in at five in the morning. The police did not need to look far to find three transmission stations. The Maillards were part of the National Front. None of the resisters they usually took in happened to be there that day.

At General Intelligence headquarters, the police decided to send the boy, who was twelve, to his grandmother's home in the north. Hugging him, Henri

Maillard told his son: "Look at me now, and remember that you're looking at an honorable man."

He was executed at Mont-Valérien on August 11, 1942.

Suzanne Maillard was sent to the cells. She stayed there until August 10, when she was transferred to Romainville with all the women arrested on the same day as she.

Auschwitz # 31 . . .

She died of typhus in the revier at Birkenau, in mid-April 1943.

Lucie MANSUY, née Caccia

Born on June 3, 1915, in Gérardmer, Vosges, to a family with four children: two girls, two boys. The parents were Italian immigrant workers.

After completing elementary school, she worked in a weaving factory in Gérardmer, where her mother was a machine operator. Her father was a master stonemason.

Lucie married Mansuy, a café waiter, on December 23, 1932. During the Spanish Civil War, he was involved in the International Brigades. A political operative, he was killed at Tortoza on July 28, 1938.

Lucie came to live in Paris in August 1940 and set up housekeeping with Maurice Quédec, a communist who worked for Renault. Both of them were involved in the Resistance from the first. Lucie made contacts, distributed underground newspapers and tracts.

They were both arrested, by inspectors from the special brigades, at six in the morning on June 18, 1942, at their home in Paris in the twentieth arrondissement; they had been tailed. In the cells until August 20, 1942, then to Romainville until the departure.

Maurice Quédec, thirty-three years old, was executed at Mont-Valérien on August 11, 1942.

Auschwitz # 31648

She held up well until April 1943, working in the marshes and on the brick detail, despite an arm dislocated by a blow from a stick. In April she caught typhus and entered the revier. She recovered and went to work in Raisko. She must have been part of a little group that was transferred to Ravensbrück on January 7, 1944, but she was held back at the moment of departure: she had a fever (others had fevers too, but one of them—Gilberte Tamisé—shook down the thermometers, something Lucie didn't have time to do). Lucie returned to the revier, recovered, then rejoined the others still in quarantine.

Transferred to Ravensbrück on August 2, 1944, to Mauthausen on March 2, 1945. Liberated by the Red Cross on April 22, 1945, repatriated through Switzerland.

On her return, she found her home stripped of all her personal belongings.

Ill as she was, she went back to work, this time at a factory: she became a metal cutter.

She suffered from the terrible fatigue that is the lot of all the deportees and from her wounded arm. And still today [1965], twenty years after the return, she is terrorized by the memory of an SS officer on horseback who reared his horse in front of her, on the construction site where we were working. She fell, tried to get up and run away, but the SS officer pursued her, excited his horse, and Lucie was trampled.

Yvette MARIVAL, née Champion

Born on August 5, 1915, in Crouzilles, Indre-et-Loire, she went to elementary school in Trogue. Her mother, widowed at twenty-eight, did not remarry. She raised her children alone, working as a domestic at the Raspail school in Tours.

Like her husband, a factory worker who was a member of the Communist Party before the war, Yvette was a fighter in the National Front in 1942. They were both denounced by a member of their group who talked under torture.

They were arrested in the middle of the night by the Gestapo on August 4, 1942.

Yvette Marival left the prison in Tours for Romainville on November 7, 1942.

Auschwitz # 31 . . .

She died in the first days in Block 14. She was not photographed. One morning, she was found dead. Her family learned of her death from Radio London in April or May, around noon.

Yvette's husband died in the deportation.

Luz Higinia MARTOS, née Goni

Born on January 11, 1906, in Ciranqui, Spain, she left Catalonia after the defeat of the republican armies in the spring of 1939 and took refuge in France. There, by now a widow, she married a Frenchman, Avestapan, acquiring his nationality. But it was under the name of Martos that she was arrested at her home in Montmartre, 22 Rue du Nord, in August 1911. She and her husband were in the Resistance.

Luz was imprisoned in the Santé until September 30, 1942, and after this date in Romainville. Luz (we used to say Loutch) was a lively woman, despite her weight, cheerful and very exuberant. She would jump up on the tables to demonstrate Spanish dances; she would sing and make everyone laugh.

Auschwitz # 31 . . .

At Birkenau, the cold, the frozen countryside immediately demoralized her. She read palms, and looking at her own she said, "It's useless for me to make the effort, useless to struggle. I will not get out. It's written in my hand," and she stopped eating. One day at work, next to Claudine Blateau, she fell in the mud. "I can't go on. Leave me here to die." The SS made her companions carry her back to the camp for roll call that evening, and she died almost immediately. This was at the beginning of February 1943.

Her husband learned of her death when he returned from the deportation.

Germaine MAURICE

Born on May 8, 1918, in Vou, Indre-et-Loire, where she was raised (by an aunt; she'd lost her mother very early), and where she completed elementary school.

Her father had a farm situated, under the occupation, on the demarcation line between the two zones. Her father immediately became part of a chain to help find passage for escaped prisoners and hunted resisters (this was the same chain Léa Kerisit [see this name] was involved in).

The Gestapo came to arrest her father on September 10, 1942. Germaine wanted to spare him: "It's my doing. My father knows nothing about it." They were both taken. Again, they'd been denounced. She left the prison at Tours for Romainville on November 7, 1942.

Auschwitz # 31788

She died in the Birkenau revier on February 23, 1943, of pneumonia.

Her aunt learned of her death from Hélène Fournier on the return. Her father died in the deportation.

Henriette MAUVAIS, née Caillot

Born on October 22, 1906, in Vitry-sur-Seine, the youngest of twelve children, seven of whom were still living at her birth.

Her parents came from a long line of truck farmers: her father cultivated a plot of ground that had been handed down from her grandmother, and her mother was also the daughter of truck farmers who had settled in Maisons-Alfort. When she completed elementary school in Vitry, her parents wanted her to learn dressmaking. She did not like dressmaking and left her apprenticeship. Very well, her father said, since that's how it is, you'll go to the factory.

She married Léon Mauvais, a turner in the Paris Company for the Distribution of Electricity, a militant union man who was elected a communist city councilor for the fourteenth arrondissement of Paris in 1936. He was arrested at the demobilization in 1940, imprisoned in various central prisons, and finally interned in Châteaubriant, from which he escaped on June 18, 1941, to join the clandestine struggle in the unoccupied zone. Henriette wanted to find him and was caught at the demarcation line in July 1941. One month in prison in Nevers under an assumed name. She had her real papers in her corset. After completing her sentence, she returned to Paris, where she served as her husband's liaison for that region. To be freer, she entrusted her two daughters to friends.

She was arrested on March 3, 1942, in the Charonne quarter, where she was going to visit her children. General Intelligence until March 10, 1942; the cells until March 23, 1942; the Santé, in isolation, until August 24, 1942; Romainville until the departure.

Auschwitz # 31674

She entered the revier as a cleaning woman on February 24, 1943. She caught typhus, recovered, then nearly died of poisoning though she never discovered the cause. The quarantine, August 3, 1943, saved her, too.

Like the others in quarantine, she was transported to Ravensbrück on August 2, 1944, where she was "NN," that is, she could not work outside the camp, and was transferred to Mauthausen on March 2, 1945. Repatriated by the Red Cross, she arrived in Paris on the evening before May 1, 1945, in time for the parade.

Her husband was not arrested. After some recuperation, she went back to work in July 1945 (she was a stenographer) but decided to stay home after her twins were born in 1948. She suffered generalized debility and nervous disorders. She, too, thought that "others cannot understand."

She died on January 13, 1970, of a stroke.

Olga MELIN, née Méru

Born on December 11, 1913, in Pont-Sainte-Maxence, Oise, the second of seven children. Her father was a baker in Pont-Sainte-Maxence, where Olga went through secondary school. She took a preparatory course for the PTT but never worked for the postal service. In 1933 she married in Larchières. Her husband made inlaid wares (chessboards and such) in Méru; the couple settled there, and Olga also made inlaid buttons, a unique local craft.

In 1942 her husband was a prisoner of war, but evidently the couple would have separated anyway; divorce proceedings, begun in 1939, were interrupted by the mobilization. Olga was living in Paris. She had left her son Etienne, aged thirteen, with her mother in Méru; the boy was disabled from polio contracted at the age of four. She worked at a printing shop.

Olga Melin and her brother, Albert Méru, were part of a group headquartered on Rue des Amandiers providing aid to Jews [see *Madeleine Morin*]. They were both arrested on September 6, 1942, in the roundup at the Gare de Lyon. They must have been transporting Jews to the demarcation line, helping them to escape into the "free" zone.

After a few weeks in Fresnes, Olga Melin was interned at the Romainville fortress at the beginning of October 1942. She stayed until the departure.

Auschwitz # 31708

Birkenau, quarantine, transfer to Ravensbrück on August 2, 1944, to Mauthausen on March 2, 1945.

One day—in the spring of 1944 in Birkenau, while the survivors were in quarantine—Olga, returning from the soup detail, dropped the soup can and raced toward an inmate working on the railroad. She acted so quickly that the kapos had no time to see her. She returned quite excited: "My husband! It's my husband!" Her husband, a prisoner of war, had attempted to escape, was recaptured, and sent to a satellite camp of Auschwitz for punishment.

"What about your divorce?" her friends asked.

"Never mind divorce. We'll get back together when we return."

She was killed in the bombing of Mauthausen on March 21, 1945, one month before the liberation of the camp.

Her son and her mother learned of her death through the Auschwitz Association on the survivors' return.

ANGÈLE MERCIER

Born on June 24, 1909, in Chaumes-en-Brie, Seine-et-Marne. She went to school in Touquin, Seine-et-Marne, until the age of thirteen, when she was placed with fruit growers who sold their produce in the local markets (Coulomiers, Provins). She was both a general maid and a salesgirl. These people felt genuine friendship for Angèle, and when she lost her father in 1930 (or '31), they made her the manager of a small working-class hotel in the nineteenth arrondissement.

This is when she got to know Pierre Landrieux, whom she lived with beginning in 1934. Pierre Landrieux was a communist. He was in the International Brigades in 1936, and Angèle, who had lost her religious faith in childhood, joined the Communist Party in 1937. She was active in helping the Spanish republicans, and entered the clandestine struggle (the FTP) in 1941 with former members of the International Brigades (Dumont, Fabien, etc.).

She was a liaison agent for Raoul Vallet, who would be executed by firing squad on June 15, 1943, and for Fabien, killed accidentally on December 29, 1944. Angèle was arrested returning from a mission on December 21, 1942, in Levallois-Perret by the special brigades. We could not reconstruct the circumstances of her arrest. She was in the same group as Jeanne Alexandre, Marie-Louise Colombain, and Suzanne Lasne. Landrieux was then a prisoner of war in eastern Prussia. They were to be married by proxy and had all their papers in order.

Kept at Intelligence headquarters from December 21 to 27, 1942, Angèle Mercier was in the cells from December 27 to 29, then in Fresnes from December 29, 1942, until January 23, 1943, when she joined the convoy in Compiègne that left the following day.

Auschwitz # 31 . . .

One morning at the beginning of March 1943, Madeleine Doiret brought her down from her tier as she was dying, and her comrades carried her to roll call. She died there.

Pierre Landrieux and Angèle's family learned of her death only on the survivors' return.

Georgette MESSMER, née Lyet ("Jo")

Born on November 20, 1913, in Besançon, the only daughter of people in modest circumstances. After completing middle school, she studied nursing while working at the Saint-Jacques hospital in Besançon. Married, then divorced, she left her profession to take over a café on the Place Bacchus, at the corner of Rue Battant, a small place with a good, local clientele. During the occupation, this clientele was so decent that the Germans felt ill at ease there and hardly ever came.

Georgette was the mother of a small boy whom she coddled and adored, but who did not prevent her from leading a rather hectic life. She liked money and was successful in a number of undertakings. We do not know who, among her numerous acquaintances, recruited her as part of a chain of escape; in any case, in 1942 she was the last contact in France for prisoners of war escaping from Germany and heading to Switzerland. On August 2, 1942, Georgette, who was busy elsewhere that day, entrusted her domestic, Marcelle Mourot [see this name] , with guiding six escapees on the road to Villiers-le-Lac. They were all caught. The Gestapo quickly discovered where Marcelle Mourot worked and boarded, and Georgette Messmer was arrested and imprisoned in Besançon. Did she manage to convince them that she had nothing to do with Marcelle, or did they release her in the hopes of catching others? She was freed a week later. She should have fled. She thought about it. But she was afraid for her son, and for her aunt who was raising the child. She was retaken around October 15 and once again imprisoned in Besançon, where Marcelle Mourot, then in Pontarlier, joined her in December.

From Besançon to Romainville, then Auschwitz.

Auschwitz # 31818

From the moment of arrival, during the formalities of tattooing, shaving, clothing, she let the *Aufseherin*—female SS—know that she was a nurse. Furthermore, she knew German. Around February 5, she was summoned to work in the revier. She died of dysentery at the beginning of April 1943. The family in Besançon learned of her death from Marcelle Mourot, who returned in May 1945.

Suzanne MEUGNOT

Born on April 28, 1896.

She arrived in Romainville at the beginning of October 1942, at the same time as Anna Sabot [see this name], with whom she had quarreled. It wasn't clear which of them blamed the other for her arrest. Or why she had been arrested.

She died the first week at Birkenau, before the inmates were photographed on February 3.

Marthe MEYNARD, née Brillouet

Born on March 29, 1912, in Angoulême, Charente.

Her mother died in 1917. Her father returned disabled from World War I and remarried. Marthe's half sister, Paulette, was born in 1924.

Marthe went to school until the age of thirteen, then worked at the Lacroix paper mill in Angoulême. In 1934 she married Gaston Meynard, also a worker at Lacroix, where eventually Paulette worked as well. Marthe, her husband, and her sister were militant communists.

On December 12, 1941, Gaston and Marthe Meynard and Antoine Emorine (visiting at their home) were arrested. Half an hour after their arrest,

Octave Rabaté, one of the leaders of the National Front, was on his way to the Meynards'; someone posted along his route warned him and he retraced his steps. Marthe Meynard was released at the end of three days, returned home, but did not move; she had to break off all contacts.

On March 2, 1942, a stranger showed up who had been to see the Sabouraults [see *Berthe Sabourault*], in Villiers-le-Roux, and was looking, he said, for the connection that was broken since the arrests of December 12. The Sabouraults had sent him to a certain M . . . , who had told the stranger: "I'm not up on these things," but had given him an appointment with *Paulette Brillouet*, Marthe's sister. The stranger was a cop. Marthe and her sister were arrested by the special brigades of Bordeaux and Poitiers. They were immediately transferred to Paris. At General Intelligence headquarters until March 10; in the cells until March 23; in the Santé, in isolation, until August 24, 1942; in Romainville until January 23, 1943. Paulette Brillouet did not leave for Auschwitz. She was ill and sent to Val-de-Grâce and deported to Ravensbrück the following April.

Auschwitz # 31675

After Birkenau, quarantine, the sewing workshop at Ravensbrück—arriving with the survivors on August 4, 1944—Marthe Meynard found her sister Paulette, who was already quite ill. On March 2, 1945, Marthe was sent to Mauthausen, where she was liberated. She returned to Angoulême at the beginning of May 1945. She waited for her sister to return.

Paulette was liberated at Ravensbrück by the International Red Cross and transported to Sweden. She died there on June 19, 1945.

Gaston Meynard, tried at Bordeaux by a French court, was sentenced to seven years' seclusion, imprisoned in France, then turned over to the Germans and deported on March 24, 1944. He died on April 16, 1945, at Mauthausen, the Gusen II detachment. Marthe was also at Mauthausen at this time but did not know her husband was there.

She was named an adjutant in the RIF.

Pierre Meynard, who was three when his parents were arrested, committed suicide in 1973, leaving four young children.

Marthe died on May 28, 1977, at the age of sixty-five.

Lucienne MICHAUD ("Nicole")

Born on April 4, 1923, in Creusot, to a family of four children. Her father was a boilermaker. She was raised in Vauzelles, in the Nièvre, where she completed elementary school.

In 1942, at the age of nineteen, she was directing an interdepartmental zone for the youth group of the National Front, acting as liaison between Chaumont, Troyes, and Paris (where she had a secret address), and transporting propaganda material.

On June 4, 1942, the train she was on was boarded by the German police at Paray-le-Monial. The police spotted her false identity card. Nicole was incarcerated in the Moulins prison with a number of people caught at the demarcation line. Tried by a German court, she claimed she was trying to reach the southern zone. She was sentenced to six months in prison and transferred to Hauts-Clos, near Troyes. But the false identity card prompted the police to investigate. They confronted Nicole with two men and a woman arrested shortly before in Troyes. These three, biased against her, recognized Nicole, giving ample details about her activity and her responsibilities. She was then sent to Romainville, where she arrived during the first weeks of October 1942.

Auschwitz # 31726

She entered the revier as a cleaning woman on February 24, 1943, recovered from typhus, was part of the group sent to quarantine on August 3, 1943, and transferred to Ravensbrück on August 2, 1944. There she worked in the earthworks detail and eventually entered the revier as a nurse. She was soon a patient. She was nursed by a female Russian doctor, also a prisoner, who gave her special treatment. During this time her comrades were sent to Mauthausen. Nicole, whose condition improved, left the revier and often had to hide to escape the selections which multiplied in the last weeks. She was liberated by the Red Cross on April 25, 1945, taken to Sweden, and repatriated by air on June 10, 1945.

She came home tubercular and spent two years in a sanatorium in Switzerland.

She found her fiancé again, who had returned from Dachau. They married on July 7, 1945, and had two children: a son, born in 1949, and a daughter, born in 1951. Nicole works in a travel agency. She is interested in her work but is always tired; she lives in the suburbs and commuting is particularly difficult. But she prefers to work. She says it would depress her to stay home.

RENÉE MICHAUX ("MARCELLE")

Born January 14, 1920. A native of La Rochelle, she was tall, good-humored, decisive, a militant in the Young Communists, and local secretary of the Young French Women of La Rochelle before the war. Her friend, André Sautel, was then secretary of the Communist Party for Charente-Maritime.

In March 1940, following a distribution of tracts in La Rochelle, the police commissioner summoned André Sautel: "Tomorrow you will bring me the machine those tracts were printed on or I'll arrest you." Instead of turning in the mimeograph machine, André Sautel went into hiding, and Renée Michaux with him.

In 1941, under the name of "Marcelle," she organized local groups of the National Front in the Gironde, acted as a liaison between the southwest and Paris, and conveyed tracts, information, and orders. She lived here and there, under various names, setting up a printing press in one place, a weapons cache in another.

She was arrested on February 15, 1942, in Paris, by inspectors of the special brigades who had come to arrest André Pican [see *Germaine Pican*]. He was moving into a room she had vacated for him. She was apprehended as she was leaving to take the train at Gare d'Austerlitz. She was carrying tracts in German meant for the soldiers of the Wehrmacht.

After several days at General Intelligence, Renée Michaux was sent to the cells until March 23, 1942; to the Santé, in isolation; and finally, on August 24, 1942, to Romainville.

Auschwitz # 31676

She had dysentery but did not want to go to the revier. She could walk only by leaning on someone's arm, and her comrades nearly carried her mornings and evenings along the road to the marshlands. She would faint during roll call. She died in the revier shortly after resigning herself to going. Her friends helped her to the door. This was around April 15, 1943.

André Sautel was arrested in Laval at the end of 1941. He was tortured, and hanged himself in his cell with a rope he had made by tearing strips off one of his pants legs. He was thirty-five years old. Renée Michaux did not know he'd been arrested.

Simone MITERNIQUE, née Brunet

Born February 23, 1906, in Senonches, Eure-et-Loir.

She arrived at Romainville at the beginning of October 1942.

Her brother, Roger Brunet, known as "Hector," was from a little village in the Tours region where, at the beginning of 1941, he had created the Hector-Touraine group, specializing in sabotage and in helping prisoners, Jews, and resisters hunted by the Gestapo. Simone Miternique and her father were at the head of the chain in Paris. Several times a week, she would lead groups with as many as sixty people to her brother, who was waiting for them at the station and helped them to cross the demarcation line. Simone Miternique and her father were arrested in Paris in August 1942. Roger Brunet was also arrested, on August 20.

Auschwitz # 31 . . .

She died in the beginning, before "the race" on February 10, 1943, in Block 14 where we then were. She had very swollen legs.

Roger Brunet was deported with his father to Sachsenhausen. He returned. The father did not.

Simone Miternique's son was taken in by his mother's uncle.

Gisèle MOLLET

Born on January 5, 1920, in Paris. Her father was a tailor in the twentieth arrondissement.

She was a maid in a hotel on Rue des Pyrénées and had a boyfriend, an Indian student who was a communist and an underground combatant sought by the police. He was arrested on March 9, 1942, by the special brigades. Gisèle Mollet, who knew of her friend's activities, wanted to dispose of the tracts hidden in her room. The police caught her before she could get there.

She spent several days at General Intelligence; at the end of the initial examination, she was sent to the cells until April 30, 1942; then to the Santé; and on August 24, 1942, to Romainville.

Auschwitz # 31 . . .

One day in the marshes, she was stomped on by an SS. She had not understood where she was supposed to carry the trague[17] to which she and Alida Delasalle were harnessed. She was able to return to the camp for roll call, but the following day she entered the revier for a long stay. She wrote to her parents in July 1943, when permission to write was granted to the survivors of the convoy. She received a parcel from home while in the revier, but she never wrote a second letter. She must have died in the first half of August 1943.

The Indian student was executed at Mont-Valérien on September 21, 1942.

Suzanne MOMON

Born August 10, 1896, in the Saint-Antoine neighborhood of Paris. Her father was foreman of a construction site. He died when Suzanne was eight years old.

---

17. Trague, from the German *tragen*, "to carry." This was a sort of hod loaded with the mud dug out of the marshes.

To help raise her four siblings, she left elementary school and worked at home with her mother, making brushes. Later, she was a worker in a paint factory, at Desfossés.

During World War I, she met Gustave Brustlein, a soldier who had been discharged with tuberculosis. Originally from a Protestant family in Mulhouse that had chosen French citizenship in 1870 (after the Franco-Prussian War), Brustlein was a socialist. He and Suzanne Momon lived together and had two children.

In 1919 Brustlein was gravely ill and, thinking he was going to die, wanted to make their union official. For the children's sake, and for his wife's. She refused: "You have time to think about it. You'll get well." He died, leaving his widow without the right to a pension and his children without the right to state aid.

Suzanne raised her children without any help. She learned the craft of tapestry-making and worked on private commissions, building up a devoted clientele in the Saint-Antoine neighborhood. She raised her children in their father's beliefs: socialist and secular. She had barely two years of schooling and was self-taught. She read a great deal, saw all the classics at the Comédie Française, wrote faultlessly, and expressed herself well.

In August 1940 her son, Gilbert Brustlein, joined the Young Communists. He was in the Youth Batallion, the first combat group, and participated in the action at the Barbès metro with Fabien* on August 23, 1941. (He is now its only survivor.) In October 1941 he was ordered to execute Colonel Hotz, commander of the Place de Nantes. In a reprisal for this attempt, twenty-seven hostages were shot at Châteaubriant.

In November 1941 Gilbert Brustlein thought he had covered his tracks and returned to Paris. Had he been spotted? One day in November, the police of the special brigades took over the concierge's lodgings in the building where Suzanne Momon lived. They cordoned off the entire quarter. They offered a reward for Brustlein, and his portrait was posted on all the walls in Paris. The concierge managed to warn Suzanne, who left the house. The whole Saint-Antoine neighborhood knew her. She went around to friends, who quickly cordoned off an area even larger than the police had done, posting themselves at all the streets where Gilbert Brustlein might enter. He did, in fact, arrive and was warned. He retraced his steps. (He was never caught, but nine members of his group were tried by a German court on March 7, 1942, and immediately executed; among them were Blancourt, Rizo, Fernand Zalkinow.)

After standing watch in vain for several days, the police arrested Suzanne. They also arrested her sister, her brother, and their children, but released them

---

*Head of the FTP. (Trans.)

after a few days. Suzanne Momon, first interrogated at police headquarters, then by the Gestapo, was imprisoned in the Santé and kept in isolation. After eight months in isolation, she was sent to Romainville on August 7, 1942.

Suddenly, on September 3, 1942, she was summoned to the fort's commander. She was released without any explanation. She suspected a trap but went home so as not to arouse suspicion. Summoned to police headquarters—the police were still looking for her son—she went. Deliberately. She preferred to give herself up rather than see her family arrested.

She was sent back to Romainville on September 8, 1942. She took her place again in the large cell, where she was jeered at. Why had she gone home? You'd have to be an idiot to do that. She said nothing. She had made her choice.

Auschwitz # 31686

She died at Birkenau in February or March 1943; there was no eyewitness report. Her family was not informed. The last sign of life they had from her was a note thrown from the train.

Denise MORET, née Cacaly

Born February 5, 1919, to a family of eight children in Pérat-le-Château, in Haute-Vienne, where she was raised and completed elementary school. Her father was a cabinetmaker.

She was married at nineteen. Her husband was an accountant. They lived on Rue Gustave-Rouanet, in the eighteenth arrondissement in Paris. She worked for a bath-and-shower manufacturer, then stopped working after the birth of a daughter in 1939.

In the autumn of 1942, Denise Moret, whose husband was a prisoner of war, was summoned to the Gestapo in Rue des Saussaies. She had no idea why, but went as instructed, and no one heard from her again. She arrived at Romainville on December 19, 1942.

Auschwitz # 31820

She died at the very beginning. No witness.

One of her brothers, Robert Cacaly, was deported to Dachau and did not return. Two other brothers, Louis and Jérémie, fighters with the Maquis, were killed by the militia.

Her three-year-old daughter, Yvette, was taken in by a grandmother.

Her husband returned from imprisonment and learned of his wife's death from the survivors of the convoy. He, too, had no idea why she was arrested.

Madeleine MORIN
and her mother, Marie-Louise MORIN, née Cribier

In July 1942, the roundups of Jews in the Père-Lachaise quarter astonished and infuriated the local residents. Trucks arrived with regional police; they swarmed through the streets, the apartment houses, and pushed hundreds of men, women, and children into the trucks. The children cried. Those who watched these scenes told each other they couldn't let it happen again. One group of young people, including Pierre D . . . —and everyone in Rue des Amandiers knew Pierrot, whose father ran a café at number 51—set up an escape network for Jews. This organization, in great part spontaneous, was unaffiliated with any known network and received no outside orders. Pierrot was a truck driver and worked for a moving company. On every trip, he transported a Jew—a man or woman or several children—hidden in a crate or in an armoire. But so few compared to the hundreds who needed saving. So the boys arranged to get fake identity cards (someone knew someone at the commissioner's office) for those who wanted to leave. They had to help them catch the train just across the demarcation line, where a guide waited for them. And thus the chain was in place. Everything was going well. On September 6, 1942, there was a roundup at Gare de Lyon. The regional police arrested a whole group of travelers whose cards were not on file in duplicate at police headquarters. Tracing back along the chain—or perhaps one of the travelers arrested told how and where he got his card—the Gestapo arrived at Rue des Amandiers, at Madeleine Morin's beauty salon.

Madeleine Morin, born on July 9, 1922, in Paris, was the youngest of three children. Her older brother and sister were married. Her mother, a widow since 1933, bought a business for Madeleine when she finished her training as a hairdresser. They lived together on Rue de Charenton and went every day to the salon. Madame Morin worked as the receptionist, Madeleine took care of the ladies; she had a boy for the gentlemen.

Madeleine was engaged to Pierrot and was part of the chain from the beginning: Jews came to her place to pick up their identity cards and train tickets. In such a mixed salon, these comings and goings went unnoticed.

When Pierrot came home on September 6, 1942, his father told him: "Don't stay here. They've just arrested Madeleine Morin and her mother. The corner is staked out. Get going." But Pierrot wanted to know where Madeleine and Madame Morin had been taken. He asked his pal at the commissioner's office: the Gestapo, Rue des Saussaies. He went there. An interpreter told him: "Madame Morin and her daughter? They're going to be released, wait for them." In fact, they did leave late that evening; Madeleine was beaten black and blue. "Okay," said Pierrot, "now you mustn't go home. I have the truck. Let's go to Fouilloux."

But the two women protested: "Why leave? Since they found nothing and released us, there's nothing to fear." And they went home to Rue de Charenton. The following day, they went back to work at Rue des Amandiers.

The Gestapo came to arrest them two weeks later, on September 24, 1942.

They spent several days at the Santé and arrived at Romainville in the beginning of October 1942.

Auschwitz # 31710

Marie-Louise Morin died at the end of February 1943. No witness.

Auschwitz # 31 . . .

Madeleine Morin died of typhus at the end of April 1943. She was only twenty-one years old.

Marie-Louise MORU ("Lisette")

Born July 27, 1925, in Port-Louis, Morbihan, the second of three children in a family that also adopted three orphans. The father worked at the armory, the mother was a fishmonger. A cheerful, close-knit family.

Lisette completed elementary school in Port-Louis and learned dressmaking. When she finished her apprenticeship in 1941, however, there was no work for a dressmaker in Port-Louis. There were constant bombings and no one thought to order a dress. Lisette went to work in a canning factory as a packer.

During the occupation, all the young people of Port-Louis contrived to defy the German soldiers and officers. Without any affiliation with a resistance network, Lisette and her friends gave resisters all the support they could, kept watch, surveyed the comings and goings of vehicles, and helped young people flee into the southern zone to join the French navy. One day Lisette was going to take flowers to the spot where an English airplane had crashed; she went along with her bouquet in her hands, telling everyone where she was going. On December 8, 1942, she was summoned to command headquarters. She went off jauntily, ready to make insolent remarks. On the way she met a comrade: "I'm going to command headquarters. They want to see me."—"I'll go with you," the friend volunteered. Neither of them returned. After several days in the prison at Vannes, Lisette was sent to Romainville until the departure.

She died in the Birkenau revier in March 1943. She was not quite eighteen years old. Marcelle Mourot was with her.

Her parents learned of her death after the war.

Marcelle MOUROT

Born in Dannemarie-sur-Crête, in Doubs, on July 31, 1918. At the age of thirteen, she lost her mother, a dressmaker, who had succumbed to bronchial pneumonia. A month later, her father, a mason, fell from a scaffold and was killed. Marcelle and a baby sister were taken in by a grandmother, who was not very well off. Marcelle never completed elementary school and went to work in a biscuit factory in Besançon. She rose at five in the morning and took the train, carrying her dinner pail with her. She returned home late in the evening. When she was fifteen, the biscuit factory, which employed many apprentices but few regular workers, let her go. She then found a place as a domestic with the Sisters of Charity, who ran a clinic. They gave her room, board, free laundry, and twenty francs a month. She stayed three years, from 1933 to 1935, then found a place with a physician, where she earned a bit more. She had to help her grandmother raise her little sister. But she was tired of being a domestic. In 1938, at the age of twenty, she was hired by a clothing manufacturer that made uniforms for the army, and took a room in Besançon. In June 1940 the manufacturer closed. Marcelle returned to her grandmother and worked here and there, depending on the few possibilities available at the time. In the spring of 1942 she happened to run into her former supervisor from the clothing factory and told her she was out of work. "My niece happens to be looking for a waitress at her café." This is how Marcelle was hired by Georgette Messmer [see this name].

The café was on Place Bacchus, in Besançon. Georgette Messmer seems to have had considerable business outside the café and often left Marcelle to run the place alone.

On August 2, 1942, Georgette Messmer said to Marcelle: "I have to go to Villers-le-Lac, but I haven't got the time. Do you want to go for me? It's to guide some prisoners of war who escaped from Germany. There are six of them. Leave first, they'll follow you at a distance, pretending not to know you. All you have to do is show them the road to Mr. X . . .'s house, and he'll help them cross the border."

Marcelle understood that her boss was involved in secret activities but hadn't speculated on their nature. She thought a moment. Transporting weapons or tracts would not have been acceptable; she would have been afraid. Going peacefully to Villers-le-Lac, two kilometers from the Swiss border, did not seem very dangerous to her. It seemed natural for prisoners of war to escape, and she thought that even if the men were caught, she was not running much of a risk. Marcelle Mourot and the six men, along with the "guide," were arrested by the regional police at Villers-le-Lac.

She was imprisoned in Pontarlier until September 1942, then in Besançon. There she found Georgette Messmer, whom she reproached for involving her in this adventure. She did not know what had become of the six escapees and the guide.

From Besançon she was transferred to Romainville (with a stopover of one day in the Dijon prison), where she arrived on December 19, 1942, and remained until the departure.

Auschwitz # 31819

She entered the revier almost immediately: her feet were injured and she couldn't walk. Then she had typhus and an ear infection, on which a Greek doctor had to operate. The operation was set for August 5, but when the group was put into quarantine on August 3, Marcelle gave up the operation. Since they were going to be freed, she thought it would be better to have the operation in France. Her condition worsened and she was sent back to the revier inside the camp. The Greek doctor operated on her in November 1943. The group was transferred to Ravensbrück on August 2, 1944, but Marcelle was still sick and stayed behind for a second operation. In November 1944 she was improving; she could join a small convoy that left for Ravensbrück, where she found the others. But having arrived on a different date, she was not "NN." She could therefore be enlisted for the factory details. She was sent to Oranienburg. Her ear infections returned, and she was sent back to Ravensbrück in February 1945. When she saw her comrades assembling for a departure on March 2, 1945, she made sure she was with them. She was liberated at Mauthausen on April 22, 1945.

Since her return, she has undergone five operations on her left ear, which is now deaf.

During the summer of 1945, at a rest home reserved for deportees, she made the acquaintance of a returnee, a *Franc-comtois* like herself, who had left for Oranienburg by the same train. Marcelle and Jean were married in 1946. They have two children.

Marie-Elisa NORDMANN

Born on November 4, 1910, in Paris, in the eighth arrondissement. Her father, after losing a good position in a Russian bank when it collapsed after the 1917 revolution, had been forced to accept an inferior post in another bank; so Marie-Elisa grew up in a bourgeois household without a bourgeois lifestyle.

She could pursue her education, however, and in 1942, as a chemical engineer with a doctorate in science, she was hired by the National Center for Scientific Research. She was divorced and lived with her mother, who was widowed in 1937, and her six-year-old son.

Beginning in October 1940, she was among those who joined the clandestine struggle against the occupation. What exactly did she do in 1942? She transported, mailed, and distributed *L'Université libre*, sheltered resisters (those who were told: "Don't go home, the cops are waiting for you"), and collected funds for the University branch of the National Front.

She was arrested at home on May 16, 1942, by the special brigades.

From police headquarters, Marie-Elisa was sent to the cells. A note written on cigarette paper, in a package, informed her that her mother, who had stayed home though she might have saved herself, had been arrested by the Gestapo on August 7 as a civilian hostage. After being beaten, the mother revealed that she was Jewish.

On August 24, 1942, Marie-Elisa was transferred to the Santé, and on September 29 to Romainville. She learned that her mother had already been there and had left on September 3. As a civilian hostage, Madame Nordmann should have been freed after four weeks (a rule rarely applied, but the rule nonetheless). But the Germans had discovered she was Jewish, and "Jewish" meant Drancy.

Marie-Elisa needed only a few days in Auschwitz to know what happened to old Jewish women: from the train straight to the gas chambers.

Auschwitz # 31687

At Birkenau, Marie-Elisa first worked on the brick and demolition crews. She entered the revier on February 28, 1943 (bronchitis, dysentery), then worked for several days in the "Canada" with Madeleine Dechavassine. She applied to work in the laboratory at Raisko, and thanks to Claudette Bloch[18] she was granted permission. On March 21, 1943, she left Birkenau to stay at the *Stabsgebaüde* with the laboratory personnel. Soon after she had typhus but managed not to be sent back to the revier at Birkenau. Three months later the scientific team set up at Raisko. Marie-Elisa worked more than a year on the *koksaghiz*.

---

18. Claudette Bloch, employed by the National Center for Scientific Research, assistant to Professor Prenant at the Sorbonne, had been arrested at the beginning of 1942, when she had shown up at Avenue Foch looking for news of her husband, an engineer with the Department of Civil Engineering (Ponts et Chaussées). When we saw her number, 7963—she had been deported the 25th of June 1942—we said to her: "Claudette, you're an archaeological find." She is certainly the only survivor of Auschwitz who had a tattoo consisting of only four numbers.

On August 14, 1944, the Raisko group was transferred to Ravensbrück. Marie-Elisa worked as a laboratory assistant at the revier, analyzing urine specimens. The killing went on, but there was a laboratory to analyze the patients' urine.

On March 2, 1945, nearly all the survivors of the convoy left Ravensbrück for Mauthausen, where, this time, Marie-Elisa became a nurse. She was liberated on April 22, 1945, and repatriated on the thirtieth.

And the return? "I was able to return to work relatively soon, in October 1945, and I readjusted rather quickly and even remarried in 1948. I had three children, which despite the fatigue also helped me to revive," she said. She added: "But I've had an awful block against research. After six years at the Atomic Energy Commission, where I directed the documentation service, I went back to teaching. It wasn't until 1960 that I republished some scientific work. My general debility, which doesn't interfere with the work of classification, inhibits creative work." Sequellae: gallstones (the result of typhus, they say), rheumatism, intestinal difficulties, general debility.

Her only brother, a teacher, the organizer of the FFI in the Morbihan and the Côtes-du-Nord, was arrested at Rennes in April 1944 and deported to Neuengamme in the penultimate convoy that left from Compiègne. He died of typhus in Bergen-Belsen on May 1, 1945, fifteen days after the English had liberated the camp.

Marie-Elisa received the Legion of Honor in 1968.

Madeleine Marie NORMAND, née Plantevigne

Born in Aigre, Charente, April 11, 1897, in a place called La Broussette, where her parents were farmers.

On September 9, 1919, she married Gustave Normand, who was also a farmer. They cultivated a pretty farm in Germeville, near Aigre: fifteen hectares of mixed farming, three horses, and sheep. Attached to the farm was a little house like a living room: you put your shoes on to go there and read. Shelves ran all along one side of the room, filled with books. By 1940, some of them were censored or suspect. The country schoolmaster also had many forbidden books. Gustave Normand bricked up one end of the classroom, and they hid everything in this double wall.

Before the war, Normand was a Communist Party militant responsible for the Charente region. He joined the Resistance at the beginning of the occupation: collecting funds, hiding resisters, helping them across the demarcation line, providing them with food and money—these were the daily activities of Gustave and Madeleine Normand.

In 1941 the Normands were targeted. They would have to leave. Gustave hesitated to abandon the farm. Madeleine dragged him off. They placed the horses with neighbors, the sheep were distributed here and there. Friends of theirs, the Gauvins, would look after the land. Madeleine and her husband relocated in a village near Saintes, where they rented a bourgeois property. But they were soon flushed out. At the beginning of March 1942, they decided to go entirely underground. They sold a horse for necessary cash and went to stay with a comrade, Poilane, while waiting for the leader of the organization to bring them instructions and false identity cards.

On March 27, 1942, Octave Rabaté arrived from Paris with the identity cards and went to the Lemassons'. The building must have been watched, since at four in the afternoon the police broke in. Rabaté and Marcelle Lemasson [see this name] were arrested. Alexandre Lemasson escaped. The police seized the identity cards, which bore the Normands' photographs.

Madeleine Normand was waiting in the public park for Marcelle Lemasson to bring cards for her and her husband. Marcelle did not come. Madeleine grew impatient and went to the Lemassons'. The police recognized her instantly from the photograph. Where was she living? She told them. The police went to Poilane's, where they found him and Gustave Normand. The two men were arrested.

Madeleine Normand was carrying 45,000 francs with her. "Did the Communist Party give you this money?" — "No," she answered, "it's from the sale of our animals." They were taken to the mayor's offices in Aigre to be confronted with the buyer of the animals. Madeleine's story was confirmed. Gustave was beaten anyway.

After four days of interrogation in Saintes, the whole group (Rabaté, Marcelle Lemasson, Poilane—who was eventually deported and returned—and the Normands) was transferred to Paris, spent several days in the offices of General Intelligence, then in the cells. From there the men were sent to the Cherche-Midi, the women, on April 29, to the Santé.

Madeleine Normand left the Santé for Romainville on August 24, 1942. There she saw her husband again, who was nearly blind from all the beatings he had suffered during interrogations.

Madeleine Normand's mother, sick with worry since her child's arrest, died the day her daughter left Compiègne for Auschwitz, January 24, 1943. Madeleine never knew.

Auschwitz # 31678

Died at Birkenau, February 23, 1943.

She was beaten to death by a *stubova* when we were in Block 26. There were no toilets or any sanitary facilities; when we got up at night, we had to take care of our needs in a metal wheelbarrow placed in front of the door expressly for that purpose. A *stubova* armed with a stick stood guard. That night Madeleine, who had dysentery, could not get to the barrow. The *stubova* beat her. Madeleine came back into the blockhouse shouting: "Marie-Claude, she's killing me," pursued by the fury who kept beating her. Her comrades pulled her up onto the tier where she lay down. Her neck was broken and she died in the night.

Gustave Normand, who stayed at Romainville after his wife's departure, was executed on October 2, 1943.

On the road from Aigre, a monument to the memory of Madeleine and Gustave Normand was erected in 1947 by Charles Tillon. Madeleine Normand was named a sergeant in the RIF. Medal of the Resistance, Croix de Guerre, military medal.

Yvonne NOUTARI, née Moudoulaud ("Yvette de Bordeaux")

Born May 5, 1915, in Bègles, Gironde, where she was raised in a working-class family; her father died young. After elementary school, she worked for a metal-box manufacturer and was married at an early age to Robert Noutari, an iron caster.

In June 1942 Robert Noutari was arrested and thrown into prison. Yvonne herself was affiliated with the National Front. She sheltered resisters. She was arrested on July 7, 1942, at her home in Bordeaux, and imprisoned in the Hâ fortress. Examining the matter, the police connected the husband's case to the wife's. Robert Noutari was executed by firing squad in Souge, on September 21, 1942. Yvonne was interned in Romainville on October 14, 1942.

Auschwitz # 31718

She experienced the whole deportation. After Birkenau, where she had a violent case of exanthematic typhus, she benefited from the quarantine. Which did not prevent her from being punished with one month in the *Strafkommando* (the disciplinary work detail) for writing in a letter to her mother: "Happy days will bloom again." She was the only Frenchwoman in this disciplinary detail, which left for work at four in the morning and returned at ten at night, and had to walk in step, chanting "alli-allo"; she held on. Her comrades each gave her a small part of their bread as a supplementary ration during the period of her punishment.

Transferred to Ravensbrück on August 2, 1944, then to Mauthausen on March 2, 1945, she was killed in the bombing along with her friends Olga

Melin and Charlotte Decock: they were at work clearing the tracks at the Amstetten train station. She died after a night of agony on March 22, 1945. During the arrival of the deportees, Yvonne's mother went to wait at the station in Bordeaux, hoping each day to see her daughter return, since she'd had news from Auschwitz and knew that Yvonne had survived. Félicienne Bierge told her of Yvonne's death.

The two Noutari children were raised by a grandmother and an aunt.

Toussainte, called "Nine," OPPICI

Born October 7, 1905, in Marseille.

Someone seemed to remember that she ran a restaurant featuring local specialties next to Place Clichy, and that she had an adolescent son. These memories were so vague that we weren't able to find further clues. She arrived at Romainville in November 1942.

Auschwitz # 31797

Died of typhus at the end of April 1943.

Anne-Marie OSTROWSKA, née Borsch

Born November 13, 1900, in Schwalbach, in the Rhineland, to a family of five children. She was raised in Frankfurt, where her father had a masonry business.

At twenty, she met Salomon Ostrowska. She loved him all her life. Her good German parents were opposed to the marriage: the young man was a Jew and a refugee. He'd come from Poland at the age of five, but since Poland did not exist as a separate country at the time, he was called a "Russian refugee." Anne-Marie braved everything. German law did not allow Ostrowska to marry her, because he would have had to prove that he was not already married in his own country; but it was impossible to obtain papers from Russia in 1920. Although Salomon Ostrowska had been in Germany since early childhood, nothing could be done: the law was the law. Anne-Marie converted to Judaism and they married in a religious ceremony. At least they had that. Anne-Marie's family cursed them. Anne-Marie and Salomon settled in Berlin. She was a dressmaker but learned leather working so they could work together.

In 1923 Hitler attempted his coup. The first Nazi groups threatened the Jews. Salomon Ostrowska, who had left Poland with his parents after the 1905 revolution, knew all about anti-Semitism. The Ostrowskas chose freedom and left for France in 1924 with their first-born son, Alfred, who was then two years old. Still considered a Russian refugee, Salomon Ostrowska, with his wife, obtained Nansen passports. She gave up any claim to her original nationality. They were married in a civil ceremony at the mayor's offices of the eleventh arrondissement in 1925. They had a second child that year, a daughter, and set up a small leather workshop on Rue Oberkampf. They were happy.

In 1939, when war broke out, Salomon Ostrowska joined the French army. Anne-Marie's three brothers were in the Wehrmacht.

Then came the occupation, the "racial" laws. Salomon Ostrowska declared himself a Jew; his wife, fearing they would one day be separated, did the same. They soon understood their mistake. Anne-Marie feared for her husband; she urged him to take shelter in the unoccupied zone in the south. Father and son left in the autumn of 1941. They were arrested by French police just as they were crossing the demarcation line. The father was sent to the camp at Gurs, the son to Mauriac.

As soon as she heard about it, Anne-Marie Ostrowska thought only of joining her husband; she would surely find a way to help him escape. She thought that moving around would be easier if she reestablished the truth; she obtained proof that she was not of the Jewish "race" and was issued a normal identity card, one unmarked with the stamp "Jew." She left with her seventeen-year-old daughter in September 1942.

The two of them were arrested in Vierzon by the Gestapo, before crossing the demarcation line. They were immediately imprisoned in Orléans. Since she was not Jewish, the mother was sent to Romainville, where she arrived on November 15, 1942. As a Jew, the daughter was sent to the camp at Pithiviers, then to Drancy.

Auschwitz # 31 . . .

Anne-Marie Ostrowska died in the marshes, the same day as Berthe Lapeyrade. Her comrades carried her back to the camp for roll call. This was at the end of March or the beginning of April 1943. One of the first days of spring.

Salomon Ostrowska was transferred from Gurs to Drancy, and from there he left for an unknown destination, "presumably Maidanek," in February–March 1943. No trace of him.

At Drancy, the daughter was recognized as "half-Jewish," which entitled her to be sent to work at Levitan's, the firm requisitioned to pack and expedite Jewish goods—especially furniture and pianos—to Germany.

Anne-Marie's son escaped from the camp at Mauriac after spending two years there. He went to Nice and joined the Resistance. He was caught in a roundup with tracts in his pocket. When he was arrested, he said, "I am a Jew," out of defiance, because the Germans had such contempt for Jews—they did not think they were capable of resistance. He was deported from Nice through

Italy, where cattle cars full of Italian Jews were added to the train. At Auschwitz, he was sent to the Jannina mine, a detail in which only eight men out of two thousand survived. He was liberated by the Soviet army on January 27, 1945, and repatriated from Odessa.

In 1946 an employee of the mayor's offices of the eleventh arrondissement went to 18 Avenue Parmentier, the family's apartment. He asked for Mademoiselle Ostrowska: "I'm here to inform you of your mother's death." No further details.

Geneviève PAKULA

Born December 22, 1922, in Poland, she arrived in France with her parents, who were employed in 1927 as agricultural workers on a farm in Bouqueval, Seine-et-Oise. She was raised there, completed elementary school, and then hired out as a domestic on a farm in the neighborhood. She wanted to educate herself, change jobs, and improve her situation, so she looked for a position in Paris.

In 1942 she was working in a small radio-electrical business in Paris. She went to night courses to learn stenography and accounting so she could handle financial matters at the shop. Her boss, a Pole, repaired transmitters that belonged to a network of resisters. She was arrested by the Gestapo on November 7, 1942, in the shop where she was working.

She was interrogated in Polish for one hour at Rue des Saussaies, then placed in solitary for several hours, and finally subjected to additional interrogation: "Who came to the shop, especially after working hours?" She said nothing. She was sent to Romainville the same day.

Auschwitz # 31794

Typhus (a week at the revier in mid-April 1943). Raisko from June 1943 until January 7, 1944. She was slated for transfer to Ravensbrück with a group of nine others, but was kept at Birkenau and rejoined those women still in quarantine because she had a fever at departure time. Only those in good health could go to Ravensbrück.

She arrived at Ravensbrück on August 4, 1944, stayed until March 2, 1945—the date of departure for Mauthausen—and was liberated at Mauthausen on April 22, 1945.

How did she make out? She married in 1946. Her husband was a taxi driver. A daughter was born in 1948, a son in 1954. She immediately went back to work, doing dressmaking at home.

She is haunted by memories: a convoy arrives, unloads near the gas chamber. SS officers, shouting and striking out with their sticks, hustle the newly arrived inmates into lines. A little boy, six or eight years old, exhausted from the journey, does not line up fast enough. The SS shouts at the mother. And the mother slaps the child.

When people arrive in the lane that leads to the gas chamber, they see a basin full of water. Given nothing to drink for the duration of the journey, which was never less than three days, they hurry over. The SS wait until they crouch over, then beat them with their sticks.

She received the Legion of Honor in July 1977.

Lucienne PALLUY

Born in Paris in the twentieth arrondissement, on January 5, 1910. The family were Parisians as far back as anyone can trace.

Lucienne took a commercial course after completing elementary school, and went to work early. She was a stenographer.

Quite naturally, we might say, she joined the Union of Women against the War and Fascism in 1936 (this was the period of the Popular Front, of the war against fascism in Spain) and the Communist Party in 1939.

When the Germans occupied Paris, she made herself scarce—knowing her own reputation as a communist—and went under cover. This was called "going into the fog." When the first groups of the FTP were formed, she was attached to Colonel Dumont, formerly of the International Brigades, for whom she became a liaison agent. But in her case, liaison agent also meant carrying black powder and cheddite [an explosive] to Madeleine Dechavassine, who used them to make explosive devices; she had to get these to Douillot and to transport kilos of explosives in shopping baskets.

In March 1942 Lucienne went to her mother's place (her mother had been a widow since 1939 and now lived alone) to get news of her brother Georges, a prisoner of war in Germany. The special brigades were watching the building—her legal residence. She was caught.

She was sent to the Santé and kept in isolation until September 29, 1942, and then to Romainville until the departure.

Auschwitz # 31689

She died of dysentery in the revier at the end of February 1943.

Her mother died at the hospice of Brévannes in 1944, without knowing what had become of her daughter. A penciled note thrown from the train on January 24, 1943, was the last sign she'd had from Lucienne.

Yvonne PATEAU, née Pateau

Born September 14, 1901, to a peasant family with four children in Angles, the Vendée. She completed elementary school, helped her parents on their farm, and in 1919 married her first cousin, Alexandre Pateau.

The Pateaus had a little farm, which included three rooms for human habitation, a stable with two cows and a horse, and several hectares of land, in a hamlet of three houses, one kilometer from the town of Saint-André-de-Cognac.

During the occupation, it was on such farms in the Charente that the FTP hid the weapons they stole from the Germans at the Jonzac quarry [see *Aminthe Guillon*]. On the eve of an action, resisters would come to take the munitions they needed and to sleep at the farm.

On July 28, 1942, at four in the morning, Monsieur Cessac, the mayor of Saint-André-de-Cognac, was abruptly awakened. He pulled his trousers on over his nightshirt so he could open up before they forced the door. Two German officers pushed him into a car. His wife threw his slippers out the window and watched him leave with the two men. Trucks filled with German soldiers were waiting further on. The officers ordered Monsieur Cessac to lead them to the Pateaus'. Once there, the soldiers, armed with machine guns, jumped down from the trucks and surrounded the hamlet.

Awakened by a knocking at the door, Alexandre Pateau opened up. A resister, in hiding there, leaped out, revolver in hand. He did not have time to fire. In an instant, he was bound and gagged. At the same time, the Germans arrested the Vaujours, neighbors and friends of the Pateaus. Yvonne Pateau quickly dressed her four-and-a-half-year-old son, Stéphane, and they were all thrown into a van that made its way toward the gendarmerie in Cognac. The car with Monsieur Cessac followed. Arriving there, Monsieur Cessac saw the Vaujours standing on the sidewalk with little Stéphane, who was crying. "Take a taxi, quick, and go to the Bajots," he whispered to them. The Bajots were friends.

That evening, Yvonne and Alexandre Pateau, along with the resister they were sheltering, were taken to Hâ. The resister, a young man from Maine-et-Loire who continued to curse the Germans and spit in their faces, was beaten with a revolver on the way.

Monsieur Cessac was confined to his parish for one month. He asked and obtained leave to go to the Pateaus' farm, which had been left untended.

On August 12, 1942, the Gestapo arrested Alexandre Pateau's brother and his wife, who were also imprisoned at Hâ.

Yvonne Pateau's family—her brother, Célestin, his wife, and their two sisters—were also arrested and interned in Mérignac.

Alexandre Pateau was executed by firing squad in Souge, on September 21, 1942. His brother and brother-in-law were freed the following October 2, after fifty-six days of internment. Yvonne's sisters and sisters-in-law had been released after eight days of detention.

From Romainville, where she arrived on October 14, 1942, Yvonne Pateau wrote to Monsieur Cessac to beg him to entrust her son Stéphane to cousins, the Guérineaus, who raised him as their own child. Monsieur Cessac was his tutor.

Auschwitz # 31728

Yvonne Pateau died at the beginning of February 1943, of acute nephritis. An official notification dated May 13, 1943, was sent to the mayor's offices in Saint-André-de-Cognac, indicating that she had died at Auschwitz, Kasernenstrasse, March 3, 1943. Monsieur Cessac not only took responsibility for all dealings with the Veterans Ministry, but after the war he recovered the body of Alexandre Pateau in Bordeaux and had it reburied in Saint-André-de-Cognac.

Yvonne Pateau was decorated with the Legion of Honor.

LUCIE, CALLED "LUCETTE," PECHEUX, NÉE LABLE

Born in the Nièvre, May 14, 1905, one of five children. The family moved to Tours when Lucette was barely six years old, probably because her father, a housepainter, had found a better job there. Lucette went to the local elementary school, then learned to make trousers, married, had a daughter, then divorced, but kept her husband's name, Pécheux.

In 1935 she joined the Communist Party and met a young militant, Pottier, a carpenter and cabinetmaker, with whom she set up housekeeping in Paris in a modest apartment under the roof of a middle-class apartment building on Rue de l'Odéon. Her daughter, Gisèle, lived with them.

Under the occupation, Pottier led the life of a militant communist: by day, he worked (in a carpentry workshop on Rue Saint-Dominique); at the end of the day he put up posters, transported brochures, and participated in actions such as the affair at Rue de Buci. The last Sunday in May 1942, a group of partisans organized a riot of housewives as the market was about to open—or rather as the line for the market was forming—in Rue de Buci. One of the organizers, perched on a little car, was haranguing the crowd. In no time, the stalls were overturned and the foodstuffs distributed. The police surrounded the quarter, four men were caught—and guillotined at the Santé in July 1942. Pottier escaped.

As for Lucette, she was working for a clothing manufacturer on Rue des Arquebusiers. At the same time, she was collecting funds for combatants in the clandestine struggle; storing brochures in a cupboard under the stairs; and, although her lodging was tiny, sheltering comrades passing through—René Despouy and others.

On June 18, 1942, at 6:30 a.m., a knock at the door: "Madame Pécheux? A telegram." It was the special brigades. Lucette and Pottier were arrested. Gisèle, Lucette's daughter, was seventeen and already working: she was part of a team that began at six o'clock. The police went to find her. All three were taken to the cells.

Gisèle was released a week later. She returned to the little rooms and, as the police had not discovered the hiding place under the stairs, she pulled out the books and brochures and burned them one by one in the stove.

Lucette Pécheux remained in the cells until August 10, 1942. From the cells, she was taken to Romainville along with the men arrested for playing a part in this affair, notably Pottier and Despouy. After spending the night in the fort's pillbox, the men were executed at Mont-Valérien the following day.

Auschwitz # 31633

She died in the revier at Birkenau around February 15, 1943. Gisèle did not learn of her mother's death until the survivors' return.

MARIE-JEANNE PENNEC

Born July 9, 1909, out of wedlock, she had been raised by a poor peasant woman from Châteaugiron, near Rennes, who had been her wet nurse. We do not know if she was married, but she had a son. After earning a living at different jobs, she was the manager of a dairy in Montreuil.

She arrived at Romainville in December 1942, and we never knew how or why she had been arrested, or by whom. All we know is that she acted as a "guide" (to the demarcation line); she said that it was very hard and that she had been "slipshod."

Auschwitz # 31817

We don't think she ever went to the revier. Tough, solitary, secretive, she had a peasant's instinct that drove her to look for anything that would serve as food, even the snails in the marshes. She was the first one to collect dandelions to eat, mixing them in the soup. She was always collecting, while she walked, while she worked, and shared her finds with the others.

At Raisko from July 1943 to January 7, 1944. Sent to Ravensbrück January 8, she was then shipped to a factory in Czechoslovakia. We do not know how she was repatriated.

After the return, she must have gone to work; she took back her son, whom she'd left with his nurse. But she began to have difficulties with the boy, an unstable adolescent who couldn't keep a job; he was unhappy with every apprenticeship and one day joined up to go to Indochina. Marie-Jeanne was deeply affected by this and suffered a nervous depression; she was hospitalized and, in the course of treatment, attempted suicide by throwing herself out the window. In 1949 she had a lobotomy. Since then she has spent several stretches in the Rennes psychiatric hospital.

GERMAINE PICAN, née MORIGOT

Born October 10, 1901, in Malaunay, a suburb of Rouen, to a family of three daughters. The father specialized in engraving the rollers used to print the calico called "rouenneries," which was typical of the region. The mother kept house, and it was a happy one. Germaine did her early schooling in Malaunay, then completed middle school in Rouen, and went on to teachers' college.

She married André Pican, a teacher as well. They both taught in Marommes, near Rouen. They had two daughters: Claudine, born in 1927, and Simone, born in 1928.

André Pican was the local Communist Party leader for the Seine-Inférieure. He was arrested for this in April 1940, interned in Neuvaines, Calvados, then imprisoned in Bonne-Nouvelle in Rouen and later in Caen, where he was liberated when the Germans arrived. He went back to the Seine-Inférieure, formed groups of the National Front and of the special organization that would soon become the FTP. He edited and printed the regional paper, *L'Avenir normand*, for the Seine-Inférieure and the Eure, and *La Vérité* for Rouen and the surrounding region. During this period, his wife Germaine stayed at her school in Maromme, acted as liaison between the regional organization her husband directed—which was clandestine—and groups that had formed in each of the localities around Rouen. The organization was active, the propaganda intense. Suspected of being the instigator, Germaine Pican was arrested on June 20, 1941, in Rouen, and interned at Compiègne, where she was joined in October 1941 by most of her comrades in the Resistance who had been caught in a roundup following a train derailing in Pavilly—an act of sabotage masterminded by André Pican. Thirty-six of these resisters were executed by firing squad or died in the deportation.

The police freed Germaine Pican on December 12, 1941, probably so she would put them on her husband's trail. She sought refuge with a teacher friend in Eure-et-Loir with her two daughters, who had been hiding out with friends in the Seine-Inférieure. The police had lost track of Germaine Pican but were still looking for her husband, and published his photograph in *Le Journal de*

Rouen. They put a price on Pican's head: 30,000 francs. But he was no longer in the region.

Germaine met her husband twice in a café in Paris, and they planned the details of their next meeting: they would live in Paris in rooms left to them by their friend Renée Michaux, who had to be transferred to the southwest. They set their third rendezvous at the home of Marie-Louise Jourdan, their letter drop.

On February 15, 1942, the day after her arrival at the Jourdans', believing she was opening the door to André, Germaine found herself face to face with six French police of the special brigades who burst into the apartment, searched the place feverishly and discovered tracts about the execution of Gabriel Péri.* They took Germaine Pican and Marie-Louise Jourdan to police headquarters, where they were interrogated.

At General Intelligence headquarters, Germaine found her husband, who had been arrested the same day a few hours earlier [see *Renée Michaux*]. They were taken to the cells. On March 21, 1942, the Germans took delivery of the men responsible for the sabotage of the train. André Pican, although handcuffed, managed to knock down the police and escape. He was pursued and threw himself into the Seine. A guard at the cells told Germaine: "Your husband tried to escape. Unfortunately, he didn't make it."

On March 23, 1942, Germaine Pican was transferred to the Santé — German division, in isolation — where she shared a cell with Danielle Casanova. She was sent to Romainville on August 24, 1942. André Pican was executed by firing squad at Mont-Valérien, on May 23, 1942.

Auschwitz # 31679

At Birkenau she was one of those rare persons who did not spend time in the revier. She had ambulatory typhus. She was part of the Raisko detail, but stayed there only two weeks. Caught stealing onions for comrades left behind at Birkenau, she was sent back to the disciplinary block. But the quarantine decree came fifteen days later, on August 3, 1943, and she benefited from it along with the others. She followed the usual route: Ravensbrück, from August 4, 1944, to March 2, 1945; Mauthausen, where she was liberated on April 22, 1945.

And then? She retired as a schoolteacher in 1955:

"With my two children, I reclaimed the little house in Maromme, which was never the same again. My Claudine, affected by the war and the loss of her fa-

---

*Péri was a Communist deputy to Parliament tried *in absentia* in 1940 by the Deladier government. He was executed at Mont-Valérien on December 15, 1941. (Trans.)

ther, died two years after my return. I gave the best of myself to what I then considered most crucial: my younger daughter, the school, my party. I was a communist and I remained one. That's what got me through. To me, my membership in the Communist Party, dating from the years of the National Front and the fight against fascism, always meant simply a necessary struggle for happiness."

Named an adjutant in the RIF.

Yvonne PICARD

She had a degree in philosophy and gave courses at the Ecole Normale Supérieure for young girls from Sèvres. The study of Marxism led her to communism.

On the notebook of a young FTP partisan arrested on May 16, 1942, the police read: "1-8-20 Athens," and from this they were able to find Yvonne Picard, born August 1, 1920, in Athens, where her father, a specialist in Greek statuary, was headmaster of the French school. She left her parents during the occupation to become involved in the clandestine struggle; nonetheless, she gave them her real address so as not to arouse their curiosity. When the police confronted Charles Picard and asked him where his daughter was, he told them without hesitation. Professor at the Sorbonne, member of the Académie des Inscriptions, he thought he had nothing to fear from his own country's police. Subsequently, he would go to police headquarters to find out what had happened and try to get his daughter released. In vain.

Yvonne Picard, arrested June 18, 1942, stayed in the cells until August 10, 1942, and was then sent to Romainville until the departure.

Auschwitz # 31634

She had contracted dysentery at the beginning and was demoralized. She said: "They'll say: a degree in philosophy at nineteen and dead of dysentery at twenty-two." She entered the revier when she couldn't hold out any longer.

"She suffered in the revier, her face was covered with lice" (Marie-Elisa).

I can see her in that dreary column we would form to carry bricks from one pile to the other, two bricks at a time. She would hold her two bricks against her chest, her left arm folded under them. "As if I were carrying books. Isn't that how we carried our books? If I could only imagine that these were books." In Auschwitz, one could not imagine anything, there was no escape into imagination, no momentary respite to play a role that wasn't real. No double life was allowed.

Yvonne Picard died on March 9, 1943.

Her fiancé, a young communist named Etiévent, was arrested along with her and shot at Mont-Valérien on August 11, 1942.

Suzanne PIERRE, née Buffard

Born May 15, 1912, in Dombasle, Meurthe-et-Moselle, to a working-class family of nine children. She was raised in Dombasle, completed her basic education there, then worked in a textile mill.

She married a blacksmith shortly before the war. Taken prisoner in 1940, he was in a disciplinary camp two years later in Ravaruska.

Suzanne did not belong to any resistance network. She worked alone to blow up a canal lock, and a telegraph pole as well. She was connected to a group of young people who had been Young Communists before the war and who, without any official organization, were fighting against the occupation on their own initiative. On November 11, 1942, they made a tricolored garland out of colored paper that they hung on the monument to the World War I dead. The police simply went around to the paper dealers to find out where they'd bought the colored paper. Identifying the buyers was easy enough in this town of 10,000. Suzanne Pierre was arrested in mid-November 1942 by the French police. After incarceration in the Charles III prison in Nancy, in isolation for a week, she was transferred to Romainville on November 21, 1942.

The young men—nine French and two Poles from Varengéville—were shot at Champigneulles at the end of 1942.

Auschwitz # 31812

She held out until August 1943. She had entered the revier in July and therefore did not follow the others into quarantine. She was probably too ill to write when permission was given at the beginning of July 1943.

Her parents learned of her death on the survivors' return.

Germaine PIROU

Born March 9, 1918, in Scrignac, Finistère, to a family of four daughters. The parents, poor agricultural workers, lived on a little farm.

At the age of twelve, Germaine left school in Scrignac and went to work. In 1942, she was a waitress in a café in Saint-Malo, Au Petit Matelot, where the sailors from the Kriegsmarine came to drink. One evening in November, after a rough day—the café was full, one of the ships was being fitted out, the men were spending their last moments on land, and she was being called from every direction—exhausted and exasperated by these customers she despised,

Germaine burst out: "You think you're going to win the war, but you won't. You're leaving and you won't come back. You'll all croak, all of you. The English are going to come and cut your throats. Every one of you. I know. I have information, I'm a communist," and she raised her fist. This was exasperation, fatigue, spite, the need to defy them, for she had never been a communist and belonged to no resistance organization. One month later, on December 17, 1942, the Gestapo arrested Germaine at Au Petit Matelot. She was confronted by two of the sailors who had returned.

From the Saint-Malo prison (with a view of the sea) she went to the prison at Rennes, and arrived at Romainville at the end of December 1942. In time for the departure.

Auschwitz # 31842

She went twice to the revier: for typhus and for an eye infection that nearly destroyed her sight. She worked at Raisko doing gardening when the detachment was formed in July 1943, but she was sent back in January 1944 because of her eyes, which were infected again. Finally cured, she rejoined the others in quarantine and followed their route: Ravensbrück from August 2, 1944, to March 2, 1945; then to Mauthausen, where she was liberated on April 22, 1945.

After the return and a period of time in Scrignac with her parents, she had to get back to work. A comrade she'd met at Mauthausen found her work at a factory in Avignon. There she met a returnee who had experienced similar hardship: forcibly enrolled in the Wehrmacht at the age of seventeen and a half, just as he was completing his apprenticeship as a mason, Simon Berger, an Austrian, fought at Stalingrad. When the war ended, he returned to his country. He found none of his family left, no work, and could expect no help since he'd worn the German uniform. He saw only one way out: to go to France, the land of freedom and plenty. But France in 1946 had little to offer him, not even a work card. What was left? The Foreign Legion. He was marked for legendary battles—after Stalingrad, Dien-Bien-Phu. He was wounded, sent back to Marseille, and discharged. He ended up in the factory in Avignon where he met Germaine.

They were married in 1956. They manage an estate, raise poultry and rabbits, live modestly, but they want their son to pursue his education. The boy is at secondary school in Avignon and is a good student.

Renée PITIOT, née Legros ("Bichette")

Born on November 17, 1921, in Paris, in the thirteenth arrondissement, she attended elementary school until the age of fourteen. Her father was a caster with Electrolux, her mother a dressmaker. She was an only daughter. In 1935 the Legroses settled in Combs-la-Ville, where they built a private home. Bichette learned dressmaking and went to work in Paris, first as junior assistant, then as chief assistant at various couture houses. She commuted by train mornings and evenings. In November 1941 she married Gustave Pitiot, who was not much older than she and was employed in the tax collection office in Brunoy, an adjacent community. He was a young communist militant. Bichette and her husband rented a place in Lilas. Gustave Pitiot was wholeheartedly involved in the Resistance under the pseudonym "Le Breton." Renée supported him. She was known under the name "Cunégonde."

Gustave Pitiot sensed that the police were on his trail. After living together less than seven months, husband and wife separated to throw the police off their track. Renée took refuge in Moret-sur-Loing with friends. The special brigades arrested her there, on June 20, 1942, two days after arresting Pitiot. At the cells, she joined the young members of the FTP arrested on June 18: Madeleine Doiret, Lulu Thévenin, her sister Carmen, Mounette, and Jackie Quatremaire, and went with them to Romainville on August 10, 1942.

Gustave Pitiot was shot the next day, August 11, 1942. He was twenty-two years old.

Auschwitz # 31629

At Birkenau she had dysentery, exanthematic typhus, the usual camp illnesses. She withstood these and was quarantined on August 3, 1943. She made the trip to Ravensbrück on August 2, 1944, to Mauthausen on March 2, 1945, and returned after the Liberation.

During a convalescent stay in Alsace, she met a former junior officer whom she married in September 1945. The new couple settled in Combs-la-Ville, near the Legros parents. Three daughters were born: in 1946, in 1949, and in 1952. They have been orphans since 1961. Bichette, ailing from the time of her return, succumbed to kidney failure. She had overestimated her strength. Forced to work to help pay for the house and raise the children, she couldn't take care of herself and rest as she should have. A resister deportee card, which would have given her the right to a better pension, was granted only after her death.

Juliette POIRIER, née Même

Her parents were gardeners in Saint-Lambert-des-Levées, in Maine-et-Loire, where she was born on July 10, 1918, one of eight children. After completing elementary school, she was hired out as a domestic in Saumur—she had to earn a living early.

In 1935, at the age of seventeen, she married Poirier, a jeweler in Saumur with a shop on Rue de la Cocasserie. In 1939 her husband was mobilized. Wounded in the battle of Dunkirk, he died in the Béthune hospital on August 1, 1940.

Juliette Poirier was arrested at her home, 46 Rue Waldeck-Rousseau, Saumur, during the summer of 1942. Her son, then seven years old, remembers only that the Germans came looking for his mother and that it was summer. He doesn't know why. He was raised by his maternal grandmother, who is dead now and probably didn't know herself. He heard that his mother had been in prison in Angers, then no one spoke about her anymore.

Juliette Poirier arrived in Romainville on October 30 or 31, 1942.

Auschwitz # 31 . . .

She died in March 1943.

Her parents were informed of her death in 1943 by the mayor's offices in Saumur. They were given a translation of the German notification that Juliette Poirier had died at the infirmary at Auschwitz, March 28, 1943, of acute stomach problems and intestinal difficulties.

MARIE, CALLED "MAÏ," POLITZER, NÉE FOURCADE

Born August 15, 1905, in Biarritz. An only daughter, she had a privileged childhood in comfortable circumstances. Her father, a great cook, had been chef at the Spanish court. After the fall of Alphonse XIII, he settled in Biarritz and did seasonal work at the resorts in Saint-Sébastien.

Maï was raised in a convent in Biarritz, and after completing her secondary studies she entered the school for midwifery in Paris. On the train home for summer vacation at the end of her first year, she met Georges Politzer,[19] who planned to make a bicycle tour through the Basque country. His bicycle was in the luggage car. But most of that summer he spent walking with Maï.

In marrying Georges Politzer, Maï discovered Marxism and became equally committed. When her husband became a militant in the clandestine struggle in August 1940, she entrusted their seven-year-old son to her parents and shared her husband's life in the underground. He hardly moved. He wrote pamphlets and theoretical articles for *L'Université libre*, the first issue of which came out in November 1940, and for *La Pensée libre*. She made contact with the outside and transported paper for the underground printers. She dyed her blonde hair brown.

---

19. Graduate in philosophy, author of *La Crise de la Psychologie contemporaine; Le Bergsonisme, Etudes d'économie politique*, etc.

They were both arrested on February 14, 1942, by the special brigades, at their illegal residence in the eighteenth arrondissement. Maï had been followed for several days.

She was put in the cells until March 23, then the Santé (in isolation). She did several stints in solitary and suffered terribly from the cold since there was no straw pallet or blanket. She said good-bye to her husband at the Santé on the morning of May 23, 1942. On August 24, 1942, she was transferred to Romainville.

Auschwitz # 31680

Several days after our arrival, on February 1 or 2, 1943, Danielle Casanova managed to get Maï into the revier as a doctor; she was only a midwife but no one stood on ceremony. Despite the horror of the revier—the dead body parts, the stench, the rats, the fleas, the pus—the life of a doctor or nurse was less arduous because there was no roll call, the place was heated, and the food was plentiful (the soup was not so carefully rationed at the revier, where most of the patients had stopped eating). Maï caught typhus and died on March 6, 1943, after only a few days of fever. She also had a large, black boil on her upper lip.

Her family learned of her death from Marie-Claude Vaillant-Couturier.

Pauline POMIES, née Lafabrier

Born October 12, 1877, in Toulouse, where she lived until the age of twelve. Then her family settled in Bordeaux, where her father was a cabinetmaker.

A laundress by profession, she married a shoemaker, and they had three children: a son, who died of illness at the age of twenty-two; another, killed in the Spanish Civil War, and a daughter, who was living with her parents in 1942.

Pauline Pomiès was arrested at her residence in Bordeaux on August 7, 1942, in the morning. Her husband was arrested returning home that evening. He had been warned and could have escaped. He did not, for fear of aggravating his wife's case and for fear that their daughter would be arrested too. They had been sheltering resisters.

Pauline Pomiès was imprisoned in the Boudet barracks until October 14, 1942, then transferred to the fort at Romainville.

Auschwitz # 31 . . .

She died on February 16, 1943. She had been caught in "the race" on February 10, but her comrades had managed to pull her out of the group of condemned and drag her back to the block. She died six days later. At sixty-five, she was simply too old.

In May 1943 her daughter received a notification of decease from Auschwitz. Her husband had been executed by firing squad at Souge on September 21, 1942.

Line PORCHER

This is the name we knew her by, but more often we called her "Mama Line." Emilie Angéline Porcher, born on January 4, 1881, in Boisville-la-Saint-Père, in Eure-et-Loir, had long been the widow of Antoine Julien Amilcar Fourmy. She had been raised in Chartres but was living in Tours, where she had settled when she was quite young. She was a communist and belonged to the same group as Fabienne Landy [see this name]. She was denounced at the same time as Fabienne. The Gestapo arrested her on July 23, 1942, at her home in Saint-Pierre-des-Corps, where they found the typewriter used for typing tracts; out of precaution, this machine was sometimes moved from one place to another.

Imprisoned in Tours, Line Porcher arrived in Romainville with the group from the Tours region on November 7, 1942.

Auschwitz # 31789

She raised her hand when the SS doctor asked those who were too old or too tired to endure roll call to identify themselves. This was between February 3 and 8, 1943. Line was taken to Block 25. Several women were certain that she left for the gas chambers with Annette Epaud on February 22, 1943, but I did not see her and doubt that she survived seventeen or eighteen days in Block 25.

The mayor's offices of Saint-Pierre-des-Corps registered February 15, 1943, as the date of death.

"Mama Line" had no family.

Delphine PRESSET

Born June 27, 1900, in Nîmes, where her father was a shopkeeper. After completing elementary school, she went to work and earned a living at various jobs, mostly as a salesgirl. When did she come to Paris? We don't know. She married, was widowed in 1942, and was employed at the factory where her husband, an adjuster, had worked until he fell ill.

She joined the Communist Party before the war, though was not politically active after September 1939; nonetheless, she maintained relations with her former comrades.

On June 18, 1942, Maurice Grandcoing, inspector of the underground newspaper L'Humanité, was arrested. In a transfer from prison to prison, the vehicle in which he was riding with four inspectors lurched and got stuck on the side of the road. The occupants were thrown out of the car. One of the policemen whispered to Grandcoing: "What are you waiting for?" He took off. Thinking where to hide, he remembered Delphine Presset's address in Villetaneuse. She took him in but thought he would be better off outside Paris. He would need papers. Delphine gave him her recently deceased husband's service record and Grandcoing set off. He was caught again by the police on August 3 or 4, 1942 (and executed by firing squad at Mont-Valérien on August 11). The police found Presset's service record and located his parents in the Savoie. "Our son? But he's dead." Delphine Presset was arrested several days later. She hadn't thought to notify the commissariat of the loss or theft of her husband's service record so as to have an alibi.

After several days in the cells, she was transferred to Romainville on August 10, 1942.

Auschwitz # 31 ...

She died in February 1943. No witness. There was no notification of decease. She had only one brother, a career soldier, who so strongly disavowed his sister's opinions that he never sent her the smallest package when she was at Romainville.

Paulette PRUNIERES, née Parant ("Pépée")

Born November 13, 1918, in Paris, in the thirteenth arrondissement, raised in Ivry where her parents were city employees and where she completed elementary school. She then took a stenography course and became a secretary.

She joined the Communist Party on March 14, 1936, and participated in the Union of French Girls.

It was natural for her to join the Resistance from the start and, beginning on May 1, 1941, to play the role of liaison agent between the organizations of the National Front in Paris and the surrounding suburbs. She was part of a technical team that published and distributed anti-German tracts.

She was arrested on March 1, 1942, at the exit of the Porte-d'Ivry metro. She had been followed for several days.

Kept under observation at General Intelligence until March 10, transferred to the cells, and from there to the Santé on March 23, 1942—German division, in isolation—and from the Santé to Romainville on August 24, 1942.

Auschwitz # 31654

She was in work details in the marshes and on the demolition crew until the quarantine. In September 1943 she had pleurisy and was treated secretly by

Doctor Hautval, who would come to the camp to tap her lungs and give her insulin shots (a female Czech doctor stole the insulin at the revier).

She left Birkenau like the others on August 2, 1944, and arrived at Ravensbrück on August 4; from there, she went to Mauthausen on March 2, 1945, arriving on March 5, where she was liberated on April 22, 1945.

Since then? She suffers terribly from nerves, has not been able to sleep without sleeping pills, and tires very easily.

She had two children, a daughter born in 1946—an extremely nervous child who has needed to be hospitalized several times—and a boy born ten years later.

Marie Thérèse PUYOOU, née Soureil

Born January 6, 1897, in Monein, Basses-Pyrénées, where she went to school.

She was married—her husband was a screwcutter and fitter—they had two children and lived in Bègles, in the Prêche quarter, where she was in business after running a cooperative. She was arrested a first time in 1941, along with her husband, then released and kept under surveillance.

Her husband was shot at Souge on October 24, 1941, but Marie-Thérèse nonetheless continued her activity in the Resistance, giving shelter to clandestine operatives.

She was arrested on July 11, 1942, at her home in Bègles. Her daughters, aged sixteen and nine, were taken in by relatives.

Imprisoned in the Hâ fortress until October 14, 1942, then in Romainville until the departure.

Auschwitz # 31720

Marie-Thérèse Puyoou died in the revier at Birkenau on March 31, 1943, most likely of typhus. The epidemic was raging at this time.

On the return of the deportees, the two children went to the Bordeaux station every day, hoping to find their mother.

They have in their possession the anthropometric photograph from Auschwitz. They have hidden it so as not to show it to their children and never look at it themselves. They want to preserve the image of their mother as they remember her.

Jacqueline QUATREMAIRE

Born October 17, 1918, in Igé, Orne, where she completed her elementary education. She was an only daughter.

Her parents settled near Paris in 1934. Her father, elected communist mayor of Noisy-le-Sec in 1936, was reelected several times in this district.

In 1936, Jacqueline Quatremaire was a stenographer with the union of pharmaceutical producers at the Labor Exchange. She worked there until the breakup of the unions in 1939.

She became politically active in 1937, directing the office of the Union of French Girls in Noisy-le-Sec. Her parents were arrested as communists by the French authorities in 1940 and interned in the camps in the southern zone. Her father escaped in 1942.

Left alone in Paris, Jacqueline was involved in the National Front and went underground. To live underground is not what readers of spy novels imagine. Twenty-year-old girls who had been living with their families suddenly found themselves alone in a small, sparsely furnished room where they spent their evenings in utter solitude, seeing no one, speaking to no one, their only human exchange workmanlike conversations with people they met for a few minutes, the time it took to pass on papers and orders. And yet, you would like to know why this and why that, the latest news, what became of X . . . , what happened to Y. . . . In addition, those living under cover had very little money, poor nourishment, and frequently received their ration cards late. And the hours of anguished waiting, the meeting when the comrade doesn't show—could he have been arrested? This was Jacqueline Quatremaire's life after 1940. Between clandestine meetings she typed texts on stencils, which she then took to a place where there was a mimeograph, etc.

She was arrested on June 17, 1942, in the fifteenth arrondissement, by inspectors of the special brigades. She had been followed for three months. Always dressed in bright colors, she seemed stubbornly defiant. The truth is that she was extremely nearsighted and hadn't realized she was being followed. Madeleine Dechavassine was arrested at the same time.

From the cells she was sent to Romainville on August 10, 1942.

Auschwitz # 31641

Jacqueline Quatremaire died of pulmonary consumption in the Birkenau revier, where she had worked as a nurse starting on February 24. An enormous abscess on her left shoulder blade seemed to consume her. Betty reported that as she lay dying, she was absolutely covered with lice.

Her parents learned of her death only on the survivors' return. A notification of decease established by the mayor's offices of Noisy-le-Sec, dated May 24, 1948, gave June 15, 1943, as the date of death, which seems accurate according to witnesses.

Military medal, Croix de Guerre with palm leaf, and the Medal of the Resistance were awarded posthumously in 1960, with the comment:

Quatremaire, Jacqueline, sergeant. Magnificent patriot, member of the internal French resistance. Arrested for acts of resistance June 17, 1942, interned until January 21, 1943. Deported January 23, 1943, to a concentration camp, died gloriously for France on June 15, 1943.

Paula RABEAUX, née Trapy

Born March 17, 1911, in Saumur, the third of six children in a family that settled in La Rochelle in 1918. She completed elementary school and went to work, first in a pharmacy, then for a manufacturer of pearl funerary ornaments, etc.

In 1931 she married Raymond Rabeaux, an industrial plumber in La Rochelle. They had a son the following year and, in 1939, a daughter, who died at the age of seven months.

During the war, Raymond Rabeaux was in a protected occupation in a gunpowder factory in the Basses-Pyrénées, and joined the Resistance when he was demobilized in 1940. Before the war he was a union militant. In 1941, too well-known in La Rochelle, the Rabeaux moved to Bordeaux, where the husband found a new job. At the same time, he was interregional head of the FTP for the area of Nantes, La Rochelle, and Bordeaux.

Paula and her husband were arrested on August 6, 1942, by the French gendarmerie: she at home in the morning, he when he left work that day. Their son, Jack, was on vacation in l'Ile-Delle, in the Vendée, staying with Paula's sister.

Paula Rabeaux was interned in Hâ fortress until October 14, 1942, then in Romainville until the departure.

Auschwitz # 31725

She died in the revier at the beginning of March 1943. Her tongue was swollen, and she could hardly eat or breathe. Félicienne Bierge was with her.

The family received a notification from Auschwitz dated May 13, 1943, indicating that Paula Rabeaux had died on March 15, 1943, at seven o'clock in the morning: no cause of death was specified.

Raymond Rabeaux was executed by firing squad in Bordeaux, on September 21, 1942.

Constance RAPPENAU

Born January 3, 1879, in Domecy-sur-Cure, Yonne, to a family of agricultural workers with four children.

Arriving in Paris very young to work as a domestic, she married there and ran a restaurant at Kremlin-Bicêtre. She divorced in 1913, had a restaurant in Vitry which she sold in 1935, and acquired another in Paris: Chez Constance, 121 Boulevard Sérurier, in the nineteenth arrondissement.

In 1941, Fabien [head of the FTP] and his partisans ate their meals at Constance's place; they called her "Mère Mie" [Mother Sweet]. They left parcels there as well. Constance did not know who Fabien was or even his name, but she knew what the parcels contained and hid them.

In February 1942—we could not establish the exact date—French and German police surrounded the restaurant where Fabien and several of his men were eating. Fabien managed to escape. The others were caught. All eighteen of them would be shot.

Constance Rappenau was imprisoned in the Santé, tried by a German court, and acquitted on September 4, 1942. Nonetheless, she was sent to Romainville on October 22, 1942.

Auschwitz # 31754

She was caught in "the race" on February 10, 1943 (she was sixty-four years old). She died in Block 25.

Her son received a notification of decease from Auschwitz: died February 17, 1943, from a liver ailment.

Germaine RENAUD

Born on July 15, 1908, in Montmorency, in Seine-et-Oise, she spent her childhood in La Roche-Posay, in Vienne. When her father, who was a teacher, took a position in Chinon in 1918, she continued her studies there. Later she went to the teachers' college in Tours. She had lost her mother when she was very young.

Germaine was a militant communist. In 1942, she set up a clandestine printing press near Tours. She personally printed papers and tracts and took them by bicycle to comrades for distribution.

On February 23, 1942, in Brèches-Bel-Air near Château-la-Vallière in the Indre-et-Loire, she was arrested by the French police at school in front of her students, and taken away on the spot. During the ride to prison in Tours, they beat her bloody to make her denounce her comrades, but never got a word out of her.

From Tours she was taken to Paris, where she was interrogated at General Intelligence, put in the cells until March 23, 1942, sent to the Santé, in isolation, until August 24, 1942, and then to Romainville.

Auschwitz # 31682

She died in Birkenau at the beginning of February 1943, though we were not yet working outside the camp. Two kapos attacked her and beat her with sticks. Why? No reason. Because she was in their way. Her skull was fractured and she was led to the blockhouse, where she died after an agonizing night.

Her family learned of her death from Hélène Fournier on the return in 1945.

Germaine RENAUDIN, née Perraux

Born March 22, 1906, in Hussigny, Meurthe-et-Moselle. Her father died young, leaving four children. Her mother divided the family, going to Belgium with two of the children and leaving the other two (including Germaine, who was four years old) with the paternal grandparents, rather well-to-do farmers in Hussigny.

Germaine went to elementary school in Hussigny until the age of twelve, then helped at the house until her marriage, in 1925, to Marius Renaudin, an iron setter.

In 1939, Marius Renaudin was mobilized. Germaine and her three children were forced back to the Gironde.

Before the war, Germaine and her husband were members of the Communist Party. In 1939, in Lesparre, Germaine abandoned none of her ideas or political activities. In 1941 she was placed in a residence under observation but nonetheless continued to distribute tracts and shelter resisters. In 1942 the police commissioner warned her that he would have to arrest her. She didn't budge. A search. The police found her husband's revolver. The judge told her: "Madame, I did not see it." When Germaine refused to sign the official report, the judge told her gently: "Madame, you are getting yourself into a serious situation." This time Germaine was saved, but judges change and dossiers remain. Germaine Renaudin was arrested on May 25, 1942, at her home in Lesparre, by a French policeman (who was shot during the Liberation) and a Gestapo agent. She was providing asylum for clandestine combatants.

After spending the night in the Lesparre commissioner's headquarters, she was sent first to the Boudet barracks, then to the fortress at Hâ, and transferred to Romainville on October 14, 1942.

Auschwitz # 31716

Germaine Renaudin held on, after resisting typhus, until July 1943. She was then recruited for the gardening detail at Raisko, and left for Ravensbrück on August 14, 1944. She followed the group of survivors to Mauthausen on March 2, 1945, and was liberated there on April 22, 1945.

She returned. She found her children, who had been fourteen, thirteen, and eleven when she was deported. Friends had taken in the two youngest; the eldest had been a farm hand and worked very hard. Her husband, a prisoner in Germany, returned at the end of May 1945. The family made their way back to Hussigny and settled in the workers' village where the mine lodged its personnel. Two more children were born: a boy in 1946, a girl in 1947.

One day a gendarme brought Germaine her certificate of demobilization. She was demobilized with the rank of sergeant. Nonetheless, she was considered a civilian victim and holds a political deportee card, as though she had never been in the Resistance; she has the right to only a minimal pension. She had a kidney removed in 1962, a breast in 1965, and died of metastasized cancer on October 4, 1968.

MARGUERITE RICHIER, née CARDINET, AND HER TWO DAUGHTERS, ODETTE AND ARMANDE

Born October 16, 1879, in Paris, where her father was a dyer and her mother kept a small hotel on Rue du Fouarre, in the Latin Quarter. Marguerite was six years old when her parents decided to return to their native province because the aniline dyes and the Paris air were damaging the father's health. Marguerite attended elementary school in Lahaymeix, Meuse, and married a local teacher. They had seven children. Only four were living in 1942: Odette, Armande, André, and Lucien.

In 1942, Marguerite Richier, who had been a widow since 1933, was living in Soissons with her two daughters: Odette, born August 10, 1911, who was not involved in any professional activity; and Armande, born November 16, 1916, who was a schoolteacher twenty kilometers away in Domiers. Odette, a communist before the war, and Armande were part of the National Front. Their mother knew what they were doing and supported them.

On October 16, 1942, Odette was on her bicycle, carrying newly printed tracts. On the way (for no apparent reason—just a gesture), she threw a handful of tracts into the air. A moment later, a carload of Gestapo passed by. The car stopped. The Germans collected some of the tracts, which were so new and clean, they could see they had just been thrown. The car caught up with the cyclist. The bundles in her baskets were visible. Odette Richier was identified, taken to command headquarters, then to her home. At the house, the police found a mimeograph, a typewriter, stencils, paper, and the address of the two brothers, who came only rarely to Soissons. The mother and daughters were arrested, imprisoned in Saint-Quentin until January 15, 1943, then transferred to Romainville.

Marguerite Richier, the mother, was sixty-three years old. She died very quickly. Several people said that she was caught in "the race" on February 10, 1943, and died in Block 25 soon after.

We have found no witness to the deaths of Odette, thirty-one years old, and Armande, twenty-six. They, too, must have died quite soon.

Anne RICHON, née Riffaud

Born on October 12, 1898, in Jusix, Lot-et-Garonne, where her parents were farmers. She went to school first in Jusix, then in Bourdelles, in the Gironde.

She was married to a blacksmith who worked for the railroads, and she worked at home, knitting sweaters.

Their son was in the clandestine struggle from the beginning, and in 1942 he was a commander in the FTP. Anne and her husband collected food and provisions for the internees at Mérignac. During the summer of 1942 they sheltered a teacher who was forced to go into hiding.

Anne and her husband were arrested at their home in Bègles in July 1942. Nothing is known about the circumstances of their arrest. One day in July their nephew, an FTP fighter, came looking for them. He found the house empty. On the table were ration cards, a few old potatoes, and some stale bread. He questioned the neighbors: they hadn't seen the Richons for a week or so. Anne Richon was imprisoned in the fortress at Hâ and transferred to Romainville on October 14, 1942.

Auschwitz # 31 . . .

She died in the Birkenau revier shortly before March 21, 1943.

She had swollen feet and legs. The edema reached as far as her hips, and her thighs were oozing. Fernande Laurent twisted strips of blanket around her legs. In a few hours, the rags were drenched. They had to be removed. Anne could not walk anymore. "You see my legs? I'm done for, it's all over," she said one day to Gilberte Tamisé. We had seen women die of edema in three days. After roll call, Gilberte Tamisé and Germaine Renaudin supported her as far as the entrance of the revier. She could not stand up. There they made her wait, sitting on the hearth. Indeed, the revier was heated: from the entrance, situated at one end, a brick fireplace extended the entire length of the barracks, as high as a bench. Anne remained sitting on the fireplace until evening. When they finally gave her a place to lie down, she was entirely burned. She died a few hours later (according to Marie-Elisa).

Her husband was executed by firing squad at Mont-Valérien on October 2, 1943, after a year in Romainville.

Their nephew, the FTP combatant who had found the house empty in July 1942, was killed in the Maquis.

Their son came out of the war alive. He learned of his mother's death on the survivors' return.

Anne Richon's mother lives in a village seventy kilometers from Bordeaux. She is eighty-six years old. In the facing house lives Anne's sister, the mother of the young man killed in combat. They are a very close family and keep Anne's memory alive.

France RONDEAUX

Her full name was Francine Rondeaux de Montbray, and she was born on December 27, 1901, in La Turbie. Her childhood was spent in Montbray castle in Normandy—the family seat since 1753, when the Rondeaux, bourgeois of Rouen, acquired the property of Montbray and added it to their name—in the Paris apartment on Boulevard Malesherbes and at Cap d'Ail where her parents had some land. Her father, a journalist, was editor of *Paris-Courses*, a horse-racing paper. She had a Belle Epoque childhood: a nanny, a private tutor, then boarding school at the Dames de l'Assomption. France married after having a daughter in 1921, divorced in 1925, kept company with artists and the elite. She was the cousin of André Gide, the writer: his mother's maiden name was Rondeaux, and he married a Rondeaux as well, his cousin Madeleine. France wrote poems, novellas, had an unrequited passion for an aviator—after the Belle Epoque came the Roaring Twenties.

In 1940, with the Germans in Paris, she did not immediately affiliate with an organized network: she helped out here and there, then became a member of the Shelburn network (which helped English aviators escape). She transformed the ground floor of her private house on Boulevard Bessières into an infirmary where wounded aviators were nursed; and she would take her car and go to Normandy to get meat and butter from her father's former tenants, sell some on the black market, and distribute the rest to friends and to the orphans of Auteuil. She also helped Jews pass into the free zone by a path her sister had shown her in Droux, in Saône-et-Loire. One day in September 1942, France Rondeaux and her friend Maggie Speed, flying along in their car, had a run-in with a Wehrmacht vehicle on Boulevard Saint-Michel. France, whose clandestine activity should have made her cautious, tried to pull a fast one. Papers, identity checks. A week later, she and her friend received a summons to appear at the Santé. Their circle of friends advised them not to go. But France did not understand: What? She should be afraid of these people? Not on your life!

As she arrived at the Santé, a sergeant jostled her; she slapped him.

During the couple of weeks the women spent in the Santé, the Gestapo established the link between them and a chain set up for helping Jews escape. They were transferred to Romainville on October 10, 1942.

On January 21, 1943, Maggie Speed, who held a British passport, was taken to the camp at Vittel, where British citizens were interned, and France Rondeaux was sent to Auschwitz.

Auschwitz # 31 . . .

She died of typhus at the beginning of May 1943. Gilberte saw her in the revier on May 1, when the disinfection took place. France, all skin and long bones— she was a tall woman—went to the bath first. She had held up admirably until then. She was a believer and prayed during roll calls. When she'd finished her prayers, she recited recipes.

Her daughter, Annette, died tragically during the same period, without knowing what had become of her mother.

Georgette ROSTAING

Born in November 1911 in Ivry-sur-Seine, where she spent her childhood. Her father was a cooper. She left school in Petit-Ivry at the age of fourteen to work for a transport company.

She was a militant communist, secretary of the office of the Ivry Union of French Girls before the war. Perched on heels so high they made people dizzy to look at her, graceful in spite of her weight, always cheerful, she was well known in Ivry and very popular.

During the occupation, she hid everything that needed hiding: resisters, bundles of tracts, weapons. She was arrested on January 6, 1943, at her place of work in the tenth arrondissement.

She was imprisoned in Fresnes and joined the convoy at Compiègne on January 23, 1943, on the eve of departure.

Auschwitz # 31850

Her good humor and her laughter accompanied her to Birkenau. In the evenings, she would sit cross-legged on her bunk and sing. In that gloomy blockhouse, where a thousand women were huddled on three tiers, her deep, rich voice soared. Georgette Rostaing died in March 1943. No one knows how. March was the worst time: everyone was sick and so weak that their minds were dimmed, and their eyes did not see.

Her family received no notification of decease from the camp. They learned of Georgette's death from letters sent by survivors after July 1943. Georgette

Rostaing was a single mother. Her little girl was raised by Georgette's mother. Her brother Pierre, arrested on December 23, 1941, deported May 14, 1944, perished in the evacuation of Dora in April 1945—beaten to death by an SS, according to some; burned to death by the SS in a barn crowded with a thousand deportees, according to others. He was twenty-one years old.

Félicia, called "Lucia," ROSTKOWSKA

Born on June 15, 1908, in Gitomiège, Poland, she studied at the co-ed lycée in Luck and was sent to France to teach the children of Polish immigrant workers in 1934–35. The last class she taught was in Potigny, Calvados.

Like her colleague Eugénie Korzeniowska, she took part in the Monika resistance network. She arrived in Romainville on October 1, 1942. We called her "Lucia."

Auschwitz # 31701

No eyewitness report of her death.

Denise ROUCAYROL

Born on December 26, 1901, in Mazamet, Tarn, where her father was a tanner. She was two years old when her mother died. Her father placed her in a Protestant orphanage in Montauban, which she left at the age of seventeen to earn a living in Paris. She worked as an aide in hospitals while taking courses in public health, and became a registered nurse in 1934.

She was arrested a first time on June 6, 1940. She had been denounced as a "defeatist" (a communist), but was released from Fresnes at the end of December 1940, after a demonstration in the women's section. Before her arrest, she had been under surveillance. The public health department at first refused to take her back, then changed its mind but transferred her to another hospital. In 1942, she was at Kremlin-Bicêtre.

She was with the clandestine organization of the Communist Party, then with the FTP. Along with Alphonsine Seibert [see this name] and five men, she created an arms cache in the attic of the hospital.

She was arrested on June 24, 1942, in the morning, coming home after a night's work. The police of the special brigades were waiting for her in the hall of the apartment house where she was living, at 9 Rue Flatters, in the fifth arrondissement.

She was interrogated at General Intelligence headquarters by the examining magistrate Piton, spent several days in the cells, was imprisoned in the Santé—

in isolation, in the German division—until August 10, 1942, then in the fort of Romainville until the departure.

Auschwitz # 31646

Denise Roucayrol died of exanthematic typhus in April 1943.
There was no notification of decease.

Suzanne ROZE, née Clément

Born August 18, 1904, in Beuzeville-le-Grenier, Seine-Inférieure, Suzanne Roze was a militant communist. In 1936, she worked in Fécamp for a clothing manufacturer that employed several hundred workers and that was owned by the mayor's offices. She created a union chapter there, the first clothing union in the region. She was shop steward, and in 1938, following a strike, she was let go. It was useless to look for work where she was blackballed everywhere. She managed to find a job at a fish-drying yard. The work was very hard. In prison, when she was asked what she had done before, she said: "I washed cod cheeks."

In 1939, too well known in Fécamp, where the Communist Party was secretly regrouping, she left for Le Havre, then for Rouen, where she lived under an assumed name. She left her son with her mother in Fécamp.

As a liaison agent in charge of supplying combatants who operated under cover and had no ration cards, she also carried out tasks that required a certain physical strength. She was a solidly built woman and less noticeable than a man would have been. She would often transport a mimeograph machine or a typewriter.

Suzanne Roze was arrested on February 20, 1942, with Madeleine Dissoubray, who had fallen into a trap set by inspectors of the special brigades. She resisted all the interrogations. Her alibi: "I deal on the black market, and I was carrying meat in my bicycle basket to a customer [Madeleine Dissoubray] I didn't know." In her pocket she had a letter from her mother. There was no name or address, but the mother mentioned a notary. The police found Madame Clément in Fécamp. She didn't know what her daughter was doing, but she did reveal that she regularly sent news of her son through Alida Delasalle.

Madame Clément was arrested, along with Alida Delasalle. Neighbors took in the child, who was twelve at the time. Mother and daughter were together. They were transferred to Paris, imprisoned in the Santé. Madame Clément was freed in July 1942. She returned to Fécamp, retrieved her grandson, and was not disturbed again. But her daughter would not return. Suzanne reproached herself for keeping this letter, she reproached herself for her mother's behavior leading to Alida Delasalle's arrest.

Suzanne was transferred from the Santé to Romainville on August 24, 1942. There she learned that her husband had filed divorce papers.

Auschwitz # 31 . . .

She arrived in Birkenau morally broken, physically exhausted from years of living underground, from months in prison, and dysentery contracted during the journey: "We'll all die here," she said. One day her comrades hid her because she hadn't the strength to work. An SS discovered her and beat her repeatedly. The following day, she entered the revier. She died a few days later, in February 1943. Before dying, she said to Alida Delasalle: "Swear to me that if you return, you won't denounce my mother; she has to raise my son."

Esterina RUJU

Born January 23, 1885.

Where was she born, where had she lived? Why had she been in Romainville since April 1942? She had a foreign accent. In Romainville, she received no letters or packages. She slept on the lower bunk of the tier where Viva slept. Viva gave her some of what she received, and Ruju—that's what we called her, as if she had no first name—was always offering to do some small task: to sew on a button, to wash out underwear. Like a miser, she hoarded everything she could find, and at our arrival in Auschwitz, Lulu helped her carry an enormous suitcase full of miscellaneous, useless things.

Auschwitz # 31838

"One day on the bricks crew, I saw her fall like a leaf, quite gently," said Poupette. This was the end of March or the beginning of April 1943.

Léonie SABAIL, née Daubigny

Born April 5, 1891, in Châtellerault.

The Sabail couple worked for the railroads: she as an office manager, he as a designer. In 1942, they were living in Bègles, on the outskirts of Bordeaux, and had a married daughter and a fifteen-year-old son.

The Sabails' house was bombed in June 1940, and this left Léonie very nervous, jumping at the slightest noise. Her husband was arrested on October 6, 1941, yet she continued to shelter resisters, among others Charles Tillon, head of the FTP for the southwest.

She was arrested on September 2, 1942, at her home, and imprisoned in the Boudet barracks, in Bordeaux, until October 14, 1942. From there she was sent to Romainville until the departure.

Auschwitz # 31745

She died on March 1, 1943, in the Birkenau revier.

Her husband was shot at Mont-Valérien on October 2, 1943.

When the deportees began to return, Léonie Sabail's children went to the Bordeaux station, on the lookout for survivors. They learned of their mother's death from one of the women in the convoy.

Anna SABOT

Born on November 13, 1898.

She arrived in Romainville between October 1 and 14, 1942, with Suzanne Meugnot. We did not know where she came from or why she was there.

Auschwitz # 31713

Arriving at Birkenau, she declared her Alsatian origins, and they did not cut her hair, a favor reserved for Germans and *Volksdeutsch*. She died very soon.

No one remembers the circumstances.

Berthe Celina SABOURAULT, née Fays

Born on June 8, 1904, at Villiers-le-Roux, near Ruffec in the Charente, where her parents were agricultural workers and where she was raised. She was the youngest of three children.

After her marriage to Raoul Sabourault, a dealer in masonry, she went to beauty school in Angoulême and set up a small salon in an annex to their house in Villiers-le-Roux.

Berthe and Raoul Sabourault were fighters in the clandestine struggle from the first. They were founding members of the National Front: they received weapons from Paris and saw to their distribution, lodged leaders of the organization, etc.

On February 21, 1942, a stranger arrived at their house who introduced himself as a member of the organization and knew the password. He said he had lost contact following a number of arrests that had taken place. The Sabouraults—perhaps out of intuition—did not agree to lodge him. They gave him lunch and he left. At around nine the next morning, the French police of Ruffec arrived and arrested Berthe and Raoul Sabourault in the presence of their son Jack, aged nine.

Berthe and Raoul Sabourault spent a week in the Ruffec prison, then were transported to Paris to be interrogated at General Intelligence headquarters. There they found their comrades who were part of the resisters' escape chain from Paris to the Pyrénées. Raoul Sabourault was severely tortured during his interrogation by the Gestapo.

Berthe was sent to the cells until March 23, 1942, to the Santé in isolation until August 24, 1942, and from there to Romainville.

Auschwitz # 31683

She died of typhus in April 1943. On the eve of her death, she was delirious and said to Louise Magadur, her neighbor at the revier: "I'm staying with you. They're going to come and take me to the crematorium," and she clung to Louise. "Her breath was on fire—I've never felt a breath as hot as hers," said Louise.

Jack Sabourault learned of his mother's death from Simone Loche on the return. He had been taken in by an uncle, a carpenter in Villiers-le-Roux.

Berthe Sabourault was named a lieutenant in the RIF, and awarded the Legion of Honor and the Croix de Guerre with red star.

Raoul Sabourault died in Mauthausen, the first of August 1944. Captain in the RIF, the Legion of Honor, and the Croix de Guerre.

Raymonde SALEZ ("Mounette")

Born on May 6, 1919, in Lilas, very near Paris. Her father was a locksmith, her mother a dressmaker. She had an older sister. Mounette completed elementary school in Lilas and then did a secretarial course. She began working shortly before the war broke out, but she was already a member of the Young Communists. From the beginning of the occupation, she was in the clandestine organization that led young people in the struggle against the occupying forces.

July 14, 1941: A student demonstration in the Latin Quarter. On Boulevard Saint-Michel, a girl suddenly unfolded a tricolor flag and raised it above her head. Mounette was the girl holding the flag. Agents arrested her. She spent twenty-four hours at the commissariat and was released.

The police verified her residence. She changed it. She rented a room in the Place Daumesnil under an assumed name and continued her activities. She participated with her group of young FTP members in the attack on the German bookstore at the corner of Boulevard Saint-Michel and Place de la Sorbonne at the beginning of 1942.

On June 18, 1942, as she was returning from a mission in the occupied zone, she was arrested by the special brigades. All the leaders of this group of young FTPs were captured that day. The young men were shot at Mont-Valérien on August 11, 1942. Among them: Bénac, Jean Compagnon, Despouy. Her fiancé, Robert Guesquen ("Bob"), had escaped. (Bob was subsequently caught and executed by firing squad on July 9, 1943, at the shooting range at Issy-les-Moulineaux; he was twenty-two years old.)

Mounette left the cells for Romainville on August 10, 1942; Romainville for Compiègne and Auschwitz on January 22, 1943; life for death on March 9, 1943, in the Birkenau revier, where she had gone at the beginning of March, exhausted from dysentery. We do not know her Auschwitz number. Her photograph was lost.

Mounette marched at the head of the column we formed when we came out of the train on the morning of January 27, 1943, after reaching the camp. She was with Jackie Quatremaire and Paulette Gourmelon. She led the others in singing "la Marseillaise." The first time and only time women entered Birkenau singing.

In July 1943, those who had held out until then had the right to send letters. Conveying the news of their comrades' deaths was their primary concern: "They have to know...." The parents who received these letters did not know how to tell the news to the families of the deceased: your daughter is dead, mine is alive.... The families of the dead did not want to believe these communications. Madeleine Dechavassine notified Mounette's sister. She waited for months before speaking to her mother, who did not want to believe it. She had not received a notification of decease. She kept hoping until our return.

Simone SAMPAIX

She was the youngest child of Lucien Sampaix, the secretary general of *L'Humanité*, who was executed on December 15, 1941, at Caen. Not even eighteen (born on June 14, 1924, in Sedan), she belonged to a small group of boys and girls who had all been Young Communists before the war. Singing in the forest in peacetime gave way to more dangerous activities. From distributing tracts in 1940, the young people went into the youth batallion, then into the special organization of the Communist Party, and finally into the FTP. Simone was particularly attached to one of her comrades. Of course, girls were not allowed in the line of fire, but they were very useful, especially when they looked like innocent schoolgirls.

On May 13, 1942, Simone Sampaix was worried because she hadn't seen her comrade for several days, and went for news to the Grunenbergers', on Rue de la Goutte-d'Or. They were not in; the police from the special brigades were there instead: they had taken over the apartments of those people known to be involved in anti-occupation activities after an attack against a hotel of informers in Place Montholon. The attack had failed; nearly all the young combatants were caught. Among them, Simone's friend.

Along with Simone Eiffes, who had been arrested at the same time, Simone Sampaix was sent to the cells; she fell ill, however, and was hospitalized in the infirmary at Fresnes. Though barely recovered, she was sent back to the cells, then transferred to Romainville on October 27, 1942.

Auschwitz # 31758

At Birkenau she was sick for months and did not leave the revier until the quarantine on August 3, 1943. She was transferred to Ravensbrück with the rest of the group on August 2, 1944, and again spent all her time there in the revier. She was liberated from Ravensbrück by the Red Cross, evacuated to Sweden, and repatriated on June 10, 1945.

She returned quite stricken. She married a young man she had seen at Auschwitz (a deportee from the 45,000s' convoy, one of the few survivors of that convoy of twelve hundred men deported from Compiègne on July 6, 1942, after the escape of nineteen prisoners: of these twelve hundred men, who arrived at Auschwitz on July 9, 1942, only a hundred and fifty were left by January 1943). Simone had a child, then divorced. She'd seen and suffered enough for three lifetimes.

Henriette SCHMIDT

Born on October 2, 1912, in Essert, in the territory of Belfort, she was one of five children. Her father was a metallurgist. After elementary school in Essert, she completed middle school in Belfort and became an employee of the city tax collection office.

We don't know how and when she became a Young Communist militant, but when she came to Paris in 1932 at the age of twenty, she was already part of the organization. Her leadership qualities must have been noticed, since she was sent to a training course in Moscow, at a school for cadres (1935–1936). At the time, she was married to Lucien Carré, a mailman's son from Belfort, but for some reason their relationship had cooled. Henriette was still in Moscow when she met André Heussler, a cabinetmaker by trade, who was there, as she was, to become a professional militant. She loved him passionately and filed for divorce on her return so they could marry. The marriage took place on August 25, 1939, in Ivry, but Henriette continued to be known by the name of Schmidt in the Union of French Girls. She was one of its four secretaries, starting in December 1936.

In 1939 the Communist Party was outlawed, along with all related organizations. The directors, the leaders, and a good number of the militants continued to pursue their ideals under cover. Henriette worked with Arthur Dalidet,[20] responsible for administrative tasks in the illegal Communist Party, and she was specifically entrusted with reintegrating comrades who had lost contact with the movement for one reason or another (return from captivity, demobilization, or being on the run). When Fernand Grenier returned to the Paris region after his escape from Châteaubriant on June 18, 1941, Henriette found him lodging and provisions, identity papers, documentation, and gave him his orders. She came and went, doing her work in a timely fashion, always on the alert. But it seems she was being followed. As a precaution, she left her residence. She returned there some time later, on October 4, 1941, just to take some linens. She waited until dark to ensure that no one was following her. She opened her door and entered. Before she had a chance to turn on the light, a hand gripped her wrist: the police had been waiting for her for nearly a week.

Henriette Schmidt was imprisoned in La Roquette, where she had the right to speak with someone once a week. One day, she was surprised by a visit from her husband, André. He was trying to disguise himself behind a pair of dark glasses, but without much success. "You're taking a terrible risk," Henriette told him. How had he managed to get there? He was in a camp and had escaped, he said. Henriette rejoined her prison companions, somewhat overexcited and also worried. Now that he was free and she wasn't with him, would he cheat on her? He was a handsome man; she loved him and tormented herself.

On the outside, however, comrades of André Heussler made some disturbing observations and were soon convinced that he had denounced his wife—to leave a free field, it seems, for another woman. In August 1942, Henriette was summoned to speak to an unexpected visitor who told her that André Heussler had been executed by his own people—those in the party—for treason. This had happened in Essert, on August 12, at the home of the Schmidt parents. As he came through the door, a bullet fired by a concealed gunman had killed him on the spot. On the kitchen floor. Henriette was dumbfounded: Was this credible? She didn't believe it.

In October 1942 she was transferred to Romainville, where she was accorded a rather tepid welcome by the communist leadership who were informed of the whole business: after all, she was the wife of a traitor. Henriette held her head up. She did not want to believe that the man she loved had been an informer.

---

20. Executed by firing squad with the Politzer group on May 30, 1942.

Auschwitz # 31699

Henriette Schmidt died in Birkenau on March 14 or 15, 1943. When she finally went to the revier, her tongue was so swollen and her throat so sore she couldn't swallow; indeed, she could hardly breathe.

When she arrived at Auschwitz, she said to Lulu: "It's not true. You understand, don't you? I have to get back. I have to get back to clear things up, to rehabilitate him. This can't be happening." A month later, she said to me: "Why do you want me, of all people, to return? For . . . what?" Dysentery broke the firmest resolutions.

On the day after the liberation of Belfort, in November 1944, the Schmidt family learned from the newspaper that Henriette had died. That is, what was left of the family. Henriette's father, Philippe Schmidt, and one of his sons-in-law, Keiflin, had been deported and both had died at Neuengamme.

Henriette was named a soldier in the RIF, but those who filed on her behalf could obtain only a political deportee card. And because she was the betrayed wife of a traitor, we cite only her maiden name. Everyone loved her.

Alphonsine SEIBERT

Born on April 17, 1899, in Paris, the thirteenth arrondissement, to a family of eight children. Her father was a shoemaker by trade. She attended the elementary school on Avenue de Choisy, and later went to work as a nurse's aide at the Kremlin-Bicêtre hospital. She married a mattress maker and had a son in 1931. She spent her life between Kremlin-Bicêtre and the thirteenth arrondissement, where she was living when she was arrested at her home on June 24, 1942, by inspectors of the special brigades. She had been part of the same FTP group as Denise Roucayrol (and had helped with the weapons cache in the attic of the hospital). The police moved discreetly and quickly.

After several days in the cells, Alphonsine Seibert was sent to the Santé; and from there, on August 10, 1942, she was taken to Romainville to await the departure.

Auschwitz # 31647

She died very quickly, witnessed by none of the survivors. Erased from memory.
Her family learned of her death only in 1945.

Léone SEIGNOLLE

Born April 16, 1901.
She arrived in Romainville on October 21, 1942. No one knew where she came from or why she was there.

On a scrap of chocolate wrapper thrown from the train by one of us we found an address: Rue de Saint-Denis, which has since become Gabriel-Péri. But the building at number 140 on this street was destroyed, the tenants relocated, and we found no trace of Léone Seignolle.

No one remembers the date of her death or its circumstances.

Raymonde SERGENT

Born August 17, 1903, in Saint-Martin-le-Beau, Indre-et-Loire. She had always lived there: after completing elementary school, she married a local boy and they ran a café-restaurant together in the town.

In 1942 her husband was a prisoner of war. She became part of a chain to aid escaping prisoners and resisters, sheltering them and helping them to reach the free zone. Like most of her comrades who did this work, she was denounced.

She left the prison in Tours for Romainville on November 7, 1942.

Auschwitz # 31 . . .

It was her idea to eat the charcoal we found in the ashes of the fires the SS made to warm themselves on the paths bordering the marshes where we worked. This charred wood was difficult to chew but somewhat effective against dysentery.

She had stored several bottles of good wine in her cellar to celebrate the Liberation. All the women from Tours and many of the others promised to gather at Saint-Martin-le-Beau. Promises made in the beginning. Then, alas, almost no one had such hopes. Marcelle Laurillou said one day to Raymonde Sergent: "Do you think we'll ever drink that nice Touraine wine again?"—"No," answered Raymonde, "neither you nor I will drink it again." She entered the revier with legs swollen from edema, her thighs torn on the inside from scratched, cracking skin, and she died there at the end of March or the beginning of April 1943. Hélène Fournier—her last surviving friend from Tours—managed to see her one evening after roll call. "Tell my husband and Gisèle [her daughter] that I've never forgotten them, that I tried to hold on." She was demoralized: "No one comes to see me."

Raymonde Sergent's family learned of her death on August 15, 1944, from a woman from Carugé, a small place three kilometers from Saint-Martin-le-Beau. We don't know how this woman got the information.

Julia SLUSARCZYK

Born April 26, 1902, in Usrzeki Dolny (Poland), raised in the village where she was born, she went to a clandestine Polish school since the official school was Ukrainian, and the natives refused to send their children there.

Her father had a pork butcher's business. It was a large family, dispersed by the two wars. There was a brother who was a butcher before 1939 and then a farmer. Julia had a daughter in 1923, in Poland, whom she could not trace.

Julia emigrated to France in 1926 and set up housekeeping with a country-man, also a butcher, at 25 Rue Saint-Paul, in Paris, and helped him in his business.

They were both arrested in their home on November 7, 1942, by German and French police, and taken someplace (she couldn't tell) for verification, they were told. She never understood the reason for her arrest: "It was the business," she said. She arrived in Romainville in mid-December 1942 and remained there until the departure.

Auschwitz # 31823

Birkenau (marshes, bricks, etc.), until the quarantine on August 3, 1943.

To Ravensbrück, where she arrived with the others on August 4, 1944, and fell gravely ill with pleurisy. Doctor Hautval nursed her in secret and gave her treatments.

Liberated on April 23, 1945, by the Swedish Red Cross, she was hospital-ized in Sweden, repatriated in June 1945, then hospitalized successfully after the return in the Hôtel-Dieu, in Pitié, in Valence, Drôme.

Her home, her business, everything had been pillaged. She had no resources. Her companion, deported to Dachau, returned in 1945 and died in 1946, the victim of an accident. Julia survived the first years after her return thanks to the generosity of friends. When she could, she did a little work several hours a day, just to feed herself. In 1960 she obtained a political deportee card and was de-clared disabled, which entitled her to a pension of around 330 francs per month. She made clothing but often had to interrupt her work because of poor health.

Hélène SOLOMON, née Langevin

Born May 25, 1909, in Fontenay-aux-Roses, she was raised in Paris with her two brothers and a sister, the children of Paul Langevin, a teacher at the Collège de France.

Hélène Langevin attended the Rue Monge elementary school, then the Fénelon secondary school, where she earned her diploma. In 1929 she married

Jacques Solomon, head of research at the National Center for Scientific Research.

Paul Langevin, then sixty-eight, was arrested at his residence on October 30, 1940, by Bomelburg, an aide to Speidel,* and imprisoned in the Santé. There were student demonstrations and protests on November 8, 1940, in front of the Collège de France to "Free Langevin," which must have given the Germans pause; they released him on December 15, 1940, and put him under surveillance in Troyes.

In 1942, Hélène and her husband were part of the University branch of the National Front; they edited L'Université libre—which came out first in November 1940—and La Pensée libre; an issue of this last publication was being prepared when they were arrested.

Jacques Solomon was arrested on March 1, 1942, in Paris. He had been followed by police of the special brigades since the arrest of Georges Politzer on February 14. Hélène was arrested the following day, just as she was retrieving a suitcase she had brought the evening before from the locker at the Saint-Lazare station; they had been preparing an emergency action in response to the many arrests of people in their group that had taken place in the past weeks.

After several days at General Intelligence headquarters, Hélène was taken to the cells on March 10 and remained there until March 23. She was subsequently in the Santé, in isolation, until August 24, 1942, then sent to Romainville.

Jacques Solomon was executed by firing squad on May 23. She had said good-bye to him at the Santé.

Auschwitz # 31684

At the beginning of February 1943, one of the polizei passed through the ranks during roll call one morning and asked if there were any biologists or chemists among us. Hélène Solomon identified herself, along with four others, and on March 21, 1943, she was sent to the Stabsgebaüde to be attached to the newly created Raisko detachment, which left the camp on July 1943. The Raisko group was transferred to Ravensbrück on August 14, 1944. In October 1944, Hélène was sent as a nurse to the Bosch and Dreilinden factories near Berlin. On April 18, 1945, following the bombings, this work detail was absorbed by Oranienburg-Sachsenhausen. Several days later, the evacuation of this last camp began. The deportees left by all routes north, through a corridor squeezed between the Russian front to the east and the Allied front to the west. Escorted by SS who killed the stragglers, the prisoners walked about ten

---

*General Hans Speidel, Nazi overseer in Paris. (Trans.)

kilometers a day, leaving their dead in ditches and on the roadside. On May 3, the SS disappeared. Hélène Solomon and a small group of Frenchwomen went ahead and met some French soldiers, who took them under their wing. It was useless to continue walking; better to await the armistice. They waited in an American encampment, a former vacation spot for Hitler Youth that had been transformed into a rest center. On May 8, the armistice was announced on the radio. The deportees could go home. By truck and van they reached a train station and traveled across Holland, arriving in France at Lille on the evening of May 14, 1945. At the rest center, there were the formalities of repatriation, clothing, identity cards, repatriation allowance (200 marks). Hélène managed to telephone her parents, who were at Gare du Nord the next day when she arrived and were momentarily bewildered: she appeared wearing a mauve-gray Luftwaffe overcoat and German army boots—it had been a very cold spring. Snow had fallen on May 1.

How did she readapt to life? Very poorly, she says: "At first I thought I could do everything: studies, militant activity, work, etc. I was elected deputy to the Constituent Assembly in October 1945, reelected in June 1946, but I was exhausted by the evening meetings, the tours of the provinces, and I had to give up standing for election again the following November. After several months of rest and a stay in Switzerland, I returned part-time at the CNRS [National Center for Scientific Research] as a contract technician, and couldn't really work full-time until 1952." She remarried in 1958.

In 1965, she still suffers, increasingly, from asthenia, abnormal fatigue, and cervical and lumbar arthrosis and decalcification.

YVONNE SOUCHAUD, née HOUDAYER

Born on April 24, 1897, in Tours, where she lived and worked with her father, a men's tailor. Her mother had died. She was married but had been separated from her husband for twenty years.

Both father and daughter were members of the Communist Party before the war and were with the National Front in 1942, distributing tracts printed by Elisabeth Le Port [see this name]. They were arrested soon after she was.

In November 1942, they were transferred from the prison in Tours to Romainville: Clément Houdayer, the father, was very ill and was hospitalized at Val-de-Grâce, where he died, and Yvonne departed for Auschwitz.

Auschwitz # 31791

She died of dysentery in March 1943. The state listed April 30, 1943, as the date of decease, but Hélène Fournier is sure she did not hold out that long.

She had no children. We have been unable to locate any family member.

Jeanne SOUQUES, née Renon

Born on November 4, 1894, in Pessac, in the Gironde, she helped her husband run a laundry in a windmill in Gradignan. Two or three times a week, she went to Bordeaux by car to deliver linens to the large hotels that were among her customers. She returned with bundles of dirty linens. Coming and going with these baskets of laundry, she also transported tracts, printed on a mimeograph hidden in the windmill, and the typewriter that was passed from one house to another, according to need. Tillon and the leaders of the National Front would come to her place when they had business in the area.

Jeanne Souques was arrested at her laundry on August 25, 1942, by the Bordeaux police, who told her: "We'll release you when we catch your husband." She did not put them on her husband's track. Henri Souques was responsible for forming the first FTP group in the area, and he was not at home that day. He was arrested subsequently, but even if the police had wanted to keep their promise to release his wife, it was too late.

From the Boudet barracks Jeanne Souques was sent to Romainville on October 14, 1942. She was very worried for her eldest son, an invalid who could not manage without help.

Auschwitz # 31739

She died at Birkenau on April 1, 1943. Typhus.

Her husband, deported to Mauthausen, returned. He learned of Jeanne's death on his return, from the survivors of the convoy.

Marguerite STORA, née Battais, and her niece, Sylviane COUPET

Marguerite Battais was born on September 18, 1895, in Saint-Hilaire-du-Harcouët, in the Manche, where the parish register records generations of Battais dating back to the late eighteenth century. Marguerite Stora made this discovery in 1941, when she needed to obtain certificates of baptism going back three generations. The last Battais left Saint-Hilaire-du-Harcouët when their two daughters were still small and set themselves up as grocers in Paris, in the eighteenth arrondissement.

Marguerite was a garment worker, and in 1926 she married Fernand Stora, a men's tailor who soon became a wealthy merchant. He had a prominent shop called *Jo et Jo*, where all the music hall stars of the 1930s bought their clothes. Jewelry, furs, travels—Marguerite Stora led a privileged life. She had everything she wanted, except a child. That is why she took in her sister's youngest daughter, Sylviane.

Sylviane Coupet, born in Paris on August 15, 1925, went to school in Algeria, in Madagascar, and in France: wherever her father was garrisoned—he was a petty officer in the colonial army. In July 1942, when her father was a prisoner of war in Germany, her mother died of tuberculosis. Sylviane went to live with her aunt, Madame Stora, on Rue Lamarck.

Fernand Stora was a Jew. He identified himself as such and wore the star. He gave his shop over to an Aryan manager and bided his time until the end of the occupation. However, his brother, Raoul Stora, and his brother's son were arrested as Jews. Fernand Stora had money. He tried to get them out of Drancy by any means possible, and began negotiations with a certain Brunet, born in Geneva on November 23, 1890, who boasted of being a double agent and of having contacts in the offices at Avenue Foch (the Gestapo department for Jewish affairs). Brunet demanded 50,000 francs. Monsieur Stora gave him 30,000 down. Time passed. Seeing no results, Monsieur Stora broke with the intermediary. Did the man decide to take revenge? Feldgendarmes came to the Storas', carried off silver and other valuable objects. The Storas did not budge—when you wore the star, you had to lie low. A few days later, the scene was repeated: again, legalized burglary. This time Madame Stora protested. Was there no way to defend themselves? Should they just take it? And how far would it go? She filed a complaint with the commissariat. Shortly afterward, she was summoned to the Gestapo: they made apologies. The thieves had been caught, they would be tried by a war council, the honor of the German uniform, etc., etc. Madame Stora pleaded on their behalf: after all, theft did not deserve the death penalty.

On November 17, 1942, Germans in uniform again appeared at Rue Lamarck. This time it was too much. Sylviane swore at them. They slapped her. This was no longer burglary. The had come to arrest Monsieur Stora. He wasn't there? Fine, they would return, but in the meantime they took Madame Stora and Sylviane, leaving Monsieur Stora's old mother, an invalid who couldn't leave her armchair.

When Monsieur Stora returned home, his mother told him what had happened. He grabbed an overcoat and bag and took refuge in a religious institution in the neighborhood. In the pocket of the coat, he found a scrawled note: "They'll get you next time." He did not return to his house until the Liberation.

Madame Stora and Sylviane were at Romainville from November 17, 1942, until the departure.

Auschwitz # 31805

Marguerite Stora died in the revier, where Manette Doridat worked as a nurse, in March 1943. Monsieur Stora did not learn of his wife's death until the survivors' return.

Auschwitz # 31804

Sylviane Coupet died in August 1943, after spending several months lying in the revier. I went to see her with Carmen several days before her death. We hardly recognized her: she was skeletal, covered with lice, her skin sallow, and in that hollow face, her intense blue eyes. She was coughing. When the fit was over, her lips were covered with pinkish saliva. Carmen kissed her and told me: "You kiss her, too." I did it. With a repugnance I'm still ashamed of today.

Gilberte TAMISE and her sister, Andrée

Their father was a boot maker in Caudéran, just outside of Bordeaux, and they were both born in a building that now bears a plaque: "Andrée Tamisé born in this building, February 28, 1922, died at Auschwitz, March 8, 1943."

Gilberte, born on February 3, 1912, was hardly more than ten years old when her mother died, leaving a baby of seven months—Andrée. Gilberte was the big sister and the little mother. She left the Jules-Ferry school in Caudéran to stay home and look after her sister and the house. She was tutored at home through her middle school diploma, then learned stenography because her father wanted her to have a profession, but she never took a job.

Andrée attended the Paul-Lapie school in Caudéran through middle school, though when the war broke out she had not yet made a career choice. But she had chosen an ideal, the same as her sister's and her father's: communism.

When the Resistance formed, they typed and printed tracts on their mimeograph machine and distributed them throughout the region. Andrée was instrumental in forming a group of Bordeaux students and young people from the youth hostels. (Out of twenty or more young men and women, only two returned after the war.) Gilberte acted as a liaison between Bordeaux, Bayonne, and Tarbes for an FTP group run by Charles Tillon.

Gilberte and Andrée were arrested at their home on April 3, 1942, by Poinsot's police. Some students had been arrested several days earlier. They'd been alerted and should have fled. But their father was interned at the camp of Mérignac. Could they leave a prisoner who needed food supplies and support? Could they leave their father, who might be subject to reprisals?

They were imprisoned at Hâ until October 14, 1942, made the journey together to Romainville, then to Auschwitz.

Auschwitz # 31714

Andrée Tamisé died on March 8, 1943. She was already weakened by dysentery when she suffered from pulmonary congestion. Yet she wanted to hold on, not to leave her sister, not to go to the revier. With Gilberte's help, she dragged herself to the marshes, the bricks, the sand. She was breathing with greater and greater difficulty. One day she said to Gilberte: "I can't follow you any more." After roll call, she wanted to get in line with those who were entering the revier. The polizei pushed her away: there were too many sick that day. She was beaten and sent back to the blockhouse. The work crews had already left. She tried to hide, to wait there for Gilberte's return. A *stubova* discovered her, dragged her outside and beat her. That evening Gilberte found Andrée, dirty, covered with mud, black and blue, and exhausted. Andrée died during the night, beside her sister, who in the morning—really the middle of the night, since we woke at three a.m.—carried Andrée outside and laid her body by the blockhouse wall, in the mud. Tenderly. And Gilberte went to roll call.

The mayor's offices of Caudéran received a notification of decease from Auschwitz in May 1943 which they communicated to the father, who had been interned in Mérignac since 1940.

Auschwitz # 31715

Gilberte Tamisé held on at Birkenau despite her sister's death, which left her dazed and empty. Her comrades did not leave her for a moment. In July 1943, she was at Raisko. She was part of a small group of eight who had been designated by the commandant of Auschwitz to be transferred to Ravensbrück on January 7, 1944. From Ravensbrück she was sent on August 9, 1944, to Beendorf, with Lucienne Thévenin and her sister, Cécile Charua, and Simone Alizon. Like them, she was liberated on May 2, 1945, after a journey of twelve days during which a thousand deportees died—of thirst, hunger, or fatigue, executed or suffocated in blankets by the kapos who wanted more space in the wagons [see *Simone Alizon*].

Gilberte was repatriated from Sweden on June 23, 1945. How has she fared since? "I came back ill, and it took me a long time to recover from the loss of my sister. I had lost my sister and my child. It was a shock coming home, where I had to explain to my father, who returned ill after years in the camp, that my sister would not return. Readapting to life was very difficult for me. Then, from 1951 to 1953, I had to nurse my father, who was tubercular. He died in 1953. I don't work, my health is too poor. Every night, waking or sleeping, I return to the camp, I replay everything we endured, and I think of all those we left behind."

Lucienne THEVENIN, née Serre ("Lulu"), and her sister Jeanne SERRE ("Carmen")

They say, "Our family was lucky." Their mother, arrested in September 1940 by the French police, handed over to the Gestapo, imprisoned in the Santé, then in Cherche-Midi, was released in January 1941. Their brother, Louis, deported to Mauthausen, returned. Their younger sister, Christiane, arrested at the beginning of 1944 (at age fourteen) by the Sabiani militia in Marseille, was released thanks to a deposit paid by her employers. Their house in Marseille was bombed, but none of the family was hurt. Georges Thévenin, Lulu's husband, sustained a leg wound trying to escape (he was a prisoner of war in Germany), but was otherwise intact. Extraordinary luck.

Their father, originally from Roussillon, was in the merchant marine; their mother, a Frenchwoman from Algeria, was a housekeeper.

Lucienne, the eldest, was born on July 16, 1917, in Marseille. Jeanne was born in Ysserville-les-Ysserts (Algeria) in July 1919.

They were raised in Marseille, where they attended elementary school. Lucienne continued her education for one year, then worked as a secretary. Jeanne left school at the age of twelve and became a folder at the Fournier-Ferrier factory. She was later a bookkeeper in a coffee-roasting plant. In 1937, mother and children left Marseille for Paris. Lucienne was a secretary, Jeanne a factory worker.

In 1939, Lucienne married Georges Thévenin, who was called up with his class in 1937 and found himself mobilized. He was taken prisoner in 1940.

In 1939, when war was declared, Lucienne and Jeanne were militant activists with the Young Communists. The organization was outlawed but continued its activity. In July 1940 they took responsibility for thousands of tracts, among them the appeal from the Communist Party. Their mother stored these materials at her apartment on Rue de la Huchette. She was arrested and released four months later. The children went into hiding.

In June 1941 Lucienne entrusted the baby she'd had the previous year to her mother-in-law and returned to the struggle. She had responsibility for the Young Communists in the first, second, third, and fourth arrondissements in Paris. The first FTP groups, formed from the Young Communists, took up arms. The two sisters were busy recruiting combatants. Jeanne was also responsible for printing. She would collect work from the printers (Daubeuf, Houdart, others). She was a plucky girl: in one year, she moved the machines, the paper stocks, and the material for L'Avant-Garde fourteen times, all alone, in a handcart that she pulled through the streets of Paris in broad daylight. Lucienne was nearly caught at the beginning of June 1942, but that day she was not at the munitions factory where the police were waiting for her. She was, in fact, delivering weapons for the attack on the Luftwaffe base at Montdésir [see *Marcelle Gourmelon*).

The two sisters were arrested at the same time, on June 19, 1942, on Avenue Trudaine, in Paris, at the home of resisters, Jean and Marguerite Rodde and their son, Edouard, who all were arrested as well.[21]

They spent three days at General Intelligence headquarters and were sent to the cells. There an agent gave Jeanne the nickname "Carmen," and it was under this name that she was generally known during the deportation. In all the camps, she registered under the assumed name of Renée Lymber, and the police never discovered her true identity. For a long time no one knew that Lulu and Carmen were sisters.

From the cells they were transferred to Romainville on August 10, 1942.

Auschwitz # 31642: Lucienne Thévenin, "Lulu"

Auschwitz # 31637: Jeanne Serre, "Carmen"

The two sisters stuck together. They always held each other by the arm to be sure of being taken together, wherever it might be. They were the only two sisters to return. As for the others, either both died (the Richiers, Noémie Durand and Rachel Fernandez, Charlotte Douillot and Henriette L'Huillier) or one did (Alizon, Tamisé, Gili-Pica). They entered the revier together on April 26, 1943, when they both had typhus (though Lulu was distraught at having to leave before Carmen); they went together to Raisko and were transferred together to Ravensbrück on January 7, 1944; they were sent together to Beendorf, to the salt mine, on August 7, 1944, and were evacuated in April 1945; finally, they both arrived in Sweden [see *Simone Alizon*] and were repatriated in June 1945, Lulu on the twenty-third, Carmen on the twenty-eighth.

Lulu found her husband again, who had been wounded trying to escape from his stalag in 1943 and was repatriated as a wounded veteran; in his barely recovered state, he took part in the fighting during the Liberation. She also found her son Paul, whom friends had kept. She took up her life again as a militant. Today, in 1965, seriously ill, constantly in danger of a retinal hemorrhage, and unable to work, she says: "I live because I force myself to live." She was named a sergeant in the RIF.

Carmen—also a sergeant in the RIF—returned to Marseille, where she married. She has three children. She lived for several years in difficult straits,

---

21. Jean Rodde (fifty-nine years old) and his son, Edouard (thirty-two), were shot at Mont-Valérien on August 11, 1942. Marguerite Rodde was interned at Romainville and freed on September 3, 1942, after the execution of her husband and her son. She died of sorrow in 1945.

which have improved since she received a pension, for she, too, did not return unscathed.

Jeanne THIEBAULT

Born on June 28, 1909, in Vandeuvre, Meurthe-et-Moselle. Her father was killed in World War I, and her mother died soon after. She was handed over to the welfare authorities, along with a brother whom she lost track of.

In 1942 she was a specialized worker for Citroën and lived on Rue d'Orgemont, in the twentieth arrondissement, with a friend, Colli, an Italian by birth, who also worked at Citroën. They were about to marry—all the preparations made, the wedding clothes spread out on the bed—when police from the special brigades came to arrest them on June 18, 1942. The police were looking for Colli's nephew, Barachi, a leader of the National Front for the Paris-North region, who had been seen several times visiting his uncle. Since they couldn't get their hands on Barachi, they took Colli and Jeanne Thiebault.

All the men arrested on June 18, 1942—printers, young FTP members—were executed by firing squad on August 11, 1942, and Jeanne Thiebault believed that Colli had been as well. But the number of men to be shot that day was set at sixty-five. He was the sixty-sixth. Left behind in the cells after his comrades' departure, he said to the guard: "I'm bored now, all alone."

"Don't complain," said the guard. "The others are already cold, you're the lucky one." He had the additional luck to be interned in France, in a camp where he survived until the Liberation.

Jeanne Thiebault was in the cells until August 10, 1942, then in Romainville until the departure.

Auschwitz # 31640

She died with no surviving witness. She had no family; thinking Colli had been executed, apparently she sent no messages. Colli's family and Colli himself did not know where she'd been deported or when she died.

Marie-Claude VAILLANT-COUTURIER, née Vogel

Born on November 3, 1912, in Paris, she was raised in the sixth arrondissement, in a family setting that was at once bourgeois, liberal, artistic, and even rather bohemian. Her father, Lucien Vogel, was a publisher and newspaper editor (he was founder of *Jardin des Modes* and, before the war, had launched some innovative publications, including *Lu et Vu*, one of the first illustrated weeklies). Her mother was a fashion editor and cookbook author; her sister,

Nadine Vogel, a film actress, was something of a celebrity; Jean and Laurent de Brunhoff, creators of the *Babar* stories, were, respectively, her uncle and her cousin.

Marie-Claude completed her secondary studies through the baccalaureate, then took a yearlong course in the decorative arts and became a photojournalist. From 1938 until war was declared, she worked for the photographic service of *L'Humanité*.

In 1934 she married Paul Vaillant-Couturier ("Paul Couturier" to the civil authorities), editor-in-chief of *L'Humanité*, who died in 1937. She then married Pierre Villon, and had a son.

She had been a member of the Communist Party since February 1934 and promptly entered the Resistance. She worked on the clandestine edition of *L'Humanité* and on other printed tracts. When she was arrested, she had for some time been acting as a liaison between the Communist Party heads and the various branches of the Resistance.

She was arrested in Paris on February 9, 1942, by the special brigades, caught in a trap at the home of an old woman to whom she was bringing food supplies for a comrade in prison. She had not been targeted, but at General Intelligence headquarters an inspector recognized her. Once identified, Marie-Claude refused to give her address. The police sent her photograph to the papers: "Amnesiac found in the street. Anyone able to provide information is kindly requested to go to police headquarters." Pleased with their cunning, the inspectors showed her the paper. And Marie-Claude was reassured: none of her contacts would keep their appointments.

Sent to the cells, she was transferred to the Santé (in isolation, alone in a cell) on March 23, 1942, and to Romainville on August 24, 1942.

Auschwitz # 31685

On February 24, 1943, thanks to Danielle Casanova, she entered the German revier as secretary (*Schreiberin*). She lost her job when she came down with typhus—a violent and lengthy bout that hit her on March 6 and did not let up until May. Back on her feet, she obtained a new position at the revier: as cleaning woman in the *Diätküche* (kitchen for special diets). Appearances were maintained at Birkenau: the dentist's office, the kitchen for special diets. Few had access to the dentist's office; and few patients were permitted to eat the white barley soup that was so appetizing compared to our usual soup made of rutabaga. For Marie-Claude, it was a privileged job, if only because of the barley soup.

After the quarantine, she did sewing and was then transferred to Ravensbrück with the majority of the survivors on August 2, 1944. For two months, she worked on the sand detail in the heart of the camp; then she was taken into the revier as secretary, but was let go after a dispute with one of the blockovas. After this, she was given responsibility for raking the streets of the camp, a job she liked very much—to walk around the camp alone with a rake in her hand was truly marvelous. Then she had a job assisting the Polish prisoner who kept the roll call register, another job she could do because she knew German.

On March 2, 1945, when all the Auschwitz survivors who were "NN" at Ravensbrück were sent to Mauthausen, Marie-Claude arranged things so she didn't have to leave—falsifying the roll call book under cover of the prevailing disarray—and could stay with the women bedridden in the revier, especially Simone Loche, who was dying. On April 23, 1945, the Swedish Red Cross came for the Frenchwomen, the Belgians, and the women from Luxembourg. They couldn't take the critically ill. Marie-Claude and Heidi Hautval reckoned on leaving with this last convoy. No one could have known what the SS would do at the last moment. They said that the sewage system of the camp was mined. The Red Cross could not make another trip—the roads were cut off. The SS abandoned the camp on April 28. It was then discovered that there were many Frenchmen among the men evacuated from other camps to Ravensbrück in the last days, and that many of them were ill. Marie-Claude and Heidi Hautval, along with several other prisoners, became responsible for the administration of the camp. There were thousands of men and women to be fed and cared for. They saw the Soviet army arrive on April 30, 1945. They remained at Ravensbrück until all the French nationals had been evacuated, helping to care for them, identify them, and organize them for repatriation.

Marie-Claude returned to Paris on June 25, 1945.

And since then? She says: "For me the deportation changed nothing. I was a militant, I became a militant again." This would sound cavalier if we were to take her literally. The truth is that she was also luckier than others: she found her whole family again, and she found Pierre Villon, who had been arrested in October 1940, escaped on January 17, 1942, and continued in the clandestine struggle without being caught, although he must have been within a hair's breadth at least three times.

She was a communist deputy. Named commander in the RIF and decorated with the Legion of Honor.

Marguerite VALINA, née Maurin ("Margot")

Born January 14, 1906, in Moings, Charente-Maritime. Her parents were bakers in Jarnac-Champagne, where Margot completed elementary school; she continued her education in Javrezac. She had a sister and two brothers.

In 1927, in Cognac, she married Lucien Valina, a Spaniard who had come to France at the age of fifteen and worked as a truck driver. They had three children: Jean born in 1926, Lucienne born in 1928, and Serge born in 1934.

In 1936, Lucien Valina joined the International Brigades and fought in Spain until the end of the civil war. Margot had accompanied him and had stayed there for some time. On her return to Cognac, she took in Spanish refugees, with whom she shared what she had. She did housecleaning.

Lucien Valina returned from Spain but was not out of armed service for long. From the beginning of the occupation, he was in one of the first combat groups that later became the FTP. As for Margot, she sheltered combatants, transmitted instructions to the Pateaus at Saint-André-de-Cognac, to the Guillons on the farm at Saint-Sévère, scouted out hiding places for weapons on the farms of the Charente and shelter for saboteurs. She sent men to stay at the farm of her childhood friend Alice Cailbault, made contact with Annette Epaud at La Rochelle and Paulette Brillouet at Angoulême. On July 28, 1942, at five in the morning (while another team was arresting the Pateaus at Saint-André-de-Cognac), the Gestapo arrested the entire Valina family: husband and wife, the eldest son Jean, aged sixteen, the daughter Lucienne, aged thirteen, and the youngest, Serge, a boy of seven.

During the ride, Margot hugged her daughter as though to reassure her and managed to whisper in her ear: "They're going to ask you if you know so and so—you don't know anyone. If they show you someone, you don't recognize them." And the little girl never flinched, even when the police said to her: "Your mother has already told us. Do you want us to kill your mother?" By early afternoon, the two youngest had been handed over to the gendarmes, who were ordered to place them in an orphanage. Instead, the gendarmes found an aunt, Margot's sister, to whom they entrusted the two children. Jean Valina, who had participated in his father's expeditions, watched for hours while his father was tortured.

The Valinas had been denounced by Vincent.[22] Lucien Valina was executed by firing squad in Bordeaux on September 21, 1942. Margot Valina was imprisoned in the Boudet barracks, then in the Hâ fortress, and arrived in Romainville on October 14, 1942.

---

22. Vincent had remained in contact with Lucien Valina since they had fought together in the Spanish Civil War. An audacious leader of the FTP, he had been arrested in May or June 1942 and had, he said, escaped. This was a police trick in which he cooperated. He led the police to his former comrades. At the Liberation, Vincent joined the Free French Forces. He was in French uniform when he was recognized in Berlin in May 1945 by a deportee who had been one of his victims. Vincent was sentenced to death by the military court of the fourth region (Bordeaux), October 30, 1948, and executed.

Auschwitz # 31732

Margot Valina died in Birkenau at the end of February 1943; her throat was so swollen she couldn't eat or breathe. Jean Valina was released after his father's execution. For a short time. In November 1942, he was arrested again and deported to Oranienburg; he did return.

Albert and Ernest Maurin, Margot Valina's brothers, were arrested in October 1942 and interned in a camp in France.

The children learned of their mother's death in 1947. Jean Valina, a subscriber to *Patriot resistant*, saw the anthropometric photograph from Auschwitz, which the Auschwitz Association had just received and published in order to locate the family.

Théodora VAN DAM, née Disper, and her daughter Reyna

Madame Van Dam, born on June 18, 1882, in Edam, in the Netherlands, was the wife of Hendrik Van Dam, secretary of the Dutch Chamber of Commerce in Paris, where the Van Dams had settled at the end of World War I. They lived in Saint-Mande with their two daughters, Reyna, born April 17, 1922, and Dorothea, born November 1, 1923.

Hendrik Van Dam belonged to a chain that helped Dutch resisters escape and find passage to England. In June 1942, when a suspicious character came to him asking for help, he sensed he was being followed by the Gestapo. He decided to leave, and set out for Portugal and London on June 30, 1942. His wife and daughters remained at Saint-Mande. On October 21, 1942, the Gestapo arrested Madame Van Dam. She was interrogated at Rue des Saussaies and sent the same day to Romainville.

Worried that her mother hadn't returned, the eldest daughter, Reyna—twenty years old—went to Rue des Saussaies to find out what had happened. Her sister Dorothea accompanied her, but just before entering the building, Reyna told her: "No, wait for me outside." At eight that evening, Dorothea went home, gathered up her things, and fled. The Gestapo were never able to find her.

Reyna was imprisoned in Fresnes, in isolation. Two months later she joined her mother in Romainville.

Auschwitz # 31749

Madame Van Dam was taken in "the race" on February 10, 1943. Reyna (we don't know her number because her photograph was lost) supported her mother. She did not want to leave her. They both died in Block 25.

Dorothea Van Dam, a supervisor in a high school in La Flèche, waited for her family to return. Her father came back. He learned through the Dutch consulate at the end of 1945 that his wife and daughter had died at Auschwitz.

Jakoba VAN DER LEE

Born January 4, 1891, in the Netherlands.

When she was very young, she married an Arab prince or sheik, who took her to his country to join his harem. She had not expected to be treated like an oriental concubine, and immediately thought of escape. She had to wait nine years, however, before returning to Europe thanks to a Dutch consul she managed to contact, using infinite subterfuge. During these nine years, she learned Arabic, and back in Paris she acquired a reputation as an Arabic scholar. She was a lecturer at the School of Oriental Languages.

She was arrested in Paris at the end of September 1942. Why? Because in a letter to her brother, who lived in Holland, she wishfully predicted Hitler's defeat. The letter was intercepted, and she was interned at Romainville on September 30. One of her cellmates was a teacher from Besançon, arrested for a similar reason, who was released a few days before the departure.

Auschwitz # 31697

Caught in "the race" on February 10, 1943, Jakoba Van der Lee died in Block 25 a few days later.

In any case, at fifty-two, she was too old to survive Birkenau.

Alice VARAILHON

Born on December 22, 1897, in Breuil-Magné, Charente-Maritime, she eventually settled in Saintes and lived there until 1942. Her family were peasants. She never finished elementary school.

She married a railway worker and had a son, Robert, who was twenty years old in 1942 and involved in the Resistance. Her husband had been arrested on June 1, 1940, and interned in various camps.

During the Resistance, she lodged clandestine fighters, and at "Mama Alice's" there was always good grub, woolens, and a pair of shoes for young men who were famished and ill supplied. She herself acted as a liaison for the FTP and collected money and food for imprisoned comrades.

Having found her name in the notebook of an FTP leader arrested in Royan shortly before, the French police arrested Alice Varailhon on September 5, 1942. "If women were shot, I'd ask for the heads of those two," said Commissioner Chiron during the interrogation of Alice Varailhon and Hélène Bolleau in La Rochelle; and the interpreter, Sutor, translating for the Gestapo agents present, answered: "We'll see about that. We have something better for them."

Imprisoned in La Rochelle until the end of October 1942, in Angoulême until November 18, 1942, then in Romainville until the departure.

Auschwitz # 31810

"We were on the demolition crew when we found the corpse of a little girl in a well. Alice made gestures which the SS took as threats, and they fired on her with a revolver, at close range. We transported her back to the camp on an improvised litter. She died shortly after roll call that evening, March 11, 1943" (Hélène Bolleau).

Named second lieutenant in the RIF.

Alice VITERBO, née Lombroso

She was an Italian, born on August 8, 1895, in Alexandria, Egypt. She was a singer and performed at the Paris Opéra. Following an automobile accident some years before the war, her leg was amputated and she wore a prosthesis. Obliged to give up her stage career, she had opened a school for voice and diction in Paris.

The reason for her arrest is unknown. Some seem to remember that she had helped members of a Gaullist network. She arrived in Romainville around December 15, 1942. She never complained, walked without a cane in the cells, sang and was generally quite cheerful. And even if she had told the fortress commander that she had only one leg, he would still have sent her off to Auschwitz.

Auschwitz # 31 . . .

She was taken in "the race" on February 10, 1943. She made a superhuman effort to run. It was extraordinary that she'd been able to stand for three hours that morning. She was trying to run, dragged along by Hélène Solomon. But she fell and was pulled out of the ranks and thrown into Block 25. She lasted longer than anyone else. For days we saw her at the window, upright and lucid. Marie-Claude went to speak to her in the evenings, after roll call. Each time Alice asked: "Bring me poison. Danielle must have some in the dental office." We had to let Alice die without help. Marie-Claude remembers still seeing her after becoming secretary at the revier, that is, after February 24. Alice Viterbo must have died on February 25 or 26, 1943. Her artificial leg lay in the snow for a long time.

Madeleine ZANI, née Davy

Born on August 8, 1915, in Mont-Saint-Martin, Meurthe-et-Moselle, to a family of ten children, seven of whom were living. Her father, a metallurgist, was killed in 1923 in an accident at the factory in Senelle. The mother raised her children by working a small farm in Mont-Saint-Martin.

Madeleine Davy completed elementary school and became a stenographer at the Société Lorraine-Escaut. She married Pierre Zani, a metal worker, and settled in Longwy.

In September 1939 the populations of the border zone were evacuated along the Gironde. Madeleine Zani, whose husband had been mobilized, was directed to Libroune, where her son Pierre was born on October 13, 1939. At the end of 1941, Madeleine Zani, a Communist Party member before the war, became politically active in the Resistance. She sheltered hunted militants—among them the husband of Yolande Gili. She was arrested on August 31, 1942, in Bordeaux, by two policemen (one French, the other German). Her son, not yet three years old, was taken in by his grandparents.

She was imprisoned in Hâ from August 31 until October 14, 1942, then sent to Romainville until the departure.

Auschwitz # 31 . . .

Died at Birkenau in March or April 1943. No witness.

The family learned of her death from survivors of the convoy.

Mado . . .

She came directly from the cells to the convoy at Compiègne on January 23, 1943, the eve of departure. Marie-Elisa, distributing bread for the journey, asked this newcomer her name: "Mado."

She was probably in the train car with a group of women who all perished. She must have died in the first few days. No one had time to get acquainted with her. None of the women surviving today remembers her.

List of Deportees

(in order of coverage)